THE MACMILLAN COMPANY
NEW YORK · BOSTON · CHICAGO · DALLAS
ATLANTA · SAN FRANCISCO

MACMILLAN & CO., LIMITED
LONDON · BOMBAY · CALCUTTA
MELBOURNE

**THE MACMILLAN COMPANY
OF CANADA,** LIMITED
TORONTO

TWENTY-FIVE YEARS OF AMERICAN EDUCATION

COLLECTED ESSAYS

WRITTEN BY A GROUP OF HIS FORMER
STUDENTS AS A TRIBUTE TO

PAUL MONROE

ON HIS COMPLETION OF TWENTY-
FIVE YEARS OF SERVICE TO
AMERICAN EDUCATION

EDITED BY

I. L. KANDEL, Ph.D.

PROFESSOR OF EDUCATION AND ASSOCIATE
INTERNATIONAL INSTITUTE, TEACHERS
COLLEGE, COLUMBIA UNIVERSITY

New York

THE MACMILLAN COMPANY

1929

Norwood Press
J. S. Cushing Co. — Berwick & Smith Co.
Norwood, Mass., U.S.A.

To
Paul Monroe
by the Authors,
His Former
Students

PREFACE

THE accompanying volume originated in a desire on the part of a number of former students of Dr. Paul Monroe to show their appreciation of his twenty-five years of service to Teachers College, Columbia University, and to American education. Few educators in this country have contributed as much as Dr. Monroe toward raising the standards of scholarship and research in the study of education. Since the twenty-five years of Dr. Monroe's fruitful activity as scholar and administrator coincide almost exactly with the completion of the first quarter of the present century, which has witnessed the development of a science of education and in which a foundation has been laid for rapid progress in education that is to come, it was considered appropriate that the tribute to Dr. Monroe should take the form of a collection of essays that would summarize the achievements in education of the past twenty-five years and that would also indicate in some measure the large field that still remains to be developed. Although the author of each essay was left free to develop his subject in his own way, the reader will find the threads of a number of common principles running through the volume. For the editor and his collaborators the task has been a labor of affection and esteem for their teacher, who with true missionary spirit now enters on a new sphere of activity and service in the field of international education.

I. L. KANDEL

NEW YORK CITY
January 1, 1924

vii

CONTENTS

ix

INTRODUCTION

PAUL MONROE — AN APPRECIATION

THE educational services of Paul Monroe now extend over a quarter of a century. The fact of long service in itself attracts attention from a world which has not yet grown indifferent to that mastery of life which is marked by the steadiness and devotion which lengthen men's labors in important places. But to point out a larger and more important milestone in the continuous industry of a scholar's mind means something more and something different to his former students and colleagues. To them the commemoration of twenty-five years of teaching and scholarship is merely a more formal and more outspoken expression of deep-seated appreciations they have long carried. Like the profession at large, they have been influenced by his mind in all the direct and indirect ways which are given to the resourceful thinker and the careful scholar. But, like themselves alone, they have shared the scholar's intimate thought as only those may who have learned the ways of discovery under his guidance. Whatever they have done in the days of independent scholarship is rooted in those hours of counsel, criticism, and suggestion when the mind of the teaching scholar and his apprentice interchange upon some problem of truth and its applications. Thus many of the young and virile leaders of American education who have passed in and out of the portals of the great Teachers College of Columbia University remember and appreciate that one mind which was specially charged to give historical perspective to personal experience, and to inculcate, in the course of the process, the distinction between reflection with and reflection without accurately determined facts.

The quarter of a century just passed encompasses no ordinary years in the history of education. It was the most extraordinary period in American educational development. No similar span of time in America or elsewhere has covered such important changes in the philosophy, the science, and the practice of school administration and school teaching. It was ushered in by the stimulating discussion of foreign educational philosophies which American students of education brought home from Germany. The United States lost for the time being that provincial and traditional point of view which had characterized its pedagogical thinking since the Civil War, at least so far as the most influential educational theorists were concerned. Experimentation on the basis of deductions from new assumptions and premises characterized many school systems. The self-satisfied stolidity of traditional American practice was broken. But conservative and less theoretic American teachers, who clung tenaciously to habitual methods, criticized the new theories, giving ground slowly and then only on the demonstrated success of the new procedures. The debate led to a comparative study of the institutions of education, for it became clear that schools served various national and social purposes at different times and places. The new study of foreign school systems was too largely contemporary in its reach to satisfy fully. A wider reaching study — the history of education — assumed a fresh importance in the professional training of leaders.

It was at this moment that Doctor Paul Monroe, a graduate of Franklin College and the University of Chicago, trained in the methods of historical and sociological study, began his career as a college teacher. It was in 1897 that he became instructor in history under the regimen of a professional school for educators, — the Teachers College of Columbia University. Two years later, he responded to the new interest in the history of education by transferring to an adjunct professorship in that field, assuming his full professorship in 1902. At an hour of propitious opportunity and at the place of greatest future influence, Professor Monroe thus began his constructive work in the training of educational scholars.

The methods of that day were not exact in educational thinking. The comparative and statistical inquiries of the educational administrators had not yet transformed that field of practice; nor had the educational psychologists begun their scientific work in tests and measurements. The one field of educational study which possessed a thoroughgoing scholarly method of inquiry was the history of education. It set the standard for graduate study and established an ideal of accurate investigation for students of education. Its demand set up a standard of respectability for every other field of educational thought. That it did so was due to the Professor of the History of Education in Teachers College even more than to the subject.

Aspirants to scholarship who had no intention of becoming teachers of the history of education wrote their doctor's dissertations in that field under this man, for the necessity of accurate method in education was already gripping the abler young men of the profession. Here and there another historical scholar or two aided influentially through publications in the history of education, but the large and continuous service was done at Teachers College under Dr. Monroe. Here was the largest body of graduate students in education and the best collections of research material. While he taught future school officers and educational thinkers he paralleled this work with his own writings. In

1901 there appeared his *Source Book in the History of Education for the Greek and Roman Period;* in 1904, his *Thomas Platter and the Educational Renaissance of the Sixteenth Century;* in 1905, his *Text-Book in the History of Education;* and, in 1907, his *Brief Course in the History of Education.* Meanwhile his students were being directed into those inquiries as to the fact of American educational history which have aided greatly in restoring the American point of view and tradition to our thinking about the public school as a national institution. Much of the solid knowledge that we possess of the historical development of American schools is the product of the many studies which have been written by Professor Monroe's students.

It would not be an adequate characterization of the scholar or the man to confine our view to Dr. Monroe's work as an historian of education. He has not been a mere historian, tracing the evolution of a particular institution. It would be far more accurate to say that Dr. Monroe is an educator with a specialized interest in the historical phases of his profession. His sociological training and bent would never permit him to look at an important social institution in a fragmentary way. He has, indeed, brought his organizing mind to the whole field of educational scholarship through his unusual editorial work, making the products of professional scholarship available to both the laity and the profession.

As editor of the division of education for the *New International Encyclopedia,* Nelson's *Cyclopedia,* and the *International Yearbook,* he has organized our professional knowledge for the public. As editor of Macmillan's *Text-Book Series in Education* and the *Source Book Series in Education,* he has collected and systematized for the profession the available scholarly information on important problems in new, scattered, or half-organized fields of knowledge. His

greatest contribution to the whole field of education is the
Cyclopedia of Education (5 vols., 1910–13). As editor-in-
chief of this ambitious work, he contributed still further
to that international reputation which he had earlier made
as an historian of education and placed under an obligation
both laymen and teachers wherever the English language is
read.

In the work of a scholar and teacher there are other and
less obvious phases of service appreciated only by the man's
intimates. The colleagues of Paul Monroe will be likely to
think of him first in the coöperative labors of university life.
The making of a successful educational institution is a joint
effort. A great institution, such as our Teachers College, is
not made by specialists seeking and teaching truth in their
own isolate ways. The other half of the tale is found in the
combined work of teachers who sit down to a common problem, recognize leadership, and follow it in the making of
some great plan which enlists enthusiastic fulfillment. No
man leaned to a common academic enterprise with more
fellowship than did the Professor of the History of Education. What his graduate students sensed in the seminar,
his colleagues in the faculty felt in the committee room, and
his professional associates knew in the learned societies of
which he has been president. It is this quality that has made
him one of those invaluable personalities which the public
always seeks for its commissions of public service. Wherever the American educational influence penetrated foreign
parts, Professor Monroe has had the impulse and the energy
to counsel, investigate, and make constructive suggestion.
Hence, his public services have touched the colonial schools
of the Philippines, the Americanization of the schools of
China, and the improvement of American Christian schools
the world over. From such accuracy and carefulness, from
such sympathy and understanding, from such energies and

organizing powers, has been compounded the personality of the Director of the School of Education in our greatest Teachers College. With its world-wide clientele no less a scholar and man would do.

It is not possible to speak the appreciation of all the far-scattered teachers of the world who have learned to be scholars, instructors, and good educational workmen under the tutelage of Professor Monroe. Each one of them would have his own angle of appreciation and his particular gratefulness for help received. What has come to my mind and been written might have been said of him by those doctors of philosophy that he trained in his seminar room, if only they might once more assemble. It is conservatively thought and recorded. What has not been expressed are those warm personal appreciations which the affection of men for a man impels them to utter upon a day of significant commemoration. Instead we present a book of modest scholarly labors, each one of which has been affectionately conceived and written by a former student of the Professor of the History of Education in the Teachers College of Columbia University.

HENRY SUZZALLO

CHAPTER I

GENERAL HISTORICAL BACKGROUND, 1897–1922

BY

EDWARD H. REISNER

TEACHERS COLLEGE, COLUMBIA UNIVERSITY

TWENTY-FIVE YEARS
OF AMERICAN EDUCATION

CHAPTER I

GENERAL HISTORICAL BACKGROUND, 1897–1922

Social Conditions Leading Up to the Political
Campaign of 1896

In 1860 the United States was predominantly a nation of
farmers. The great bulk of the population — 83.9 per cent,
to be exact — lived in the open country or in places of fewer
than eight thousand inhabitants. In 1890 the cityward
trend of population, which is one of the most important
social phenomena of our times, was already well under way,
with 29 per cent of the entire population classified as urban
on the basis of the definition followed above. In 1860 the
total value of goods manufactured in the United States was
something under $1,900,000,000, while in 1894 the total
was five times that amount. In 1860 the building of railways was only in its infancy, there being a total mileage of
about 30,000 miles. In 1890 over 163,000 miles of railway
extended from the Atlantic to the Pacific and spread over
the entire country in closely woven network.

Such facts as the above are but symptomatic of the
fundamental changes that were going on in the nation.
They mean that the industrial revolution which had already done much to change social conditions in Great

Britain and on the continent of Europe was during the post-Civil War generation beginning to make a great difference in American life as well. The changes from small- to large-scale industrial production, from domestic to factory organization, from hand- to power-driven machine manu-facture, were accompanied in this country, as in others, by the increased employment of women and children, by a calamitous harvest of industrial accidents, by oppressively long hours of labor, and by other disadvantages to the work-men that were hardly less significant. They were also ac-companied by the efforts of the workingmen to organize in order to secure the strength that comes from collective bargaining with respect to all the details of their employ-ment.

The history of the industrial revolution in this country reflects the traditional English *laissez-faire* economic theory combined with a characteristically American individualism. Moreover, when the industrial situation first came to be a matter of common interest and control, the solution of the complex industrial problems was placed before a population that was predominantly agricultural, and largely unsym-pathetic with the labor viewpoint because unfamiliar with the conditions which labor strove to have remedied.

Both cause and accompaniment of the industrial revolu-tion in the United States was the tremendous increase in railway mileage mentioned above. The railways increased the scale of business operations and made possible the or-ganization of industrial corporations whose business was not confined to the borders of one state or to those of two or three states, but was nation-wide. The railways, too, were typical forms of big business engaged in interstate trade. The peculiar form of organization which business followed at this time was that of limited-stock companies. As the expensiveness of unlimited competition was realized, there was a general tendency for companies engaged in the same line of industry or trade to combine, or for the largest and strongest of them to engage in bitter competition with their smaller and weaker rivals with the object either of making the smaller competitors come into the general combination or to eliminate them altogether. The railways in the same way passed through a stage of destructive competition and ended by creating great combinations of smaller railways which were able to restrict competition to larger units or to reach agreements regarding rates and the sharing of traffic.

The tendency to form trusts and systems had not reached its fullest development before it was seen that these great companies, almost monopolistic in their control, were able to exert pressure upon smaller competitors — the shipper, the manufacturer, the ultimate consumer in general — that was inimical to the principle of free and unrestricted competition in business. The railroads, in particular, were able to oppress the shipper and the traveler with rates that were considered exorbitant, or that were known to be unequal for different shippers. Under such conditions the people asked relief through legislation, which it was difficult to secure. In all too many cases the railroads made it their business to block legislation aimed at controlling them, through the manipulation of legislatures, and even when such legislation was passed, it was found that the relief to be gained through state laws was efficacious only in so far as it related to commerce carried on wholly within the state.

The conviction that the form which big business had taken was bad and that aid was needed in the form of federal legislation came to a definite expression in the passage of the Interstate Commerce Act of 1887 and the Sherman Anti-Trust Act of 1890. The former measure prohibited a number of the practices which had been regarded as unfair and called into existence an Interstate Commerce Commission, which was given power to pass upon the justice of rates, after investigation of the facts in the case, and to lay penalties upon the railroads for failure to live up to its decisions. The latter act forbade as illegal every contract, combination in the form of trust or otherwise, or conspiracy, in restraint of trade or commerce among the several states or with foreign nations, and provided penalties for infraction of the law. Owing to judicial decisions which curtailed the application of the acts, and partly to the indecision of the federal administration, the relief that was hoped for upon the passage of these acts was long delayed. Indeed, it was only with the coming of a new spirit into federal politics after 1900 that any appreciable headway was made in the policy of governmental control of big business.

The big stakes for which large combinations of business were playing made it financially profitable for them to expend vast sums in the control of elections. They entered into unholy alliances with political bosses to control the selection of candidates at the primaries, in order thus to insure that city councils, legislatures, state administrative officers, the judiciary, and the federal congress might be amenable to orders, or at least susceptible to financial considerations. The venal use of money in politics was made easier by reason of the large immigrant populations in the growing cities, but even among native stock the liberal distribution of money to carry an election was common political procedure. Back of all this degradation of the principle of government by the people lay a conviction held by many business men that it was essential that property should be protected against the attacks of radical reformers. Many men, otherwise honest, condoned the fact that very vile means were being used to attain, as they thought, thoroughly justifiable ends.

The early phases of American material development were largely dependent upon an uncontrolled and unchecked exploitation of natural resources. Of all these the most extensive was the abundance of rich agricultural land that might be had almost for the asking. The announcement of the Commissioner of the Public Domain in 1890 that the end of the frontier was in sight and that the best of the free land had been taken up marks in a very real way the beginning of a new epoch in American life. It was not accidental that in 1889 the Department of Agriculture was made one of the separate departments of the federal administration and its secretary given a seat in the President's Cabinet, for now it was recognized as essential to continued national prosperity that wasteful methods of cultivation be superseded by efforts to preserve the fertility of the soil. As yet, however, nothing had been done to protect the great resources in forest and water course, in mine and quarry, for the benefit of the entire people and for succeeding generations instead of turning them over to the enrichment of private individuals.

In face of all the unfavorable political and economic conditions which have just been recalled, there was in the country at large during the eighties a feeling of shame at the failure of liberal political institutions to result in better government, and a degree of interest in political and economic reform that was destined in the near future to bring about appreciable improvement. Considerable progress had been made before 1896 in establishing the federal administration upon a basis of competitive examination and merit. Ballot reforms had made it more difficult for the bosses to deliver a bought electorate, and occasional legislation indicated a developing consciousness on the part of the public that the uncontrolled development of the factory system of production had wrought unjustifiable hardships upon the industrial worker.

Meanwhile certain combinations of specific circumstances were setting the stage for the spectacular political campaign of 1896.

The Political Campaign of 1896

An extended period of poor crops, at a time when prices of agricultural products were at the lowest point reached after the Civil War, had made it impossible for farmers generally to pay the interest on the mortgages which rested on their properties. To them it seemed desirable that there should be a cheaper and freer currency. More money in circulation would tend to raise the price of their produce, would provide cash for interest payments, and, at the same time, relatively lessen the debt. The employees of the industrial system had felt all through Cleveland's second administration the pinch of an acute financial depression in the form of low wages and unemployment. They, too, desired to see more money in circulation for the effect they thought it would have on business in general and on their own private financial circumstances. Then there were the silver states that desired a better market for their chief commodity.

The demand for a freer currency was, however, by no means the only plank in the platform of general political revolt which culminated in the campaign of 1896. There was a well-defined feeling among the farmers that they were being exploited in more ways than one, and this feeling was shared by the great number of workingmen who were smarting under their inability to get redress for their grievances through the courts or through progressive industrial legislation. These two groups believed themselves to be under the unjust domination of capital, and they undertook to develop a political régime more sympathetic with their point of view and more immediately responsive to their will.

The agrarian-labor revolt took definite form in the organization of the People's Party, while for a time the Populist group was in complete control of the Democratic Party. After a campaign of unexampled enthusiasm and activity, William McKinley was elected President with a Republican Congress to support him, but it is worthy of note that William Jennings Bryan received a larger popular vote than had ever before been given to any presidential candidate, in spite of the fact that he was defeated by more than a half-million votes.

The demand for a freer circulation of currency through the unlimited coinage of silver came to be the central issue in the campaign of 1896, because that was thought by the various disaffected groups to be the immediate panacea for the ills that troubled them. However, as it has turned out, that issue was largely a temporary one, the occasion for which was almost immediately removed by the return of industrial prosperity, good crops, higher wages, and better prices. The remainder of the Populist program, on the other hand, has been of much more enduring significance. The demand for government ownership of railways, telegraphs, and telephones was prophetic of the largely increased control which the government has since that time come to exercise over the utilities by which the public is served. The demands for conservation of the wealth in public land, for ballot reform, direct election of United States senators, a shorter working day, an income tax, and other political and economic changes of like tenor indicated that a considerable portion of the population had become convinced that the policies of unchecked individualism and governmental unconcern with economic matters would no longer serve the needs of society. There was abroad in the land an insistent proposal that new social controls should be set up for the protection of the many against the power of the financially intrenched few, and that political power to that end should be placed more directly in the hands of the people.

New Functions of the Federal Administration

For so long as McKinley remained President, the federal administration followed closely the counsels of men intimately connected with big business, with complete indifference to the demand for reforms of various kinds which had been indicated by the election of 1896. No legislative action was taken to strengthen the hands of the Interstate Commerce Commission, which had been considerably shorn of power by judicial decisions, and no action was taken by the administration to control the operations of industrial combinations under the powers given in the Sherman Anti-Trust Act. On the contrary, a high protective tariff was installed to the evident advantage of the business interests. A period of unexampled prosperity was in full swing, and for the time being the social critics were silenced. What is equally important in explaining the delay in taking up the solution of industrial and social problems after the election of 1896 was the shift of attention to foreign and military affairs, which were prominent in the public mind from the very beginning of McKinley's first term. The war with Spain (1898) substituted patriotic for critical attitudes. Prosperity having continued, the chief issue in the campaign of 1900 was whether or not the United States should follow the path of empire upon which she had set out with the acquisition of Porto Rico and the Philippine Islands. It was only with the accession to the presidency of Theodore Roosevelt, after the assassination of President McKinley in 1901, that a new conception of the powers and responsibilities of government in social and economic affairs became influential in the federal administration.

After the end of the business depression which lasted from 1893 to 1896, a new and spectacular period of industrial development took place in which the tendency toward combinations in business became more pronounced than ever and followed broader patterns. Instead of representing combinations of firms or corporations engaged in the same phase of business, the newer tendency was for combinations to be perfected that would control the entire range of industrial processes from the production of raw materials to the sale of the finished product. Typical of this sort of combination was the United States Steel Trust, organized in 1901 with a capital stock of $1,400,000,000, of which amount, according to various estimates, $400,000,000 to $700,000,000 was "water." The increasing importance of elaborative industry in the economic life of the country during the period since 1890 is shown by the increase in the proportion of the population dwelling in the city from 35.4 per cent [1] in 1890 to 51.4 per cent in 1920. Between 1889 and 1914 the value of manufactured products increased from nine to twenty-four billions, while between 1890 and 1920 the value of the output of mines, quarries, and oil and gas wells increased from six hundred six millions to six thousand seven hundred millions. Coincident with the business revival after 1896, there was a campaign of publicity in the magazine and newspaper press that thoroughly aroused the reading public to some of the evil practices of big business. The time was ripe for a champion to declare for government interference and control in the matter of business practices that so closely affected the public welfare.

In his first presidential message Theodore Roosevelt took up, as the first subject of consideration, the proper relationship between the federal administration and business. He advised the creation of some agency that might

[1] According to the changed definition of the 1920 census.

gain accurate information about corporations to the end that a properly constituted body with adequate powers might eliminate those abuses of corporate organization and management that were inimical to the common welfare.   To attain this end a Department of Commerce and Labor was created, the Secretary of which was to have a seat in the President's Cabinet, and in which there was to be a Bureau of Corporations, with the function of gathering the desired information about the corporations.   The trial of government cases under the Sherman Anti-Trust Act and the Interstate Commerce Act was expedited by Congressional action, and the Interstate Commerce Act was strengthened.   Power which the Government had possessed, but had not applied, was now directed toward the dissolution of some of the most conspicuous industrial combinations.   In his public utterances the President declared openly for the "square deal," and in his public acts he applied the principle of the subordination of private business interests to the public good.

In other important connections Roosevelt identified himself with an aroused and enlightened public conscience, of which none was more noteworthy than his espousal of the movement for the conservation of the country's natural resources.   His activities in this field resulted in the passage of the Newlands Reclamation Act of 1902, which had as its object the reclamation of the arid lands of the Rocky Mountain region through irrigation, and in the appointment of the National Conservation Commission.   Due again to his initiative, vast tracts of public land were saved to the public as forest reserves and sources of water power.

When William Howard Taft became President in 1909, he was committed to the progressive policies of his predecessor, and it was thought that he would continue along the lines which had brought so generous public approval to the administration of Roosevelt. Early in his term, however, misunderstandings arose over the tariff and over the conservation policy of the administration, and successive events threw Taft upon the support of the leaders of the party who were less responsive to the popular demand for enlightened social legislation. The result was a split in the Republican Party, with the "Old Guard" representing the attitudes of the Republican Party in its halcyon days of the McKinley régime, and the "Progressives" claiming that upon them had fallen the mantle of Roosevelt. The party misunderstanding became so grave that President Taft, the regular party nominee, was opposed in the election of 1912 not only by Woodrow Wilson, a Democrat of proved liberal tendencies, but also by Roosevelt, who received the support of "Progressive" Republicans. The result was the election of Mr. Wilson.

In the opening years of the first Wilson administration, a great deal of legislation was passed which represented not only the intention of making big business and the transportation companies operate within the fair limits of common honesty and fair competition, but also an appreciation that the rules according to which the industrial life of the nation was to expand must be comprehensible and definite and not of such a nature as to result in the crippling of business initiative. The Federal Trade Commission was created in 1914 with powers and duties looking to the prevention of unfair methods of competition in commerce. In the same year the Clayton Act declared in detail what constituted such unfair methods. The Esch-Cummins Act of 1920 represented the culmination of the Wilson legislation with respect to the control of Interstate Commerce. It created a Railroad Board of Labor Adjustment to pass upon matters of controversy between employers and employees, gave the Interstate Commerce Commission power to establish rates designed to provide the railways a fair return upon their real valuation, and recognized as necessary and legal the combination of railways subject to the approval of the Commission.

Expansion of Federal Administration

For the present purpose, the foregoing sketch may be taken as indicating the general trend of the federal policy with respect to the interference of the government in economic affairs, — a field to which its activities had been largely foreign in the earlier history of the country. And now, without any effort at completeness, some additional details may be given which will indicate how much the business of the federal government has expanded in what had previously been considered no field at all for government action or the exclusive province of state sovereignty. The creation of the Department of Commerce and Labor has already been mentioned as one of the early indications of a new intention of the federal government to concern itself more actively with the concerns of the industrial life. The division of that department in 1913 into the separate departments of Commerce and of Labor showed the growth of the work of the original department and the recognition of the problems connected with labor as being of sufficient complexity and importance to have a separate administration. The Bureau of Labor Statistics and the Children's Bureau in the Department of Labor have been collecting data that are invaluable in the determination of wise social policy. The Naturalization Bureau of the same Department has carried on an important work in connection with the Americanization of immigrants. The work of the federal Postal Department has also greatly increased with the universal development of rural free delivery, the establishment of the parcel post, and the operation of the postal

savings bank. The Department of Agriculture has undergone a rapid expansion of its work and been given many new
functions through the increased participation of the federal
government in the educational work carried on by the states.
Among these may be mentioned the experimental work
carried on in the state agricultural colleges under the Hatch
Act (1887) and succeeding acts which have increased the
federal contributions for experimental purposes, the extension work in agriculture and home economics under the
Smith-Lever Act (1914), and the county-farm-bureau and
county-agent work. The great expansion of the work of
the federal Department of Agriculture conducted in connection with the several states led in 1915 to the creation of
the States Relations Service to have charge of the work
carried on in common by the national and state governments.
The Treasury Department has experienced a large development of its activities through the tremendous financial
operations of the World War and has been brought closer to
the people of the entire country through the multiplication
of holders of government securities. The activities of the
same department in the field of public health have been
greatly expanded as well. The creation of the Federal
Reserve Bank has made the federal government a much
more active participant in national financial operations
and policies. The establishment of the Farm Loan Bureau,
the passage of the Federal Aid Roads Act (1916), and the
passage of the Smith-Hughes Act for the promotion of
vocational education, each involving the appropriation of
millions of dollars to be expended or administered within
the states, the passage of the Prohibition Amendment, the
levying of a federal income tax, and pure food and narcotics
legislation have multiplied the number of federal servants
necessary for efficient administration and have brought the
existence, the significance, and the power of the federal

government home to every citizen in a way that was simply not thought of in the year 1897.

A New Theory of Social Justice

The general awakening of the public conscience to the need for special legislative control of the activities of big business, which we have seen as characteristic of the last twenty-five years of our history, was accompanied by a new sensitiveness to the hardships which the industrial system had brought to the human factors of production. The long hours of the working day, the appalling frequency of industrial accidents, the unhealthful conditions under which a great deal of labor was performed, the unsatisfactory legal status of the workingmen's organizations, the prevalence of child labor, the inadequate wages in certain industries, and the petty oppression under which many groups of employees suffered were only some of the items in a sweeping indictment which was placed before the public in those years. The result has been an almost complete reversal of the legal or political philosophy which had hitherto been applied to the settlement of labor litigation. Efforts to correct abuses of the industrial system had, in the earlier generation, encountered the doctrines of the common law, which had arisen through the decisions of judges under the much less complex circumstances of the period preceding the industrial revolution and which had continued under the inertia of the common law into a time and a set of circumstances for which they were inadequate. Much of the early industrial legislation had been declared unconstitutional as interfering with the constitutional guarantees of liberty and enjoyment of property. The common-law doctrine that an employer could not be held responsible for an industrial accident that had been caused by the negligence of a fellow workman long resisted the demand for compensation to workmen in the case of injuries that occurred in the normal course of occupation. The new conscience, however, insisted that the new conditions of industrial production made the application of much old common law and many constitutions unfair to the men employed and dangerous to the future welfare of society. It demanded that the technicalities of this age-old law should be brushed aside and that the courts should participate in giving present-day justice in the light of present-day conditions. The result was the appearance on the bench of a new type of judge and the discovery of new constitutional sanctions which have made it possible for society to get its will observed in the improvement of the conditions of labor and in a distribution of the risks of production. The result has been the passage of laws and the application of those laws to the ends of lessening the hazards of industry, of providing compensation for industrial accidents, of improving the sanitary conditions of factories, of eliminating child labor, of limiting the hours of employment of women, of providing means of industrial conciliation, and in many ways besides. The problem as to what share of the return of his labor the laborer shall receive, as intricately tied up with all the details of his relationship with his employer and the public, is at present far from a satisfactory solution and constitutes one of the live issues of public policy. The mental attitude, however, which promises constructive thinking in an effort to solve this complex problem, or set of problems, has become increasingly prevalent during the last twenty-five years, and we may face the future with a certain degree of confidence that orderly progress toward a better equilibrium will take place.

Extensions of State Administration

One of the most striking developments that has come about since the epoch-making campaign of 1896 is the increase in the functions of government assumed by the states for the protection and the enhancement of the common good.   Agencies have been provided to see that insurance companies shall be managed on sound principles, that the investment securities that are offered for sale in the state shall be on a sound basis, that the food we buy shall be pure, that the hotels we lodge in shall be sanitary, that the milk we buy and the ice cream we consume shall contain a certain proportion of butter fat, that the public halls in which we sit shall be properly constructed, that the houses we live in shall be provided with proper fire escapes, that our public school children shall be vaccinated, that factories shall observe the provisions of the law regarding the safety and health of workmen, that our children shall go to school, and that the public utilities that serve the people with light, heat, and transportation shall give adequate service at fair cost.   The state is now spending huge sums in aid of local communities in the building of roads and bridges and other public works, and in aid of public health, public education, or other forms of social service where twenty-five years ago it spent for those objects in comparison practically nothing.

Government Placed More Immediately in the Hands of the Voters

With all this multiplication of the functions and agencies of government, both federal and state, the trend of political evolution has been in the direction of placing the control of public officials and public policy more immediately in the hands of the people.   The adoption of the secret ballot had been almost universally accomplished before 1897, but since that time the adoption of the direct primary system for all officers short of the presidency has been accomplished.   This change of the machinery of political control was designed to take away from the party bosses the last remnants of their power through putting the nomination as well as the selection of public servants directly in the hands of the voters. It remains a potent means to efficient and honest government, but unfortunately the application of the instrument has been faulty in the extreme and reveals a degree of civic lethargy that is, to say the least, disquieting. In some states the initiative and the referendum in state legislation have been developed, while to a limited extent the principle of the recall of public servants has been put into effect. Of outstanding significance in the political history of the period under consideration is the admission of women to the full rights and responsibilities of citizenship.

Improvements in Rural Life

Any account of the domestic history of the United States during the last twenty-five years would be inadequate which did not at least mention the great change which has come over rural life in that time. The poor financial condition of the farmer passed with the general business depression that came to an end in 1896, and from that date until after the close of the World War his economic position was highly favorable. It was a period of high prices for his products and of relative decline in the cost of the things he had to buy. The trend of farm values was upward and he reaped the advantage of this increment. He had ready money to buy the labor-saving equipment which made his labor less exacting and his output greater. He could take advantage of the offerings of an especially inventive generation and apply them to the greater efficiency and comfort of his farm and home. The internal combustion engine was harnessed to supply water for barn and house, to provide power for a wide range of backbreaking work, and, mounted on wheels, it gave him an untiring means of eliminating to a large extent the isolation which had constituted the greatest social limitation of life in the open country. The telephone put him in instant touch with his neighbors and with the world outside, and the rural postman brought him his daily mail. Sometimes out of his own resources unaided, but more often with the advantage of improved administration and the bounty of the larger state community, he has supplied his family with educational opportunities the equal of those enjoyed by children living in the towns and cities.

To be sure, the picture drawn above of the improved status of the farmer is by no means universally applicable, for there remain large rural areas in the United States in which the conditions described are woefully unfulfilled. It is equally true that at the present time, owing to some of the influences of the World War on our complicated and sensitive social organization, the farmers as a class in this country are experiencing a period of acute financial depression. But notwithstanding all the qualifications that have to be made, one of the most favorable developments that has taken place in American life in the last quarter-century is the improved condition and prospects of the rural population.

The United States Accepts an International Rôle

No less prominent a characteristic of the changed nature of American life than the increased complexity of its domestic affairs is the extent to which this country has swung out during the last quarter-century into the current of international politics. The connection between industrial changes and the new international relationship is very close, for the industrial revolution, with its new problems of markets for finished products and of supplies of raw materials, has been the underlying cause of the intensity of international competition which has characterized the political policies of the Western World during the last century.

The war with Spain in 1898 and the consequent accession of colonial possessions represented the more or less accidental precipitation of a change in the international policies of the United States which the development of her industrial life had made inevitable sooner or later. Nevertheless, the protectorate over Cuba and the possession of Porto Rico and the Philippines represent important landmarks in the history of our diplomatic policy. These steps into Spanish America emphasized the interest of the United States in Pan-American affairs and have been followed in quick succession by others no less significant. In 1902 the United States intervened in the dispute between Venezuela and some of the European powers; in 1903 it recognized the Republic of Panama and entered into contracts with that new republic which paved the way to the construction of the Panama Canal; in 1905 it established a protectorate over Santo Domingo, and in 1915 and 1916 respectively it entered into the same sort of relationship with Haiti and Nicaragua. The general interest which has been shown during the last fifteen or twenty years in cementing closer and more friendly relations between our country and the Spanish-American republics is a reflection of the march of commerce, while our difficult relations with Mexico have been related to the expansion of American investments in that country for the production of some of the raw materials essential to our developing industrial life.

In the Far East the United States became involved in the Boxer Rebellion of 1900, and in the diplomacy connected with the settlement of the disputes which arose was insistent upon observance of the principles of the open door and the territorial integrity of China. The part played by President Roosevelt in the negotiations leading to peace between Japan and Russia in 1905 indicated our interest in the Far East, while during the last six years our diplomatic relations with

China and Japan have very frankly recognized the Far Eastern situation as being of the greatest concern to this country. We are interested in the Far East primarily because it is essential to the free development of American trade that our commercial participation in that part of the world should be untrammeled.

Many other events of the last twenty-five years have indicated that the period of comparative isolation of America from the politics of the world at large was coming to an end. Among these may be mentioned the enthusiastic support that was given by the government of the United States to the two Hague Conferences and to the Permanent Court of Arbitration organized by the second of the Hague Conferences (1907), and also the efforts made by the administrations of Roosevelt, Taft, and Wilson to draw up agreements between the United States and other individual powers providing for the peaceful settlement of disputes between them. But the supreme proof of the thoroughgoing interdependence of our national fortunes with those of the rest of the world lies in the events of the last nine years beginning with the outbreak of the World War. At first news of war, public opinion held that the hostilities in Europe were just a recurrence of the conflict of national interests of which the preceding centuries had been full, and that it would be possible for the United States to stand by in its traditional policy of aloofness from entangling alliances with foreign powers. But as event followed upon event, it came to be seen that the war was after all our war. It was not a far-off conflict, but one that came home to our very doors, involving our material fortunes and enlisting our sympathies in an unmistakable direction. The news of the war ceased to be foreign and became home news, and we found ourselves neutral neither in act nor in attitude. The definite entrance of the United States into the war came as a natural and inevitable step.

Educational Developments of the Period

We have found the chief characteristic of our national life during the past twenty-five years to be a rapidly increasing complexity of economic and social conditions. This factor has called for the elaboration of new social controls in which both the federal and the state governments have participated. It is very natural that the public agencies for education should have received a great deal of attention in this time, since the schools must serve as the fundamental social control in a democratic society, and it may be said that education has made greater progress in the period under consideration than in any period of equal length during our history as a nation and, perhaps, than in all the years of our history preceding. Within this period, for the first time, there has come about a persistent effort to make the schools serve society in terms of the intelligence, right attitudes, and formed habits of the children who were to become the citizens of the future. The scientific study of the curriculum, of the methods of teaching and learning, of the correlation of the school experience with the life of society, of the adaptation of curricula to the economic and social needs of children of various probable walks of life, of the desirable course of study to be followed in the preparation of teachers, of the correlation of high school studies with effective college work, — these are only some of the aspects of the renewed determination to make of the school an efficient agency of social development and control.

The intensified interest in the content and quality of the school experience has had its correlate on the institutional side in the spectacular development of the high school, the commanding growth of technical and higher education, the development of college departments and university schools of education, the change of the normal schools to degree-granting teachers' colleges, the reorganization of secondary education through the development of the junior high school, the extensive supply of opportunities for vocational preparation through the modification of the curricula of secondary schools and the supply of part-time and continuation schools, and the very extensive adoption of the kindergarten as a part of the public-school system.

No less significant of a deeper appreciation of the importance of public education than the changes mentioned above is the intensive development of the agencies of school administration. Within this period the federal government has, step by step, added to the duties of existing departments social functions that are either educational or inseparably related to education and has at the same time enlarged the work of the federal Bureau of Education and entered into coöperative plans with the separate states for the fostering of special kinds of education. The states likewise have enlarged the staffs of their departments of education to meet the needs which have been brought about through standardization of the educational work done in the states, more extensive financial contributions on the part of the state governments, more general establishment of minimum requirements, and more active leadership in the direction of improved buildings, better salaries for teachers, better enforcement of attendance regulations, better adaptations of educational opportunities to the vocational needs of the pupil and the economic needs of society.

More might well be said to indicate the scope and the vitality of the educational rebirth which this nation has experienced during the past generation, but that is properly the burden of the pages which follow.

REFERENCES

HOWLAND, HAROLD J. — *Theodore Roosevelt and His Times;* Yale University Press, 1919.

KENDRICK, BURTON J. — *The Age of Big Business;* Yale University Press, 1919.

LINGLEY, CHARLES R. — *Since the Civil War;* Century, 1920.

PAXSON, FREDERIC L. — *The New Nation;* Houghton Mifflin, 1915.

CHAPTER II

University Study of Education

BY

I. L. Kandel

TEACHERS COLLEGE, COLUMBIA UNIVERSITY

CHAPTER II

UNIVERSITY STUDY OF EDUCATION

Introduction

The most significant development in the whole field of education in the United States has been the organization of facilities and opportunities for its study. It is difficult to realize, however, that this development has taken place in less than the twenty-five years that have just passed. By the close of the nineteenth century grudging recognition had already been given in a number of colleges and universities to the study of pedagogy or education, but the subject either was treated as an appanage of the chair of philosophy or, where it was taught in a separate department, was given only by one or two men. The view of Josiah Royce, expressed in 1891, was shared by many who professed the long, or even the recently, established subjects considered worthy of college or university study. "To sum it all in one word," wrote Royce, "teaching is an art. Therefore there is no science of education . . . But, on the other hand, if the teacher wants aid from the scientific spirit, and counsel from scientific education, there stands ready to his hand such assistance as, above all, psychology has to offer to the educator who desires to become a living observer of the minds of children, and such assistance, too, as ethics may suggest to the man who is strong enough to grapple with deeper problems."

The next thirty years were to disprove Royce's statement and to establish the fact that, while the practice of education is an art, the foundations for its successful pursuit rest on scientific bases. In spite of the discouraging attitude of colleges and universities to the study of education, the view was soon accepted that a modern university must be an "institution where any person can find instruction in any study," and that from the standpoint of the public the scientific study of education is as urgent as the study of law, medicine, and engineering. It was still necessary, however, and at the beginning of the period no easy task, to prove that the study of education included more than the mere preparation of teachers. The keynote of the new movement was probably sounded by Dean J. E. Russell when in 1900 he wrote that "University departments of education have as their special function the investigation of educational foundations, the interpretation of educational ideals, the invention of educational methods, and the application of educational principles. The science of education . . . needs to be developed and made over to fit modern conditions." In 1896–97 the material was not available to carry out such a program. Although 220 out of 432 institutions were reported by the United States Commissioner of Education as offering courses in pedagogy, these consisted only of "elements of theory and practice of teaching," or of "psychology, history of education, child study, and school management," or of "the science, art, and history of education." At best the work hardly rose above the standards of the regular normal schools. Not only did the subject lack content and rely on borrowing extensively from other fields of science, themselves still young, but few specialists were available to teach it. So long as the subjects consisted mainly of theory which was little more than sophisticated practice, or was based on a few principles of psychology which on the whole had little bearing and applicability in the classroom, or derived its aims and ends from a metaphysical philosophy unrelated to the needs of a developing society, its claim to scientific character could not be established. Neither the formalism of Herbart nor the mysticism of Froebel furnished the basis for further progress, but that progress was demanded is indicated by the prevalence during the last decade of the nineteenth century and the early years of the twentieth of a kaleidoscope of changing fads and fancies, each guaranteed to solve the problem of education — until the next appeared. That the subject of education did ultimately emerge from the realm of tradition and vague expectations and fulfill the vision that was in those who, like Dean Russell, early saw the possibilities of a scientific basis for it, was due largely to the stimulus derived from the faith of the American people in education.

The Public and Education

The most striking difference between the administration of education in the United States and in European countries is the absence of a centralized authority. Constitutionally the direction of education is left to each state. Since, however, this direction was, and in many states still is, but lightly exercised, education becomes a matter of local concern. To this fact is due the great variation in educational progress throughout the country, but while it is responsible for standards in certain sections lower than those that prevail under more centralized governments, it has also been responsible for the attainment of standards considerably in advance of those that prevail elsewhere. This point was shrewdly brought out by Sir Joshua Fitch, who wrote, in 1901,

There is no uniformity in the methods or machinery of education in the states. But in its stead there prevails much of the local patriotism, which makes each of the leading communities proud of its own institutions, and keenly solicitous to produce such examples of good work as may prove worthy of imitation in other states and cities . . . Hence America may be regarded as a laboratory in which educational experiments are being tried out on a great scale, under conditions exceptionally favorable to the encouragement of inventiveness and fresh enthusiasm, and to the discovery of new methods and new truths.

Such experimentation and enthusiasm, however, are due not to the desire for novelty; they have their roots in the popular attitude to education. Without a centralized authority to which to look for direction and guidance, local communities were compelled to seek their own educational salvation. Out of this variety of standards and experimentation based on local initiative and independence, leadership in education went from time to time to the most progressive and resulted in a search for and encouragement of a more scientific study of all phases of education.

Democracy and Education

Fundamentally the essence of American education rests on a demand for equality of opportunity for every boy and girl for the best possible types of education. The absence of social stratification, with opportunities for advancement through education mainly, furnishes for the American educator one of the most searching problems with which the European educators have not been called upon to deal until recently. The system has to provide not merely two or three types of education, but types to suit the needs and abilities of each individual. The absence of one type of education for the masses and another for the leaders has made it incumbent on the student of education to make every year of schooling as rich and fruitful as possible. The problem of education is thus to train good citizens and at the same time to furnish freedom for individual development. In the secondary field the fact that the secondary schools are open to all has given rise to a new situation to which the traditional conceptions of a liberal education are no longer applicable, a problem that is further complicated by the fact that such education must look to the needs of an industrial and commercial society. The traditional views on culture are thus in the melting pot, and a new conception must be evolved suited to modern needs and modern conditions. Both elementary and secondary education have in their recent development demanded a new orientation of educational aims and values and a sounder and more reliable psychology of individual differences, new principles of curriculum-making, and more effective methods of instruction.

Professionalization of Education

A further problem was set by a demand from the public for better results. It was felt with the increasing cost of education, which set in at the beginning of the present century, that the schools did not accomplish what they set out to perform. Many pupils did not advance through the schools; many dropped out before completing the minimum expected even in elementary education. This demand directed attention to a reëxamination of aims, processes, and methods, and in turn posited the development of a scientific attitude and scientific methods of investigation and research. Allied to this problem and equally influential in leading to a similar demand for scientific inquiry was the changing attitude on discipline. A society founded on faith in individual freedom refused to tolerate a type of discipline in the schools which rested on obedience to authority. Hence the task devolved on the educator to discover a substitute to replace external pressure and the imposition of the teacher's will.

From another aspect another influence was brought to bear on the student of education to approach his subject scientifically. Education rests on popular control and free discussion with great local freedom. The faith in education is widespread, but the educational administrator can only turn this to account if he brings to his task not merely a knowledge of education but an equally sound and thorough equipment in the principles of administration. Since educational progress rests on popular will and consent, the administrator must understand his public and educate it up to new standards, and in a society where business efficiency is one of the cardinal virtues he must be no less efficient in the conduct of his office than the director of a large industrial concern spending an equal amount of money. Education has become one of the largest enterprises of the country for the management of which mere empiricism and routine will not suffice. A new field has thus been opened in the second half of the period under discussion, which requires a sound equipment not only in framing educational aims and policies but also in the principles of management and administration.

The attitude of the American people to the universities, and especially to those that are maintained by public taxation, has resulted in a demand for service which has given them a new status in national life, barely realized in the European universities during the War. The agricultural colleges and experiment stations have for many years devoted themselves to the task of bringing their scientific knowledge and equipment to bear on the practical work of the farmer. A similar function has been expected of the departments or schools of education in colleges and universities, a task which has had the advantage of keeping such departments in close touch with practical everyday problems of the teacher and administrator and has provided them in turn with extensive laboratories both for experimentation and research. The study of education was thus saved from becoming academic and cultivating idols of the den.

Finally, as a result of improving standards in the training of teachers, higher salaries, greater security of tenure, and the establishment of pensions, the occupation of teaching has changed from a craft to a profession. It may at once be admitted that improvement in these respects has not been uniform, that many thousands of teachers are still inadequately prepared, that annual appointments still prevail, and that salaries are grudgingly paid, but the fact remains that the tendency is strongly in the direction of professionalization. This development has been at once the result and the cause of the improved status of education as a professional study. Nowhere is this more obvious than in the recent program of educational associations, national, state, and local, which have assumed an increasingly technical character and, as was recently noted by an English observer, give little attention, as contrasted with English organization, to questions of group welfare. The absence of stratification within the different grades of teaching and the opportunity open to every serious student of education have both stimulated progressive study of education as the chief avenue for advancement. The same effect has been achieved by the slow but gradual disappearance of "politics" from the conduct of educational affairs. At the same time the teacher is being given greater participation in the administration of professional matters; even though this may be provided legally in but few systems, the day when courses of study and methods are prescribed from above is gradually disappearing. Such encouragement of initiative, with promotion made dependent on improved training and study, has stimulated the establishment throughout the country of institutions for the advanced study of education.

Teachers in Service

The past twenty-five years have witnessed a radical change in the improvement of teachers in service. At the beginning of the period the teachers' institute was still popular, though ineffective. Offered for but a few days each year, the courses of such institutes were haphazard, unorganized, and unconnected frequently with the requirements of class-room procedure, with inspirational lectures and entertainments to offset the meagerness of the programs. Their professional content and value were slight because teachers came unprepared and were not expected to show any results. While the short-period institutes have survived, their character has changed; the work has become more highly technical and specialized to meet the needs of particular groups of teachers and with a special bearing on the problems in which the teachers are daily interested.

Institutes are, however, being replaced by opportunities for more intensive study conducted in some cases by teachers' associations, in others in connection with local normal schools, teachers' colleges, and education departments of universities. The work here offered, while not restricted to professional studies, largely revolves round these. It may include cultural courses, but in general covers courses in methods in special subjects, the organization of the curriculum, training for positions as principals and supervisors, and professional studies in general, such as principles of teaching, philosophy of education, psychology, and tests and measurements. While much of this work is of an undergraduate character, it serves not merely to improve the service of the teacher but to promote a professional attitude, and to prepare for further advanced work.

The effect of such organizations for the improvement of teachers in service becomes obvious in the increase of teachers attending summer schools maintained by normal schools, teachers' colleges, and universities. The long summer vacation combined with a growing practice of local boards to subsidize the attendance of their teachers either by scholarships or bonuses or by increases in salary contingent on successful work in the courses pursued, has increased the enrollment of summer schools in many cases beyond the capacity of the institutions to deal satisfactorily with the large numbers that present themselves. In 1921 a total of 253,111 students, the majority of them teachers, attended summer schools in 410 institutions; of these 241 were universities and degree-granting colleges, attended by 143,154 students. Here again the work is predominantly of an undergraduate character, although a large proportion of the students attend for graduate study. The majority of the courses selected are professional. Whatever the nature of the studies, however, and whatever the standards, the distinguishing feature is that the teacher acquires the habit of further study and the supply of students serves both to raise the standards of professional attainment, and by its wide ramifications in which practice and theory react upon each other, the professional study of education is constantly vitalized and compelled to justify itself by its practical applicability. As in engineering and medicine, the pressure of practical situations, which are brought to a focus in the needs of teachers in service, has prevented the professional study of education from becoming too academic. It would be difficult to find in any other profession or in any other country, except in England and Scotland where similar work has recently been begun, such intense desire, as shown by teachers in summer schools, to keep abreast of the latest developments in their subject.

The stimulus obtained from the "refresher" courses in summer schools, local institutions, and extension work is further strengthened by the enlistment of teachers in the revision and improvement of courses of study and in other ways in which their practical experience is helpful, by the increasingly frequent publication of official circulars and magazines dealing with current movements in education, and by the coöperation of teachers with local or university bureaus of research.

The greatest obstacle to the development of a profession of teaching at the beginning of the period under consideration was the absence of anything to encourage the exercise of initiative on the part of the teacher. Originating at a time when the facilities for training were inadequate, a system of local centralization developed in which the superintendent undertook to prescribe with meticulous detail not merely the course of study but also the methods of instruction. The result frequently was rigid uniformity within any one system, a tradition, which like the system of payment by results in England, long hampered educational progress even after the requirement of normal school training had been established in the larger areas. The change came but gradually and is not yet generally prevalent. Teachers are, however, being given more opportunities than formerly to coöperate in the drafting of courses of study and greater initiative in the employment of methods of instruction.

Although formal agencies have been established in eighty-six school systems for the organization of such channels of coöperation, the informal selection by the superintendent of committees of teachers of recognized ability for specific purposes has been found more effective than the elected teachers' councils. The important contribution of such systems of coöperation lies in the improvement of professional standards and in the promotion of professional study. If teachers are to enjoy opportunities to make available their knowledge and experience, it follows that such contributions can only be of value and carry weight if based on a thorough appreciation not merely of the problems involved but of the need of a scientific attitude in education.

It may be objected that, with more than 150,000 untrained and relatively unprepared teachers employed in the schools of the country, it is premature even to-day to talk of the professionalization of teachers. But, as Sir Michael Sadler has pointed out, democracy in its advance presents a ragged edge; the great hope of a democracy, and particularly a democracy without a centralized authority, lies in experimentation and variation, and the advance so far made by those teachers who are in the van of progress marks the route yet to be traveled but free from the handicaps and obstacles encountered by the pioneers.

Agencies for Research and Investigation

The absence of a centralized national authority, while it has had the advantage of placing the responsibility for educational progress on local bodies, meant also the absence of an agency for setting standards and for investigation. The only guidance and direction available were afforded by a comparison of the efforts and results of the work achieved by the local systems themselves. The great service of the United States Bureau of Education, handicapped though it is by a lack of compulsory powers, has lain largely in the collection of information on the progress of education throughout the country and in directing attention through its reports and bulletins to progressive movements in all branches and fields of education both here and abroad. Early in the course of the past quarter-century the need was felt for something more than generalized reports and statistics to enable the school systems to evaluate their achievements and defects. Professor Royce had already advocated, in the nineties, the appointment of consulting psychologists to devise and recommend better methods of instruction; and this suggestion was repeated by Chancellor in one of the earliest books on school administration. In 1905 Professor G. H. Locke urged the importance of the investigation of school systems by outside agencies — "a thorough study of the system of schools in a city, its organization and administration, its curriculum, indeed the methods by which the city undertakes to afford opportunities for education to its boys and girls." Such investigations, he suggested, might properly be undertaken by departments of education in colleges and universities — a practice which would at the same time keep such departments in close touch with practice. A similar suggestion was put forward in 1907 by Professor M. V. O'Shea — "What we need to do is to see to it that departments of education are first of all investigating institutions."

Excellent though these suggestions were they were compelled to wait for their success for the development of an adequate technique that would raise the results of any investigations above the level of mere personal opinion. Nothing had as yet been done in discussing in the field of educational administration such questions as the standards of buildings and equipment, the selection of textbooks, reports and accounting, educational finance, rating of teachers, and similar questions. Statistical technique in educational psychology was in its infancy and little had yet been accomplished in devising standard tests and measurements. Nor was there any definite agreement on the aims and purposes of education, although guidance was to come shortly from the work and writings of John Dewey. Investigations by external authorities were, however, beginning to be demanded, in some cases by the public in order to discover the status of their school systems, in others by the superintendents and teachers, in self-defense. The first survey, made in Montclair in 1911, represented the personal opinion of one expert; within less than four years the character of surveys was changed and personal opinion, however expert, yielded to objective standards based on a completely developed technique of tests and measurements; quantitative methods were substituted for qualitative methods and personal opinions, and while the results are not yet sufficiently exten-sive and advanced to furnish the basis for a clearer state-ment of educational aims and ideals, the procedure of the classroom has been greatly affected by the movement.

The development of the survey as a method of educational accounting and control is dealt with elsewhere in this book. From the point of view of the present chapter its signifi-cance has lain in the stimulus that it has given to and the demands that it levies upon the student of education in all its branches — administration, psychology, methods, curric-ula, and so on.   Educational theory can no longer be based on authority and tradition ; it must be related to practical needs and must constantly be infused with a critical and inquiring attitude of mind.   The survey movement is the American substitute for governmental inspection ; but sum-marizes in itself all the differences that distinguish a system of education centrally organized and slowly responsive to changing conceptions and requirements in education from a system that is based on variety and local initiative, that is self-critical and perhaps too alert and too sensitive to the varying demands of rapidly changing social condi-tions.   Whatever the weaknesses, however, the survey method has changed the professional study of education from an academic and theoretical study to a laboratory science. In a more real sense than was ever dreamed of by Sir Joshua Fitch in 1900, the schools and school systems of the country have become the experimental stations of a vast array of organizations for the study of education ; and experimenta-tion by trial and error methods is being replaced by experi-mentation under the control of scientific methods.

The conduct of surveys was in the early stages intrusted to a few individuals, but in the later development it has be-come an important coöperative enterprise, requiring a large force of collaborators, a long period of time, and the expenditure of large sums of money. These requirements were in many cases met by the entry into the field of educational inquiry of wealthy private foundations. Thus the General Education Board, established in 1902, has conducted a number of local and state surveys and has contributed considerably by a wise expenditure of funds to the improvement of education in the South ; the Carnegie Foundation for the Advancement of Teaching, established in 1906, has conducted important surveys in a number of fields — standardization of colleges, legal and medical education, the professional preparation of teachers, and the organization of education in a state. The Russell Sage Foundation, established in 1907, very early gave a much-needed impetus to the quantitative and objective study of education and has made several important surveys. Finally, one of the youngest of these foundations, the Commonwealth Fund, established in 1918, is subsidizing valuable studies in educational finance, the organization of the content in several subjects, and investigations in educational psychology. The developments of the last decade have justified the anticipation of Professor J. H. Tufts in 1909 that "if we can show that we want to do something worth doing, that we know how to set about it, and that we are broad enough in our vision to look beyond our machinery to the larger personal and social welfare, means for investigation will not be wanting."

Such foundations, however, are interested in the main in pointing the way and in opening up and stimulating new fields of inquiry. There still remains the desirability of establishing permanent agencies of investigation and research. The more progressive communities in the United States are ready to welcome the scientific collection and interpretation of statistical and other data referring to schools, while trained educators are equally ready for opportunities in the practical field for scientific research, the results of which may be utilized for the formulation of educational policies. The occasional survey, while it was of great value, only pointed the way to the creation of permanent local bureaus of reference and research. New York City was the earliest to establish such a Division of Reference and Research in 1913 and has been followed by a number of other important centers, both city and state. The character of the work of such bureaus varies; in some cases the whole field of education is covered; in others only the administrative and statistical aspects; in others again only measurements and tests. The university departments of education, particularly in the state-maintained institutions, have also recognized their opportunities and obligations in this direction and both informally through individual members of their faculties and through formally organized bureaus have entered the field of coöperative research in education. In this way they serve as centers for the direction of inquiries into problems submitted to them by local school systems, for the collecting and interpretation of data, and for the publication and dissemination of results; in a number of instances opportunities for purely experimental work are furnished by schools attached to such departments. The first bureau of this type was established in 1913 at the University of Oklahoma and has been followed by the creation of bureaus in other universities and in teachers' colleges.

The work of both city and state bureaus and of university bureaus of research culminated in the organization in 1916 of a National Association of Directors of Educational Research, now the Educational Research Association, whose aims are the promotion of the practical use of quantitative methods in educational research and the improvement of the efficiency of educational administration, supervision, and teaching by means of scientific methods.

Only a reference is necessary to the numerous professional associations for the promotion and discussion of educational research. A comparison of programs of the societies that were in existence at the beginning of the past quarter-century and at the end of this period will serve to indicate the road and distance that the study of education has traveled. The Proceedings of the National Education Association, of the Department of Superintendence, and of the National Society for the Study of Education tell their own story. More recently there have been established the National Society of College Teachers of Education, the Educational Research Association, Section L, of the American Association for the Advancement of Science, the National Conference on Educational Method, and numerous local societies, all devoted to the advancement of the study of education on a scientific basis, to the improvement of all branches of education, and ultimately to placing the vocation of teaching on a professional footing.

The Formal Study of Education

The account of the study of education up to this point has dealt in the main with the factors that contributed to its development as a result of the public attitude to education, and of the practical demands of the schools themselves. It is difficult in dealing with any applied science to disentangle the share contributed from practical needs and situations and the share derived from pure science. So in the field of education it is not a simple matter to apportion equitably the stimulus that has been given to its development in the last twenty-five years by the necessities of classroom procedure and of administration on the one hand and the formal organization of and research into the different branches of the subject that have taken place in the universities. It is not necessary here to indicate the growth in the number of graduate schools of education, the number of courses offered, and the enrollment of students. From the point of view of this chapter, greater interest attaches to the development of the content and subject matter subsumed under the general term of education.

At the beginning of the period under discussion the study of education, whether in normal schools or in colleges, was limited to a few fields and with very little differentiation. Virtually the only specialization possible was between preparation for service in the elementary or in the secondary field. The subjects of study were included sometimes under the blanket term "pedagogy," sometimes "school management and pedagogy"; in a few places courses in history of education and psychology or child study were gradually beginning to appear. No provision was yet made for training the supervisor, principal, superintendent, or any of the other specialized workers in education; training for these fields was to be obtained by experience. The courses offered by Teachers College, Columbia University, for 1897–98 may be taken as an adequate and representative summary of the status of education as a special study at that time:

Psychology and General Method
Advanced Psychology and General
  Method
Child Study
Primary Methods
History of Education (2 courses)
Philosophy of Education and
  School Management
School Supervision and School
  Management
Elementary Methods
Principles of Art Education
Methods of Teaching English
  Literature

Methods of Teaching English
  Composition
The Teaching of History in
  Secondary Schools
Methods of Teaching Mathematics in Elementary and
  Secondary Schools
Kindergarten Department
  (11 courses)
Methods of Teaching Domestic Science
Methods of Teaching Sewing

Within ten years these courses had become so differentiated that the following list could be compiled in 1905–06:

Child Study
Genetic Psychology
Mental Development
Educational Psychology
Principles of Education
Philosophy of Education
Educational Theory
History of Education
Educational Classics
General Methods

Special Methods
School Management
School Supervision
Elementary Education
Secondary Schools
School Systems
Contemporary Education
School Law
School Administration
School Hygiene

With these were continued the courses in methods of special subjects.

Five years later it became possible to consider seriously the problem of research within the field of education. Hitherto the various studies were isolated and unconnected subjects within the larger field.   After 1910 the field gradually became so wide and its subdivisions so highly specialized that no student could be expected to master them all.   The rapid development of facilities for the graduate study of education leading to advanced degrees may be said to have begun at that time.   The reasons have already been suggested in other parts of this chapter.   The publication of Monroe's *Textbook in the History of Education* in 1905 had already indicated the possibilities in that field and had stimulated a number of special studies and contributions, which gradually led to the expansion of the subject into a number of highly diversified courses, including new research into the historical development of education both in this country and elsewhere and establishing the value of the historical outlook as an important method of approach to the study of principles.   The work of John Dewey opened up a new field of inquiry into the philosophical and social bases underlying education and, while it has not stimulated any considerable contributions in philosophy of education, it has influenced most of the investigations made in the last decade or more on principles of education, the course of study, and methods of instruction. At the same time this field of study and inquiry has been compelled to take into account the extensive contributions which have been made since 1902 by the psychologists, for whom a new field was opened up by Professor Thorndike both in educational psychology and in educational statistics. An entirely new subject has been added to the list, as a result of Dewey's emphasis on the social aspects of education, under the title of Educational Sociology — an inquiry into social and group life and its effect on educational aims and purposes.

The same period has also witnessed the development of a specialized study of educational administration, which resulted from the revelation of the general ignorance of such matters as the classification of pupils, retardation and elimination, school finance, adequate accounting and reports, and in general the absence of a suitable relation between the hours spent for education and the products of the schools. The practical demands for expert guidance, as revealed by the surveys, have led to the development of specialized training for expert administrators and superintendents in such problems as the following:

Problems of teaching, involving the study of methods employed with a view to improving the results achieved; problems of supervision with the confident expectation that the efficiency of teachers might be increased through the methods which were employed; the classification of children; the fiscal administration of schools, including cost accounting, budget-making, salaries and salary schedules, the distribution of state school funds; the development of adequate systems of taxation; the development of building programs; studies of equipment to be provided; the setting up of an adequate attendance service; the methods of handling school publicity; the installation of an adequate system of records and reports; the development of a set of rules for boards of education; the revision of sections of city charters dealing with education; the codification of state laws for education; the development of an adequate health service; the reorganization of curricula for the training of teachers; the organization of a rural community in relation to a modern rural school; and the like. (Based on G. D. Strayer, in *Studies in Education*, Educational Monographs of the Society of College Teachers of Education, Number XI, 1922, p. 98.)

The opportunities for specialization in elementary, secondary, and rural education have similarly been expanded and fructified by the recent developments in psychology, philosophy of education, and social studies. Each field has been analyzed in turn, its needs and problems have been appraised, and technical courses have been elaborated for the specialists. In another direction, the practical-mindedness of the American public and a desire to give a suitable equipment to each boy and girl for a life career have led to the development of specialized training for teachers and organizers of vocational and agricultural education and in home economics, all of which have been specially stimulated and fostered by federal subsidy.

The emergency created by the War was for the nation as a whole more revealing than any survey; the mass of facts collected in connection with the organization of the army and other activities revealed deficiencies in American education, hitherto suspected, perhaps, but not statistically verified. The lack of preparation of a large percentage of the teachers, the importance and needs of rural education, the prevalence of physical defects and inadequate provision for health education, the problems of immigrant and adult illiteracy, and the low standard of education in general were revealed, and, while alarming, have had the effect of emphasizing the need of further study and improved training both of teachers in general and of experts in the different fields here mentioned.

What this specialization in the various branches of education has resulted in may be indicated by the organization of the College of Education of the University of Minnesota, which may be regarded as typical of the organization in other state universities and a number of the larger private institutions, offering both undergraduate and graduate work. The following departments are there maintained: history and philosophy of education; educational administration; theory and practice of teaching; trade and industrial education; agricultural education; home economics education; art education; physical education; public school music; bureau of educational investigation.

The following list of courses offered by the School of Education of Teachers College, Columbia University, is presented for purpose of comparison with the courses listed earlier and to indicate the ramifications in the professional study of education as organized to-day. The various branches may be found in many other institutions, and, although the number of courses is not so extensive elsewhere, the general range and scope are representative.

History and Principles of Education
History of Education
Play Materials for Young Children
Experimental Playground
Plays, Games, and Dances of Early Childhood
Beginnings of Music for Young Children
Beginnings of Fine and Industrial Arts
Biological Materials for Elementary Schools
Regional Studies in Science
The Library in the Modern School
Teaching English to Adult Immigrants
Teaching English to Foreigners
Literature of Upper Elementary Grades
Literature of the Primary Grades
Geography for Teachers and Supervisors in Elementary Grades
Phonetics
American History for Elementary Teachers and Supervisors
Teaching of Civics in Secondary Schools
Household Arts for Rural Communities
Industrial Arts for the Elementary Grades
Industrial Arts for Social and Religious Workers
Industrial Arts for Special Classes
Teaching Industrial Arts in Elementary Schools
Mathematics of the Elementary School
Teaching Applied Mathematics
Teaching Applied Mathematics in Evening Schools
Educational Hygiene
Health Education
Practice Teaching in Connection with Education

Hygiene of Childhood and Adolescence
Principles and Practices of Scoutcraft
Recreational Education
Recreational Leadership and Games
Clubcraft
Club Leadership
Principles of Education Administration
Consolidation and the Rural High School
Democracy and Education in Europe
Problems of Advisers of Women and Girls
Educational Publicity
Theory and Practice of Teaching in Elementary Schools
Principles and Practice of Teaching in Elementary Schools
Measurement and Experimentation in Elementary Education
Illustrative Lessons in Citizenship
Supervision in the Elementary School
Socializing the Elementary School Curriculum
The Technique of Teaching
Methods of Teaching in Special Classes
Observation Experimentation and Teaching in Special Classes
Organization and Supervision of Special Classes
Subject Matter and Methods of the Primary School
History of the Family as a Social Institution
Education of Women
History of Education in United States
Observation of Teaching of Young Children
Fundamentals of First Grade
Practice in Teaching of Young Children
Conservation of the Child and the Home
Philosophy of Education
Foundations of Method
Ethics and Educational Problems
Educational Psychology
Psychology of Childhood
Psychology of Adolescence
Psychology of Exceptional Children
The Psychology of Thinking
Introductory Course in Mental Tests
Psychology of Habit, Skill, Practice, and Memory
Mental Measurements
Methods in Religious Education
Field Work in Social-Religious Centers
The Use of the Bible in Religious Education
Problems in Missionary Education
Rural Education
Rural Education and Country Life
Field Work: Rural Education and Rural Sociology
Rural Sociology and Economics
Field Work in Rural Community Surveys

The Preparation of Rural Teachers
Rural School Supervision
General Methods for Secondary Schools
Teaching in Junior High Schools
Supervised Observation and Teaching
Teaching Secondary School Subjects
Experimental Teaching in Secondary Schools
Improvement of Instruction in Secondary Schools
Problems in Administration for Heads of Secondary School Departments
Administrative Problems of the High School
Organization and Administration of Secondary Education
Organization and Administration of the Junior High School
Extra-Curricular Activities in Junior and Senior High Schools
Social Organization of the Secondary School
Field Studies in Extra-Curricular High School Activities
Introduction to Sociology
Introductory Educational Sociology
Practical Applications of Sociology
Sociological Foundations of Civic Education
Education in Citizenship for Foreign-born
Fundamentals in Civic Education
Vocations for Girls and Women
Vocational Education
Vocational Education in High Schools
Administration of Vocational Education
Vocational Guidance
Prevocational Training in Junior and Senior High Schools
Science in Secondary Schools
Teaching Biological Science in Secondary Schools
Teaching Physics in Secondary Schools
Laboratory Projects in Automobile Mechanics
Teaching General Science in Secondary Schools
Teaching Chemistry in Secondary Schools
Problems in Teaching Science in Secondary Schools
Teaching English in Secondary Schools
Teaching English in Elementary and Normal Schools
Practicum.   Teaching English in Secondary Schools
Supervision of English in Secondary Schools
Experiment and Research in Teaching English
College Teaching of English Composition
Development of Theory of Composition
Teaching French in Secondary Schools
Teaching and Supervision of Geography in Secondary Schools
Regional Geography
Teaching Foreign Languages in Secondary Schools
Problems in Modern Language Method
Teaching History in Secondary Schools
Experimental Lessons in History
Education for Citizenship

Teaching History in Normal Schools
Practicum. Literature of American History
Practicum. Industrial and Social History in Schools
Teaching and Supervision of Latin in Secondary Schools
Advanced Course in Cæsar and Vergil
Teaching Algebra in Secondary Schools
Teaching Geometry in Secondary Schools
Advanced Course in Teaching and Supervision of Mathematics
Practicum in Health Education
Administration of Hygiene and Physical Education
Major Course for Superintendents of Schools
Research Course for School Superintendents
Practicum. Cost and Financing of Public Education
Practicum. Comparative Education
Major Course for Elementary and Primary Principals and Supervisors
   and Critic Teachers in Training Schools
Criticism and Supervision of Instruction in Elementary Schools
Measurement and Experimentation in Elementary Education
Experimental Supervision and Teaching of Classroom Studies
Supervision in Primary Grades
Major Course for Normal School Teachers, Supervisors, and Administra-
   tors
Research Course in Elementary Supervision
Research Course in Professional Education of Teachers
History of Education
Historical Development of Modern Elementary Education
Historical Development of Public Education
Practicum. History of Education in the United States
Historical Study of the Problems of Secondary Education
Practicum. Current Problems in Supervision and Training of Teachers
   of Young Children
Study of Curricula for Young Children
Philosophy of Education
Practicum. Philosophy of Education
Practicum. Historical Relations of Philosophy and Education
Major Course in Mental and Educational Tests
Practicum. Statistical Methods in Education
Advanced Educational Statistics
Clinical Psychology
Mental Adjustments
Mental and Vocational Tests
Reconstruction of the Elementary School Curriculum
Reconstruction of Junior and Senior High School Curriculum
Psychology of the Elementary School Subjects
Educational Psychology — Advanced Course
Practicum. Problems of Social-Religious Work
The Curriculum of the Church School
Supervision of Religious Instruction
Principles of Religious Education

Practicum in Religious Education
Introduction to the Psychology of the Christian Life
Problems in Missionary Education
Major Course for Rural Community Workers
Major Course for Directors of Rural Education in Normal Schools and
    Teachers Colleges
Major Course for Supervisors of Rural Schools
Major Course for High School Principals
A Research Course for High School Principals
Administrative Problems of the High School
Practicum. Educational Sociology
Community Socialization
Applied Sociology : Special Education for Adults and Community Groups
Public Opinion. Adult Education
Sociological Foundations of Curricula
Problems of Curricula
Training Supervisors for Americanization of Foreigners
Major Course in Administration of Vocational Education
Research Course for Administrators of Vocational Education
Practicum. Vocational Guidance
Seminar. Historical Foundations of Modern Education
Seminar. Elementary Education
Seminar in Normal School Education
Seminar. Philosophy of Education
Seminar. Educational Psychology
Seminar in the Teaching of Mathematics
Seminar in Religious Education
Seminar. Rural Education
Seminar. Rural Sociology
Seminar. Secondary Education
Seminar. Educational Sociology

The study of education has emerged from its swaddling
clothes in the period covered by this chapter ; neglected and
hidden under the ægis of other subjects or departments,
education has become in most universities the field through
which the greatest service is done to society. Statistical
presentations might have indicated the number of students,
both undergraduate and graduate, engaged in this study
and the amount and cost of buildings and equipment devoted to its pursuit, but nothing speaks so eloquently as
the list of courses here given of the vast field for human endeavor that has been made explicit in the past twenty-five
years. The schools need well-prepared teachers, but society

needs still more the guidance and direction of specialists and experts, and if faith is to be cultivated in them, it can only come, as it is more and more coming, through the existence and cultivation of a scientific study of the subjects that they profess.   This has been made possible in less than half of the twenty-five years here discussed.   If only passing reference has been made to the dark spots that still exist in education in the United States, this has not been done to glorify the advances made in the study of education, but in the belief that the instruments already perfected will remove the deficiencies that still remain, and find new fields to conquer.

REFERENCES

College and university catalogues.
MONROE, PAUL — *The Cyclopedia of Education;* Macmillan, 1911–13.
     (See article under "Education, Academic Study of.")
National Society for the Study of Education — *Yearbooks.*
National Society of College Teachers of Education — *Monographs.*
United States Bureau of Education — *Reports of the Commissioner of Education.*

CHAPTER III

TENDENCIES IN EDUCATIONAL PHILOSOPHY

BY

WILLIAM H. KILPATRICK

TEACHERS COLLEGE, COLUMBIA UNIVERSITY

CHAPTER III

TENDENCIES IN EDUCATIONAL PHILOSOPHY

Introduction

The philosophy of education will here mean the determined effort to find out what education should do in the face of contradictory demands coming to it from the deeply rooted but relatively distinct interests of life. As life presents ever new phases, so education will face very varying demands. The philosophy of education will accordingly vary much with the times. Since each decision, however, must take due account of the whole of experience, the philosophy of education will seek to base itself as best it can on such views of the functioning of experience as will furnish a maximum of guidance. In spite, then, of the great variation due to shifting problems, there will be for any one system of such philosophy a relatively abiding body of attitudes and points of view which will enter largely into the consideration and solution of each new conflict as it arises. Finally, to the degree that a consistent point of view can be attained, the school system should consistently exemplify this view. The history here undertaken will accordingly take account of three intermingling constituents: of the new problems that have successively arisen during the period under review, of the new points of view that have emerged, and of the effort to develop a unified and consistent system of thought and procedure.

The Traditional Background of the Study

Before tracing the successive demands and consequent changes, it will be well to ask, What was the situation at the opening of our period, the last decade of the nineteenth century? What were, at the time, the dominant points of view? The answer is not difficult. The oldest substratum point of view of American education was of course the common stock of custom and procedure brought from the old world. In this the school was closely associated with the church. The coercive measures of school discipline and the stress on memorizing fitted well with the prevailing doctrine of total depravity. Naïve and uncritical acceptance of established custom was perhaps the dominant note. Beginning about a century ago and lasting well-nigh to the nineties Pestalozzianism in varying form broke into this established custom and in some measure dissipated the prevailing uncritical attitude. Thus it was increasingly demanded that pupils "understand" what they "learned." For this "object lessons" were devised. Education was conceived as a process of "leading out," not of "pouring in." The conception of "methods" and devices as aids to teaching became common. From various causes the harsher measures of coercion were being mitigated; but so far there was no deep-lying reconstruction.

The Beginnings of a Scientific Attack

The decade before our period opens saw a variety of influences and movements tending powerfully to break up the uncritical acceptance of custom. Herbert Spencer's fame, then at its height, called emphatic attention to his previously published essays on education. His insistence on science and on the theory of punishment by natural consequences influenced many. His discussion of comparative values helped largely to introduce a term and conception destined to have great influence. Froebel's writings, by their striking opposition to the existing ideas and practices, had effects more far-reaching than the number of the kindergartens then established would indicate. Whatever else may be said, Froebel had a point of view, an inclusive system based on a philosophy, in other words a philosophy of education worked out into a correlative system of procedure. The very idea challenged thought. Even those who reacted most violently either against Froebel's philosophy or against his educational system must be impressed with the connection between the two. In so far as this was true, here was an ideal which even his opponents could enjoy. Peculiarly stimulating also was Froebel's idea of a school without books. Education and schooling separate things? Once the idea was clearly disengaged, it would not down. Something must be done about it. The almost holy zeal of the Froebelians assisted much to increase these effects.

Two American reformers stand out in this seed-bed decade, and later, as forces which helped greatly in the ferment — Francis W. Parker and G. Stanley Hall. Both had studied in Germany, and so had got outside our customary point of view. Each in his own way began to stir American education, each calling attention to a factor increasingly embodied since in the American viewpoint. Colonel Parker, first near Boston and later in Chicago, roused great enthusiasm by showing what could be done if child nature were treated sympathetically. President Hall was more the scholar. He emphasized the study of psychology as a practical agency in education. Child study, the psychology of childhood and adolescence, the accumulation of life data, even his emphasis on recapitulation — these had their due part in putting the study of education on a scientific basis. To appraise his scientific contribution is for present purposes not necessary. But America believes, as does no other country, that education must be based on a study of psychology. That this is so is due in no small degree to the influence of President Hall. These two men thus from different angles helped materially to make education an object of serious study, which is perhaps the greatest single achievement to be recorded in this account.

Herbartianism

Among the formative influences of the period under consideration none is more pronounced perhaps than Herbartianism as it was brought to this country by Charles De Garmo and the brothers Charles and Frank McMurry. Each had studied abroad at Jena and Leipzig, the great centers of German "pedagogy," at the time when the prestige of German thought stood probably at the zenith of its influence in our history. The doctrines of interest and apperception, the culture-epoch theory, and the five formal steps, which these men brought back with them, offered in the aggregate a body of educational thought as simple in conception as it was attractive in theory. Moreover, it worked. If the culture-epoch theory lacked somewhat of supplying a complete curriculum, it helped greatly to enrich the work of the lower grades. And what could be more practical than the five formal steps? Can we wonder that the normal schools, almost with one accord, accepted these as the basis of their lesson plans? As for apperception, it was so evidently true that men only wondered that they had not always preached it. The doctrine of interest too, how simple it all was and how true!

But here came the rub. These things were obviously true only if one looked at them in certain ways. The stiff-necked just wouldn't look at them from the right angle. Disputes arose. In the end it appears clear that the service rendered by the Herbartian movement was not to contribute a permanent deposit of educational theory—no single item of their doctrines remains as they taught it — but rather to stimulate thought. Attacking squarely, as this movement did, so much of what then prevailed, it brought conscious attention to almost the whole range of theory regarding the educative process. To settle the disputes thus raised resort was had to new material. Biology as remade by the doctrine of evolution offered perhaps the richest single source of supply. In the utilization of new materials, as is later indicated, education here made significant advance.

Hegelianism

Hegelianism was another contributing factor in the beginning of our twenty-five year period. Its fame, however, was greater than its influence. Rosenkranz was the outstanding author, as William T. Harris was the outstanding American defender. It seems rather probable that the translation of Rosenkranz made under Dr. Harris's direction gave the term "philosophy of education" its first strong hold in America. The association with "metaphysics" was, however, in later years nearly sufficient to drive the very name "philosophy of education" from American institutions of learning — so great was the reaction when it came. The actual influence of Hegelianism in American study of education was at all times limited, although Dr. Harris was for years probably our most outstanding student of education. He is called by a contributor in Monroe's *The Cyclopedia of Education*, Vol. III, p. 220, "America's first great educational philosopher," and it is there stated of him that "he developed such insight into school problems as was enjoyed by none of his predecessors and by few if any of his contemporaries." Both statements may well be admitted; but it is in this day difficult to understand how one could so stand out in his own time and yet leave so little permanent impression on the present existing body of accepted thought. To say the least, Hegelianism is radically out of harmony with the prevailing temper of present-day inquiry. Certainly among educational students of the present, few seem disposed to acknowledge appreciable indebtedness to this movement.

Dr. Harris did, however, exert influence and certainly for good; but it was with him as with the Herbartians — he contributed more to the ferment of ideas, more to the stimulation of thought, than to the present accepted body of educational theory. His clashes with the Herbartians furnished not a few of the occasions where, as he might have said, it was necessary to transcend both in order to mediate the conflict. The famous dispute over "interest" and "effort" thus called forth Professor Dewey's monograph, *Interest as Related to Will.*[1]

One of Dr. Harris's chief interests was the kindergarten. With the collaboration of Miss Susan E. Blow, there was elaborated a theory of Hegelian Froebelianism which for a goodly number of years virtually dominated in that field. The use of symbolism that was retained in this system and the general metaphysical basis of the system were again points of attack and sources of stimulation to opposed thought. It is a justified anticipation of results, coming in the latter half of our period, to say that in the end the opposition to any and all Hegelianism and symbolism has won the battle and now holds almost undisputed sway. A scientific psychology and the general American rejection of "metaphysics" have carried the day for a theory in keeping with the dominant ideas later to be discussed.

To ask why Hegelianism failed to gain a permanent footing in American educational thought offers an easy introduction to the present prevailing philosophic theory relating to education. No pretense at completeness at this point is made, but two outstanding features will help the further discussion. First, prevailing American thought is suspicious of any system that does not manifest the most cordial rela-

[1] Later rewritten as *Interest and Effort in Education.*

tionships with experimental science and with its immediate and derived procedures for reaching positions worthy of belief. Anything approaching an *a priori* attack is, rightly or wrongly, discredited in advance. Second, the prevailing American temper demands that the ideas presented for its serious consideration shall be such as promise directly or indirectly to help in the solution of its insistent problems. That some regret this tendency is true. That many conceive our insistent problems narrowly is equally true. That most are averse to any sustained effort to take into systematic account all pertinent data is still further true. But the main tendency seems undeniable. Intellectual America has on the whole accepted both these attitudes. It is mainly interested in meeting life's problems. It accepts the procedure of verifiable science as its safest road to reliable thinking. Second only to making education an object of serious study, the gradual acceptance of these two positions as a conscious philosophy constitutes the outstanding feature of the development herein discussed.

The Problems of a Philosophy of Education

With this somewhat lengthy introduction, let us now approach our problem, the tracing of the development of the philosophy of education in the United States within the past twenty-five years.

As defined at the outset the philosophy of education will differ in important respects from any one of the sciences. Such a philosophy functions essentially at conflict points only, and these will change with the march of events. The philosophy of education will thus seem to the scientist to shift its interest with astonishing rapidity ; and what is to him even more disconcerting, its specific decisions will often undergo consideration and perhaps revision. While such shift and revision are inherent in a study that attempts to deal with the contradictory demands of life in a growing world, it does not follow that there is no accumulation of valuable points of view. The contrary is distinctly true. Many of life's problems are both permanent and ever varying. Man remains practically the same. The conditions under which he lives change. Our study then will consider principally two phases, the successive major problems that have presented themselves during the period under consideration, and the accumulation of points of view helpful for their solution. The problems that have presented themselves may in turn be conveniently divided into two groups, those that have come to education from the outside, especially from the world of affairs, and those that have arisen from the inside, particularly from within the world of thought, which has all the while functioned in the philosophy of education, whether consciously or unconsciously. Of course no sharp separation here is either desirable or feasible. The presentation of the problems here made will be so directed as eventually to place in review before us the content of the study as it now presents itself. We begin with the demands that have come from without.

External Influences: Economic Changes

Since the school has come into existence largely to prepare each rising generation for its more adequate participation in society and life, practically every line of human interest and endeavor will make demand on the school. Among the movements characteristic of the modern world none is more outstanding than industrialism and its attendant changes. Its influence on the school was long delayed, but during the period under review this influence in American life came at length to consciousness in a new sense and degree. The growing urbanization of the American people, the steady movement of historic industries from home to factory, the increasing complexity of life meant, on the one hand, new and more numerous demands for adjustment from the young. They meant, on the other hand, the gradual removal of opportunity which first-hand participation and easy observation had formerly granted to youth for making its needed adjustments. Greater demands on the young and fewer opportunities in home and community contacts mean in effect a greatly changed demand on the school. Both the content of school learning and the character of school experience would have to be greatly modified if social life were not greatly to suffer. Curriculum and method must change.

Immigration

But this was not all. The immigrant complicated the situation. History has nowhere else seen a peaceful invasion so numerous, so varied, or so long-continued as that to which this country has been subjected. How to unify the never-ending stream of newcomers into the social body had always been a concern with theorists. Now the problem became acute. Even the man in the street must notice. In the industrial centers school buildings could hardly be erected fast enough to house the incoming numbers. But the real problem lay deeper. Increasingly did the newcomers aggregate themselves into relatively compact masses, in many respects merely transplanting their old life, but often under less healthful social conditions. Transplanted church and newspaper generally used the language of "the old country." A parochial school was introduced, often as a conscious rival to the public schools. The question of unification had become obviously difficult.

Industrial Stratification

Nor is the picture yet complete. Industrialism easily means extremes of wealth and accordingly of culture and outlook. The ever greater immigration increased these differences. Democracy became increasingly difficult of practice. In industrial centers, crowded particularly with the more recent and poorer immigrant workers, there was socially less and less commingling between old and new stocks and both politically and economically more and more opposition between "mass" and "class." Private schools for the wealthy made, from another angle, further inroads on the public schools. These conditions, aggravated by an unusual arrogance of "big business" near the beginning of our period, raised for anxious thought some of the most fundamental questions of life. What about our boasted American democracy? Can it survive the passing of the frontier and the industrial urbanization of our people? What in fact is democracy? Should it not include all social relationships and among them the industrial? What does socialization inherently mean and what is the relation of education? What is the relation of labor and leisure to life itself? Is there a dualism here? What, after all, constitutes the good life; and what can education do? What in fact is the relation between the two? And what about progress? Can we any longer believe in inevitable progress — that easy compound of benevolent theology, easy-going evolution, and pride in a gloriously painted national history?

It is literally true that the conscious philosophy of education as here to be traced largely originated for America just at this tide in American history. Complacency was jarred, as a century and more ago, "out of its dogmatic slumber"; and thought in this country awoke to ask these far-reaching questions. Education became in a new sense and degree self-conscious. In the attempt to answer these questions new points of view were attained, as later discussed, which constitute a worthy addition to the world's stock of ideas. The study of the meaning and function of education in the experience process and in relation to the social progress assumed a new dignity.

Vocational Education

Among the influences of industrialism on social life, few seem more natural, once the idea is suggested, than its demand for "vocational" education. The argument seems easy and convincing that the young should be trained to take their parts in the great economic system. Each person should not only carry his own weight but add besides something to the common economic stock. Productive occupation is obligatory on all. But preparation is necessary, at any rate for many lines of endeavor. Let us then have trade and other vocational schools. But here questions begin to arise. What shall be the relation of such schools and their educational programs to the general programs of the existing public schools? At once demands of "efficiency" and "culture" and citizenship come forward. Are trade schools to turn out "hands"? "Hands" or no, surely they must be efficient. And the advocates of efficiency, questioning whether the needed preparation can be intrusted to the ordinary school system, propose a dual system with business men in charge of the new schools. Their opponents rise and question whether children are to be exploited for the advantage of industry and, more fundamentally still, whether we are trying to perpetuate the *status quo* in industrial relationships. So that what began seemingly as a simple matter of industrial demand and supply turns out to have far-reaching complications, a question that cannot be settled simply by asking the needs of one life interest. The character of the good life, equal participation therein, equal opportunities in education, progress, socialization, the existing economic order, — these are some of the questions implicated. Clearly no partial inquiry by specially interested groups could do justice to such a subject as this. Philosophy of education finds in this one of its insistent current problems.

Social Unrest

Along with a growing industrialism and the fact of great immigration were other factors, some more or less independent, others obviously related. The passing of the frontier — land for settlement practically free for the asking — closed an outlet hitherto available for certain expanding, or "outbreaking," spirits, and increased the pressure especially upon our economic institutions. Equality of opportunity was in a true sense lessened. One main prop of our historic democracy had been removed. It is highly probable that in this we find part of the intenser demand for "radical" treatment of our economic system. These considerations do not mean that the quality of injustice had been changed. From the earliest colonial days great and exasperating inequalities had been present to plague social life. But in the passing of free land a "safety valve" had been removed. The increased pressure here from the one side brought its reaction in opposition, and American "practical" thought began to consider coercion and suppression in a way that seemed to many others a clear reversal of the traditional American attitude. The assassination of President McKinley by a crazed anarchist of outlandish name had already directed attention to a situation that seemed to call for special treatment, and the steps then taken had paved the way for a new and wider acceptance of "strong" measures in the line of legal control. The fact that the unpalatable doctrines were frequently taught by foreigners and generally were aimed at economic reconstruction served to increase the feelings of separation and opposition already described. Constructive opinion turned more consciously to the need of unifying measures and leaned more strongly than ever upon the school as the best agency to accomplish this end. At first this was often a blind and almost mystic faith, but at any rate a common consciousness was being aroused, and more specific thought was being directed as to how the needed unity might reasonably be attained. The problem of the school as a conscious agency of social unification had been added to the pressing problems of a wider and deeper educational theory.

The World War and Social Control

While this was going on, the World War came and increased greatly certain aspects of the strain. All who contemplated the entry of this country into the war on the side with France and England saw the critical danger of divisions here due to the continued maintenance of old world allegiances and antagonisms. The cry against "hyphenism" was raised and much social pressure resulted. With our actual entry into the war, this pressure assumed legal (often illegal) and military forms. Into this situation a further complication was added by the effort of certain "radical" labor groups to profit by the general unsettled condition of affairs. This allowed the advocates of coercion to assume the cloak of patriotism; and under this guise there was an increasing acceptance of the doctrine that forcible suppression is a proper method of social control in dealing with unpalatable doctrines. "Military necessity" opened the door, and legal control of ideas entered. The demand arose that the schools not only be purged of any "improper" doctrines but become actual propagandists of "sound" positions. Bills were passed in various states requiring the teaching of "democracy" or the "constitution." New York went furthest in expelling Socialists from its legislature and in passing the "Lusk bills" aimed to close a socialist school in New York

City and to expel from the public school system any teachers who had ever advocated any change in the form of government of the state or nation.

Thus was given to the philosophy of education one of its most insistent and most complex problems. The problems of "freedom of speech," of "freedom of teaching," in short the whole problem of social control in a democracy, assumed a new dress and insistency. The effort to solve these gives to the world-old problems of curriculum and method added complications: What shall we do with current controversial questions? Shall we ignore or take sides or present both sides? Shall we let children remain in ignorance of such problems, leaving them to the indoctrination of partisan homes? Or shall we tell them what to think, indoctrinating them with the ideas of the group in control for the time being of the schools? Or shall we raise the disputed questions and see that the pupils feel the opposed issues, and teach them primarily methods of attack? It would indeed be hard to find a problem that promises more trouble ahead than this. Almost every deep-rooted interest makes its demand, and widely opposed are the proposals severally advocated.

The Position of the Public School

While our problem has so far been treated as if the controversies lie only in the political and economic realms, a conclusion to this effect would be unauthorized. Religious controversies also have recently assumed a new dress and a new insistency. The general question of the' proper unification of the American people, the question of "assimilation" of the "hyphenate" has raised for education a most difficult and bitter controversy. Certain of the churches maintain parochial schools, and this they do partly because of well-established European practices, partly to insure the continued adherence of their natural population increase, partly because of a very deeply rooted philosophic (religious) position.   The effect of such schools, their opponents urge, is to hinder a proper unification within the body of American citizenship.   The fact that some of these schools have been conducted in languages other than English aroused during war time a resentment that allying itself with other deep-seated feelings has maintained itself in perhaps increasing degree since.   One result has been a movement to require all elementary school pupils to attend public schools; and one state (Oregon) has by legal enactment taken this stand. Involved in this, in greater or less opposition, are the deep-rooted ideas that the parents in the family have the inherent right to decide what shall be the education of the child, that the state must not interfere in religious matters, that the state must safeguard its own preservation and is the final agent of society to care for the rising generation.   Surely a complicated problem.

Education and "Indoctrination"

Involved still further in the foregoing is the very funda-mental question as to whether in a democratic society any adults, whether major part or minor part, have the right of "indoctrination," that is, of using educative processes with the as yet helpless young in such way as to fasten in them irrevocably (or practically so) beliefs on one side or the other in a controversial question.   It would seem out of the question for a mind so warped to face adequately a changing world.   To raise this question is to cut deep.   Of existing institutions the deepest rooted perhaps of all, the family, is thus called to the bar to answer the charge of hindering efficiency, of obstructing "progress," and of failing to respect the right of the child to become an independent thinking person.   That the church and the state seem involved and often on opposite sides adds importance to the controversy.

Few problems so typically illustrate the subject matter of the philosophy of education as it has here been defined. For while education must act, it apparently cannot so act as to meet all the contrary demands made simultaneously upon it.

The pressing existence of just such a knotty problem as the foregoing requires that effort be made to lay bare the issues involved and if possible to find conceptions that promise help in the solution. We can see at once that the relation of the young and immature to society as a whole is involved, as also is the relation of such institutions as the family and church and state to each other and to the social whole. The philosophy of education will frankly go to ethics or to sociology or to political theory for any assistance they can render. What pertinent and useful conceptions these may have formulated are factors that must be taken into account. The fact that educational policies do actually affect life at all its many points means that a thoroughgoing philosophy of education must take account of whatever has been worked out in the many fields of human interest. As a practical discipline, one of its specific functions will be to build up in the future practitioner a useful stock of sensitivities to the more important aspects of life likely to be involved in the doubtful and difficult educational situations that lie ahead.

National Self-Consciousness

The demands of one further situation will probably suffice to marshal the major external influences that we should consider. When, in ancient days, Persia loomed threateningly on the horizon, Athens began in self-defense to study her impending foe and by making contrasts became in turn most fruitfully conscious and critical of her own ways, not only in matters of war but eventually in almost every respect of life. So, in lesser fashion, it eventuated with the United States and the World War. Especially during the years when we were onlookers, we studied Prussia, her strengths and her weaknesses, as never before. The actual war itself and its disheartening aftermath, together with the final debacle of that old Prussia, have in a measure lessened interest in the comparison and study. But the relation of an educational system to its dominant social scheme was during this time added, in degree at least, to our list of permanent problems. How did the Prussian school system in its many details express the Prussian philosophy of life? And how did it, in actual practice, incarnate this philosophy in the Prussian youth? If the Prussian educational system could so well succeed in its aim, why should not ours? Questions of first importance thus arise which we must hold before ourselves till we more adequately solve them. What is America's philosophy of life? Wherein can it be improved? In so far as we have an acceptable philosophy of life, is our school system consistently furthering it? Or does our philosophy point in one way and the features of our school system point varyingly in other directions? Thus there come to clearer consciousness two permanent problems in any philosophy of education: What philosophy of life should we hold and embody? What changes should be made in our school system that it may adequately and consistently embody and express the philosophy we accept? The ramifications of these two problems in the thought and the practical realms are as infinite as life itself. But consciously or not, adequately or not, each educator placed in any position of responsibility answers in his every act both questions. It is then not a problem of whether one shall or shall not have a philosophy of education, but solely and exactly of what kind of philosophy one shall have, whether each one of us is to absorb his philosophy unquestioningly by tradition from the prejudices of his chance associates, or whether under competent guidance he is to make a conscious and determined effort to build a philosophy that shall correlate his educational activities with the best that has been thought by man.

This completes our consideration of the demands made externally upon education. The list of these demands is perhaps not long, but the demands themselves are serious. Industrialism and immigration have made, it appears, at once the most far-reaching and the most pervasive demands. A correlative reorganization of school curriculum, school method, and school aims has in consequence been forced upon education. Economic stratification and a correlative social unrest, following largely in the wake of industrialism and immigration, have added most searching inquiries regarding the institutions of general social life and the bases upon which they should be founded. The effect here has been still deeper questioning regarding school aims and the effects of school procedure. Additional to all the foregoing the World War came to accentuate many older problems and to add new ones. Among these, most significant perhaps of all, are those having to do with freedom, that is, the relations of the individual and of sub-groups with the rest of society. The necessary correlative of all these varied demands has been, as has appeared, on the one hand a reëxamination of the assumptions underlying our total educational effort and on the other a reconsideration of our total procedure. What should follow in the way of remaking aims, curriculum, and method we postpone until we have considered the demands upon education coming now rather from the inside.

Education as a subject of study is but part of a larger thought world; and this thought world is constantly engaged in maintaining a satisfactory self-consistency as new elements are successively introduced. To understand our twenty-five year period and the thought movements in it, we must go much further back. Probably the most fundamental char-

acteristic of the modern world as distinguished from the
ancient and medieval is the growth of a body of tested
thought (or science) and its application to the affairs of men.
Industrialism as earlier discussed is but one outgrowth of the
applications of science.   The influence of this tested thought
within the thought realm itself has been no less great.
Science and its processes now give us the norm and ideal of
truth and its determination.

The Demand for a "Practical" Philosophy

The reflex influence of tested thought as thus furnishing
the norm and ideal of truth has been profound.   Prior to
this acceptance of science man's powers were counted, in
theory at least, to be wholly unreliable, needing to be
amended and supplemented from without in order that man
might know anything reliably.   And this external supple-
mentation only prepared him to receive what must still come
to him from without.   Man as man could not originate
anything trustworthy.   The day of thus despising man's
powers may to some seem too remote to bear on our story;
but the fact is that during our very period philosophic thought
began to shape itself in a new sense and degree on this basis
of science and faith in man.   Perhaps in the movement called
"Pragmatism" this tendency found its clearest expression.
In this point of view truth is conceived as the quality we
ascribe to an hypothesis which scientifically stands the test.
Ideas as expressed in terms are taken to mean only and
exactly the consequences that flow from them when, as
guides to conduct, they are put to work.   Ideas are thus
formulations coming from past experiences and existing to
control future experiences.   Experience becomes then the
stuff of life and consequently the sole object of study, the
guidance of which to more satisfactory levels sums man's
endeavor.

Democracy and Progress

Another characteristic of our times, caused in part by the growth of science, is what we may, for short, call "the democratic tendency." Some of its demands on life have been indicated in the preceding part of this discussion. At this point, however, we are concerned with its thought correlative. Feudalism, or whatever we term the system in which men are by the accidents of birth given prearranged places in society, through its long continuance shaped thought in conformity with itself. Thus Aristotle held that some men are by nature slaves; and the idea persists even to-day not in term but certainly in substance, so ingrained is feudalism in our social customs and thought habits. In like manner the still prevailing ideas of labor and leisure seem to find their origin and continued support in a scheme wherein labor is a burden engaged in only by those not fortunate enough to be able to avoid it. In other words, a stratified society with its lines of cleavage makes it easier for thought to entertain dualisms, and even demands such dualisms as the intellectual support of the existing stratification. In this way not only the opposed ideas of slave and freeman, work and leisure, but many other antitheses, as, culture and vocation, practical versus intellectual activities, pure versus applied sciences, man and nature, mind and body, have been introduced. It is at once clear that some of these are the immediate outgrowth of caste antitheses. It is less obvious, but probably no less true that even the more philosophic of these conceptions in fact originated under like conditions and were introduced, as intimated above, because they were needed for the defense of a stratified social system.

As concerns the world of affairs, the democratic tendency has become manifest by the gradual dying away of the characteristics of feudalism. Many still remain, but many have gone. Old customs, however, die slowly. Indeed they often show surprising powers of resurrection as after a decline they find some new support. Thus we see new wealth reviving, in America, feudalistic practices that had supposedly died out in this democratic environment. Among the customs and habits that hold on after their reason for being has gone, some of the most tenacious are found in the thought realm, particularly as thought is embodied in processes and formulations for the school; for, hitherto at any rate, the school has admittedly dealt in matters that had no vital connection at the time of learning with the lives of those who learn them. Moreover too frequently in the past and even yet school people have been set apart from vital contacts with life. For this and other reasons the school has hitherto lacked the selective influence that would discriminate what was dead from what was alive. Democracy and feudalism have in fact clashed in their thought correlatives as truly as in outside matters. But the school has lagged behind the world of affairs in eliminating feudalistic remains. Both in its practice and in its thought many such have remained intrenched.

Professor John Dewey, America's foremost student in this field, has felt more clearly than anyone else this conflict in the thought realm, and has given much of his effort on the one hand to hunting down and exposing these remains of feudalism and on the other to elaborating a democratic philosophy which should drive them out. It is not flattery but simple fact to recognize in him the outstanding figure in the development of the philosophy of education during the period under discussion. It is chiefly his position that is here developed.

The Doctrine of Evolution and Philosophy

When we seek formative influences on thought in the last half century, or, perhaps better, ask what sources have given suggestion for needed new conceptions, by all odds the greatest influence and source is the doctrine of evolution first brought convincingly to the world's attention by Charles Darwin. It seems not too much to say that the foremost task of thought during recent decades has been to elaborate the implication of this doctrine. Thus to the study of biology is the thought world indebted for two of its most influential conceptions. Aristotle introduced the one and Darwin the other. The development seen in the seed gave to Aristotle the conception of change which governed thought for two thousand years. This, however, was a limited change, hedged in, decently bounded. Moreover the goal was fixed in advance, so that "Reality" did not after all change. Now such a combination of limited change and fixed order is a very comforting line of thought to vested interests of every kind. We accordingly find that in the Middle Ages both feudalism and theology, if for the moment we may separate the two, cordially accepted Aristotelianism; and on this basis the thought of the Western world by incessant argumentation made itself at length into thoroughgoing consistency.

Thus when Darwin startled the world by upholding the "origin of species," the clamor and conflict that arose was, contrary to common opinion, not so much between science and theology as between two philosophies that differed in their views regarding the place of change in the world. If Aristotelian change returned always on itself and accordingly harmonized with a fixed order and conservatism, clearly Darwinian change must point to some other view of order. All the vested interests so far as they were consistently alert acted wisely to ask what sort of world this evolutionary hypothesis contemplated. Some at once began to say that what is e-volved must of course have been previously in-volved, so that after all nothing really new comes into existence. But the opposed idea of the intrinsically new, once it was disengaged and offered to the world, would not down. What does it lead to?

One of the primary results of the study of evolution has been an insistence on continuous change as opposed to catastrophic leaps. Existing forms seem to have come into existence slowly, step by step. So that two existent forms now widely different may in fact trace their descent from one common ancestral stock. This would mean that these two "kinds" differ really in degree rather than in kind. Continuity thus offers itself in place of antithesis as a way of conceiving the things of the world. Human physiology is thus understood in the light of comparative physiology. Human psychology is but the extreme in a continuous distribution reaching from the lowest organism upward. In this conception, dualisms lose their hitherto firm support. The fixed distinctions needed for feudalism are no longer so obvious or convincing. Democracy finds in evolution a thought-world ally.

But Darwinian change interpreted in the sense of creative evolution reaches still further. When once we entertain the idea of movement without goals fixed in advance, we face what has been called, perhaps irreverently, a "universe with the lid off." Many will ask in bewilderment where then can they find support for cherished opinions; and they meet the answer that it is not the business of thought to find support for ideas or positions or practices that ask to be accepted first and supported afterwards. Such "rationalization" is but the prostitution of thought. Thought is properly creative. Its business is to resolve for us the situations of difficulty that confront us and find solutions. True enough thought consolidates its positions creatively won, but in so doing it remains true to the scientific ideal. It holds everything tentative and subject to revision as further testing may demand. To the statement just made most perhaps will give assent. But when some begin to see that ethics, and the existing social and economic order, and existing governmental institutions and conceptions are to be included along with everything else in the scope of this tentative attitude, they falter. To such the foundation of the moral universe seems broken. They fear lest they be forced to yield what they now wish to believe.

The New Philosophy of Experience

The considerations thus reached carry us still farther. In the general idea of evolution and particularly in the evolution of human affairs we face a process tending not toward some externally fixed goal, but one guided and controlled from within the process. And here a new difficulty arises. On such a basis what can guidance mean? What does it mean, many will ask, to steer a course when there is no outward and fixed goal toward which to steer it? That man is peculiarly adapted to control, they may willingly admit. That thought is the prime means of control, they may likewise admit. But how to determine direction whether good or bad without some fixed goal by which to measure, this they do not see.

The answer indicated by the line of thought we have been pursuing is to look at the experience process itself — and from within. Are all experiences equally "good"? Common sense says, No, there is great diversity. Then let us begin, as science has always done, where practical common sense has brought us, and apply more thorough thought. The comparison and determination of goods leads by one path to what we call ethics, or perhaps by a small shift to democracy broadly considered. Yet another point of view here concerns us.

When we compare experiences as to their effects on subsequent experiences, they obviously cover a wide range.

Some lead fruitfully to subsequent experiences that we call good, others lead as truly to subsequent experiences we call bad. Two conceptions here emerge, education and the valuation of experiences. Clearly, education is at least one important means through which one experience may influence subsequent experiences; namely, by changing the agent himself. Now as to the valuation of experiences. Whatever else may be true, experiences differ in worth; so that the power to control the character of experience one is to have is at least an instrumental good. But meanings are the stuff of which control is compounded. Whatever other value any experience may have, it should have then this additional value that it yield meanings — meanings that show the relation of part to part within this experience, meanings that relate this experience to other experiences. Only on the basis of such meanings may control be exercised to raise the experience process to "higher" or "better " or "richer" levels. All other "goods" in life are at least more efficiently and more consistently cared for by acquiring such meanings. But to get meanings is, in so far, to get education. So we may conclude that life is enhanced when experiences are educative.

Common experience corroborates this judgment. We apply the depreciatory term "mere pleasures" to those experiences which merely please and leave otherwise no good effect, and we say, also disparagingly, that one "indulges" himself who engages often in such. More generally we conclude that happiness is impossible on a basis of "mere pleasures," because they do not sufficiently engage the active powers of the individual and they leave unsatisfied the deepseated demand that one, upon consideration, finds one's self to be progressing. Whatever else may be said about it then, the "good life" is one which engages meaningfully more and more of the individual's powers, that is, the good life is essentially one of growing.   Since the individual's good is on the whole either self-contradictory or meaningless apart from the good of his fellows, we reach the conclusion that the good life will include such growing in each as contributes to the continued growing of all.

The conception of evolutionary as opposed to Aristotelian change yields then the conclusion that education, which is of course one with growing, lies at the heart of the good life. Herein is the answer to the problem of steering the experience process from within.   We should constantly seek to increase in the experience process the number and use of meanings and the sharing of interests.   If these demands be met, we are living the good life so far as control can effect it.

The implications of this conclusion are far-reaching.   For one thing education becomes, in Professor Dewey's phrase, life itself and no longer a mere preparation for life.   Subject matter finds its rightful place in increasing here and now in and through each experience the number and use of meanings and the sharing of interests.   What this further means in the reconstruction of curriculum and procedure is a tale too long to tell here.   But seldom in the history of thought does a single conception demand more.

Biological Psychology

It was stated earlier in the chapter that Herbartianism, Hegelianism, and the old order conflicted at many points, and that in the clash progress was made.   The bearings of evolution proved most important at this point.   Out of the new study of biology a new psychology was born.   The conception of behavior, of reaction to situation, gave an entirely new shift to the study of education.   James and Dewey led.   "Education is for behavior and habits are the stuff of which behavior consists."   This sentence from James's *Talks to Teachers* indicates the new outlook.   The need for activity is henceforth on a new basis. Dewey's *How We Think* gave classic expression to the functioning of thought in the educative experience process. The famous Chapter VI on the complete act of thought has given the problem an entirely new place in American conception. It is no exaggeration to say that biological psychology has remade our notion of the educative process and its function in the life process.

Tests and Measurements

We have now studied the more fundamental problems and answering conceptions that have characterized the development of the philosophy of education during the period under consideration. It may not be out of place to consider a few very recent developments. The most striking single movement in education of the present decade has been the development of more scientific tests and measurements. At first this brought few problems to the philosophy of education, but more recently two lines of questioning have been raised. The published results of the application of the Army Intelligence Tests to upwards of a million men during the World War have been interpreted by some to call in question the possibility of running society on a democratic basis. Emphasis of this has raised the fear that intrenched privilege, availing itself of unwarranted deductions, might for a time at least successfully discredit democracy. As democracy is a perpetual experiment, it would be as unfortunate for anything to lessen interest in equality of opportunity for development as to lower faith in warranted endeavor. That theories of society and programs of action must of course square with the facts no true modern will deny. The philosophy of education must and will take its facts from whatever source they come, but it will insist first that reported facts be real facts and second that no narrow or hasty interpretation of the facts shall determine action. **For the** time, at any rate, we face in this a serious problem.

The other difficulty raised by tests and measurements is more technical. As was inevitable, the measuring of achievement began with the matters that lent themselves best to measuring, which so far has generally meant the more mechanical of educational outcomes. As was further inevitable, these measures have been put to work in the service of accepted theories as to the educative process. The results along both lines have in many places been to hamper a broader and more human type of educative procedure which had begun to grow up in answer to other lines of development as herein discussed. We find then a conflict between two aspects of education, that having to do with the aims and values and that having to do with means and achievement. Such a conflict according to our conception comes before the philosophy of education. The resolution of the difficulty seems to hang upon the problem of the nature and functioning of subject matter — at present one of the debatable issues. In the meanwhile, disheartening drill on what is needed for future use finds in the present application of the tests a frequent ally.

The Individual and Society

The bigness of organization in American education as in American life raises questions as to how the individual shall be related to the group. When any one person is set in authority over others, democratic considerations have to be taken into account. Particularly is this true when the work is, like education, of a kind that refuses to be mechanized. And herein lies a most knotty problem. One set of considerations demand that the curriculum be made objectively by scientific experts, but other considerations demand that it be made on the spot by teacher and pupils. How can the latter be possible with so many incompetent teachers in the field? Again, democracy expects group decisions; how are such feasible under existing conditions? Are we not in danger of losing expert leadership? Still even in factories the output is influenced by the "human factor." How shall the school system meet the questions so raised? Here again the philosophy of education finds an insistent problem.

The Nation and Education

A recent problem in American education connects itself most vitally with the historic American problem of "states' rights." What shall be the attitude of the federal government towards the education of American children? Leave it to the states, in spite of the consequent gross inequity of opportunity? Or shall the federal government subsidize elementary and secondary education? And if so, what measure if any of control shall follow? How on any basis of subsidy can we avoid the blighting effects of a centralized bureaucracy? And consider the nature of the opposition to the movement. Does it arise from fear of centralization or of greater taxation or of a more efficient rival in the public schools? So complicated a question demands serious consideration; but it will be hard to escape the conclusion that the wealth of all the people should underwrite the education of all the children. If the public school has logic to stand on, it leads straight to this conclusion. Support and control, however, stand on different bases and should accordingly be treated differently. Here a problem superficially administrative involves philosophy before it can be settled.

Thus ends the survey of the twenty-five years from 1898 to 1923. The definition of the philosophy of education as given at the outset has been vindicated. The life of our people has in this period been seen to make from varying angles many opposed demands upon education. To act at any time in the face of such demands and with due consideration of all the complex results has meant the kind of thought we have called philosophizing, and this has been true whether the needed deliberation has been made by philosopher or by administrator. The more immediate demands have often involved deeper demands. So that education has been called on to face problems that involved the bases of all associate life and action. The answers that have been made to these questions have naturally been various, but during the period under discussion there has been in this field an unmistakable trend. In this movement the most influential leaders have been William James and John Dewey — especially the latter — in the philosophy of education.

Educational Sociology

In keeping with this trend there came in the first half of our period, as has been discussed, a pronounced reaction against "metaphysics." One result of this was to lead Professor (now President) Henry Suzzallo in 1909 to propose, in effect, to abandon the name "Philosophy of Education" and substitute instead that of "Educational Sociology." To many this has seemed a happy suggestion, and not a little has been done under this title both in the way of publishing books and of conducting courses. A dispute about terms easily becomes the most futile of discussions. In this instance it seems to the present writer that educational sociology may well be admitted to have an entirely proper place as an effort to discuss and determine scientifically certain sociological questions that present themselves to education. But it seems equally clear to the writer that as educators we shall still need and shall always need to face conflicting demands made on education from various angles; and accordingly in the sense herein discussed there must always be the philosophic approach to many insistent problems. What choice then between the terms? Since thinking of the higher kind will go on according to the taste and ability of the thinker, the question of any bearing on productive thought is probably not involved. The practical problem would seem to be that of courses for students. For the less advanced students, quite possibly neither term will be used. For more advanced students, some schools will offer a choice between both kinds of courses, others will offer only one line emphasizing the material treated according to the taste and inclination of the best available instructor. Whatever else may be said, it will hardly be denied that the actual philosophy of education of the practical schoolman is a matter of fundamental importance. In the making of this, no conscientious instructor will willingly exclude any helpful point of view.

The Resulting Philosophy of Education

The philosophy of education as actually formulated has greatly emphasized democracy. This has been the conception most obviously involved in the many demands that have confronted education. The effort to understand democracy, to make the conception consistent amid all the varying demands of modern life, and to apply the conception consistently in education — these almost sum the major problems that have presented themselves during the twenty-five years under consideration. For furthering the solution side of the work, the doctrine of evolution and the conception of experience have proved most fruitful. From these have grown a biological and instrumental psychology and accompanying new conceptions of human nature, of thought, and of value. Out of it all, has come the conception of growth as perhaps the most inclusive single formula for directing education.

This conception of growth is at once so difficult and so important as to demand a few words of special consideration. It will perhaps help us to think of this growth as life based especially on the continual increase of meanings in experience and on the continually increased sharing of interests. Imagine any group of people with its present wants (interests) and its present means of gratifying them. If each new experience is so lived as to bring with it the practical increase of meanings and to lead as much as is feasibly possible to continually wider and varied sharing of interests with others, life it appears is then enhanced for all concerned and in all feasible directions. But this practical increase of meanings and shared interests is exactly education in both its intellectual and its moral aspects and these of a kind to include the whole of life. So education is at once life and the means to richer life. In paradoxical brevity education has thus no aim beyond itself, that is, beyond more of the like thing.

Democracy then becomes the kind of society that most encourages this kind of growing. The fixed distinctions of feudalism, ancient or modern, have no abiding place in this conception. But the consistent application of the conceptions of democracy and growth to education involves more reconstruction than has thus far been realized. Such a democracy should make its school system a conscious agency of progress, in particular trying to set its rising generation free from the hampering prejudices which the old have accumulated. Curriculum and method, as is indicated below, get in this a new spirit. Equally will democracy strive for all its members, whether rich or poor, urban or rural, old stock or new, and wherever found in our country. The talk that too many are being educated must die as a kind of blasphemy. The spirit of democracy must more fully pervade the school system itself. Expert knowledge will be sought and utilized, not, however, in superintendent or supervisor only, but as far as feasible throughout. In every relationship will each person's growth and the sharing of interests and responsibility be positive ends. Among the children individual differences will be studied in order that fullest correlative opportunity may be accorded to each. Here again do democracy and growth make demands both on curriculum and method.

The curriculum must be richer and better adapted to the life of the present and future. On no other basis can all the manifold complex demands passed in review be met. No reactionary prating about "fads and frills" or "burden of taxes" must be allowed to stay the process. Again, since the demands are very numerous, time cannot be given to the relatively less significant. Everything must count.

But here other considerations enter. Best teaching and best learning demand that teacher and pupil have a vital part in making the curriculum. It is exceedingly doubtful that any precisely prepared curriculum made and imposed by authority can adequately educate. For education, being life, is a process of growth for both teacher and child, and in this growth all the aspects of life must enter. Steering such a process means, as we saw, to increase with experience the meanings of the world about us and to give to life an increasing social content. Increasingly also must the child take over his own steering. In these respects is experience to be continuously remade. By our newer psychology these things are possible only as the child exercises with satisfaction what is to be built into his character. Purposeful activity in a social situation and under wise guidance seems best to promise the accomplishment of these ends.

So we come to method. For method has now a much richer meaning than how best to make a child learn specific subject matter chosen in advance. Method, the teacher's method, is primarily a question of how to stimulate and guide the child so that he shall best call forth and exercise all his possibilities. This conception fits with the demands of democracy and growth. For democracy to succeed in the ever growing complexity of modern life, our children must be able and disposed to adapt themselves unselfishly to a situation ever shifting in unexpected ways. It is then methods of attack rather than specific solutions to life's problems that we must teach. That our children shall think rather than what they shall think must be our first concern. This is not to deny that some solutions will persist. Some will persist and these we shall teach, but always with care so as not to hamper our children by our prejudices. A chief concern must be the social attitudes that underlie any successful social life. These must in the main come inherently in the living. It will be accordingly necessary to give up our factory-like discipline and provide a school life richer in social opportunities. Again does our psychology tell us that only as we practice may we hope to grow. With method then as with curriculum and administration and architecture and all the rest, each item of procedure must be the correlative of the democratic theory of life consistently applied. This is the last word of the present-day philosophy of education.

REFERENCES

KILPATRICK, WILLIAM H. — *Syllabus in the Philosophy of Education;* Teachers College, Columbia University, 1923.
———— *Source Book in the Philosophy of Education;* The Macmillan Company, 1923.

CHAPTER IV

DEVELOPMENT OF EDUCATIONAL PSYCHOLOGY

BY

DANIEL B. LEARY

UNIVERSITY OF BUFFALO

CHAPTER IV

DEVELOPMENT OF EDUCATIONAL PSYCHOLOGY

Psychology and Philosophy

The formation, in 1895, of the National Herbart Society for the Scientific Study of Education marks an important date in the development of educational theory in general, and educational psychology in particular. For the papers, the debates, and the general principles which were formulated in the early days of this body, before it became, more simply, the National Society for the Scientific Study of Education, have ever since influenced the course of evolution of educational thought and practice in this country. The five Yearbooks with supplements, largely on purely Herbartian themes, are still full of live issues; the authors, almost without exception, became and still are leaders in the educational world; the papers, themselves, reflect a sincerity and an earnestness as well as a willingness to see broadly that is still an inspiration. That these early speculations are abstract, is true; that they are metaphysical, at times even to absurdity, is also true; but that they yielded a rich product of more concrete material is shown by the almost abrupt way in which the Yearbooks, under the new name which the society took at the end of its fifth year, begin to talk about such things as teaching, the progress of geography, courses of study, the relation of theory to practice, the education of teachers, vocational subjects, and so on. The haste with which such general and philosophical topics as concentration, isolation, and unification, the doctrine of interest, and the social aspects of moral education are dropped for more concrete and pragmatic interests and researches is almost startling. Not until many years have passed do we again find general discussions comparable to the early ones.

It is difficult, even theoretically, to separate the psychology of education from the philosophy of education; particularly is this true of the early debates of the Herbart Society. Indeed, it does not clearly appear that all those who took part in these early debates were sure of the nature and the field of psychology. To quote one remark, "One's metaphysics forms a basis for his psychology." But as we read on it becomes apparent that two trends of thought, two different crystallizations of experience are being formulated : one more concrete, based on experience in the sense of science in general, looking for facts first and theories only as a legitimate generalization from them; the other more mystical, more moral in the popular sense of that term, more deductive than inductive, not particularly keen about concrete observation, prone to argue about technicalities, and inclined to worry about words. The former might be personified in such people, say, as James, Dewey, and Thorndike; the latter, more truly Herbartian, in De Garmo, Harris, Van Liew, Parker, and perhaps Hall. That the first stream of thought is not entirely an inner product of the Society is true; James is an intrusion from without; but as one reads even Dewey's first paper, in the *First Yearbook* (1895), one is struck by its outstanding modernness, its concreteness, as contrasted with some of the other less tangible, less practical speculations.

That educational practice was going on all the while is, obviously, a fact to be reckoned with. Indeed, one may think of the history of educational psychology for the past quarter of a century as the gradual modification of highly metaphysical doctrines by the insistently intruding and unanswerable facts of classroom experience, plus, finally and characteristically modern, a new attempt at generalizations and ultimate theories. Thus, for example, the doctrine of general discipline, a favorite with the Herbartians, has arisen again with us, changed by the knowledge of new facts, but much the same in its hopes and promises. Interest, apperception, unity, continuity, will, character — in all these we are still interested, though sometimes under new names, and always with a new approach and a better knowledge of the actual psychology involved. Again, the present discussion of instincts, in so far as there is any attempt to read into them anything more than an unlearned mode of response to a stimulus, recalls the earlier discussions on the Herbartian soul.

Herbartian Psychology

Our first need, then, will be to outline roughly the nature of the psychology prevalent in the early nineties. First of all, the general, "popular" psychology, used more or less uncritically in the schools, was committed to a "faculty" type of mind — an aggregation of different, separate, infusible "powers." Courses of study were more or less definitely designed to affect and mature these separate abilities ; the senses were trained, the memory strengthened, the reason disciplined, and so on ; and since these things could be done as well, apparently, by one subject as another, a considerable debate waged about the relative appropriateness of competing subjects for the curriculum. That this was not Herbartian is quite evident ; indeed one function of the Herbartian psychology was to install another concept of the mind in the educators of the period. To Herbart, psychology is based on three different but interrelated foundations — metaphysics, mathematics, and experience. It is interesting to realize that, however much we may disagree with the concrete results of such a platform, in the long run his psychology was productive of rich fruit.   One may trace the mathematical suggestions through the German experimentalists down to present-day tests and measurements, with Thorndike, of course, as the mediating link between purely laboratory studies and their concrete application in the schoolroom.   Likewise, one may trace the metaphysical strain through successive forms and find emerging, with James and again Thorndike, the concept of original nature.   The experience side becomes more and more exact and concrete, the technique of scientific procedure entering more and more into the analysis of child life until there emerges, finally, such a generalization as, say, the laws of learning, as stated in present-day terminology.

Of Herbart's metaphysical foundations we need say little. To him the concept "soul" represented a necessary presupposition for any dealings with human nature.   He arrived at this concept by the elaboration, in thought, of the facts of experience in such way as to remove all logical contradictions.   Any assumption necessary in order to bring harmony into this thought process was apparently permitted.   Thus, the soul is real, is a monad, is simple, and has only ideas as its one form of activity, directed universally toward self-preservation.   Thus there are certainly no faculties.   Though we may not care to use any longer either this metaphysical method, nor yet accept his presuppositions or conclusions, still the idea of unity was of untold value for the period.   It turned attention in a new direction; one, moreover, destined to be more fruitful, for in spite of its *a priori* origin it was still an honest attempt to gather from experience some of the facts necessary as the basis for an educational psychology.

In his mathematics, as we have seen, Herbart finds another basis.   Ideas, he teaches, are passive in their primary state; but through relation to one another they become forces. Ideas are thus a system of mental stresses and strains, the statics and dynamics of which may be theoretically and perhaps actually calculated quantitatively, thus establishing a determinism in the psychological field. That his particular mathematics were, at times, fanciful is doubtless true; but the conception has led, when freed of the underlying somewhat mystical implications, to some of the most important developments of the modern period.

The third basis, experience, proved more immediately fruitful. He applied the general term "apperception" to that assimilative function or ability of the soul or mind whereby it sees or understands all that it does experience in terms of prior experience. As we have seen, to Herbart the one original tendency of the soul is to preserve itself; beyond this there is nothing said about original nature in the present sense of that term. Or, putting it differently, the individual grows and matures through the acquisition of an ideational content, assimilated through a constantly more richly apperceived experience, instead of through the maturing development and modification of a complex set of capacities, abilities, and tendencies to respond to situations. There is little or no idea, in Herbart's psychology, of correlated structure and function; there are no laws of learning in the sense of generalizations arrived at through concrete experiment and observation. From this point of view, Herbart's psychology is not a psychology of experience at all; he really uses the word in a secondary sense, meaning that experience is the medium of learning, not the medium of our knowledge of learning.

It is interesting to note how Kant and Herbart differ in respect to this. Kant was particularly interested in the constitutive abilities and characteristics of mind, prior to and independent of all experience; Herbart, in what happens to the mind because of its nature when deluged with ideas. Apperception with Kant meant an original synthesizing

power of the mind; with Herbart it meant the interpretation of ideas in accordance with ideas received earlier.   To
be sure, each solution has its own peculiar difficulties.   Of
Kant one may ask, How may a mind function with nothing
to function on?   Of Herbart we may ask, How, then, was the
first idea apperceived?   That all this is metaphysical and
speculative and quite without practical interest at the present
moment, is true; the pertinent point is that we have solved
the problem by a radically different approach from that of
either Kant or Herbart and with a radically different conception of the whole nature of the human mind and body.

This doctrine of apperception leads, of course, to many
concrete classroom rules and principles of procedure, some
of which we will examine later; for method, as a reflection
of educational psychology as such, is as inextricably bound
up with the history of the latter as is the philosophy of education.   But there are yet several general and theoretical
considerations that deserve attention.   First of all, while
Herbart's psychology insists on the unity of the mind, it also
insists equally strongly that it is essentially or preponderantly
intellectual, a nexus of ideas, or, at any rate, a system in which
ideas are of primary importance.   Feeling, for example, is
thought of as due to a relationship pertaining between ideas.
As Lindner puts it: "A feeling is the consciousness of a furthering or an arrest of the movement of thought; when a
furthering, a feeling of pleasure; when an arrest, a feeling of
pain.   The life of the soul is one of ideas; every furthering
of them is at the same time a promotion of the life activity
of the mind; every arrest of ideas is also an arrest of soul
life."   This may, to be sure, be translated into more modern
terms, but in doing so it loses the predominant intellectual
coloring.   Thorndike's concept of "satisfying" and "un-
satisfying" is related, but neither speculative nor ideational.

Again, "Desire is in general a state of mind which strives to bring about some other state of mind not now present." Compared with the idea of "readiness" this is very deficient in both clarity and practical application. Still further, "An object of desire is attainable when it appears as the final member of a series of changes which are related as cause and effect, the first member of the series proceeding from the ego that wills. If such a causal series comes to the support of any desire, the desire is transformed into will; the object is not only desired, it is willed. Will, then, means the desire for a certain result and certainty, or at least a belief in the certainty, of its attainment." Thus, will, desire, and feeling are thought of as reflections of the nature and relationships of ideas. Ideas, content, information, provided that they be properly apperceived, make for will, character, attainment. That the ideo-motor theory is naturally derived from such a metaphysical situation is apparent; such definitions of will and feeling require that acts necessarily follow thoughts of them. Even if concrete motor experience and learning should appear theoretically necessary, concrete practice did expect from such presuppositions that proficiency in act would follow on harmony and the proper content of thought.

Transitional Period

It must not, however, be thought that there was anything like universal agreement with either the metaphysical assumptions and generalizations of Herbart's psychology or its concrete application to classroom practice. An interesting occasion of expression of growing doubts in both directions is found in the paper by Frick and Friedel in the supplement to the *Third Yearbook* (1897), and in the discussion of that paper as contained in the report of the discussions at Chattanooga, February, 1898. Some extracts from the authors' own summary of their paper will indicate the direction of change. "Herbart's theory of the soul is rejected. . . . Knowledge exercises, indeed, a strong influence upon the will, but it should not be regarded as the essential source of will." These quotations indicate the growing tendency to doubt the current conception of original nature as well as that of a specifically intellectual will; both are, in time, to be replaced with more substantial ideas. The soul becomes a group of endowments, the will something connected with habits, motor and otherwise. But the ideomotor theory was, even here, subjected to criticism. "Not knowledge, but interest is the purpose and aim of all instruction." It must be noticed that interest, in this connection, is something resulting from instruction, not something, as in the modern sense of the word, leading to learning. The authors indeed remark, "interest is commonly turned about and falsely regarded as a means and a condition for instruction." . . . "Ordinarily," says Herbart, "teachers try to interest pupils so that they may learn. Pedagogically correct is the opposite. They should learn so as to establish an interest for later times." To connect this idea of interest with will, we note, "Such an interest leads to the threshold of will. Interest is that condition out of which will grows. Interest builds everywhere the necessary transition to will."

In the discussion at Chattanooga, however, there was even more of interest to us, as showing the gradual evolution of educational psychology, than the above slight modifications of Frick and Friedel. Dean Russell, of Teachers College, remarks that "we must believe that whatever is true in primary instruction will be true in secondary instruction." While this is primarily a remark on method, it shows also the conscious realization that an educational psychology, if valid at all, will be universal and applicable to all stages of learning. L. H. Galbreath, of the School of Pedagogy of the University of Buffalo, in commenting on the psychology and pedagogy of the report, remarked . . . "this paper states that pedagogy is based upon psychology. . . . It is not true as a matter of fact, it is not true as a matter of theory." This is comment on the original statement to the effect that while it is doubtful if any then existing psychology could be made the basis for pedagogy, still Herbart's system would be "least objectionable"; indeed, many of his propositions (pedagogical) might well be adopted by psychologists of a rival school. This is, truly, light on the state of the subject some twenty-five years ago. W. T. Harris, United States Commissioner of Education, remarked, "(it) is my suspicion that there is not a good psychology or ontology underlying Herbartianism. . . ." Later on he apparently involves himself in an impasse when he defends free will and yet holds to the formative powers of schooling and education. The discussion then wanders off on this point, both Charles McMurry and Frank McMurry answering Dr. Harris. All this, quite evidently, shows the almost entire absence of a psychology of such nature that there was no difference on fundamentals. Here are not minor shades of opinion regarding some phase of the subject, but almost diametrically opposed points of view. That this is always the necessary result of speculation may be true; but it is noteworthy, as we have said, that many of the speculative visions, when changed a bit by time and new evidence, yielded solid and more practical results.

Froebelianism

The Herbartian movement, as we have seen, was both philosophical and, by implication, psychological. It led both to immediate methodological classroom results, as well as speculations that later, with the addition of a more scientific approach and more concrete evidence, crystallized in the form of present-day educational psychology. Froe-

belianism, on the other hand, while it was in part responsible for an increased interest in child nature as such, as
contrasted with the earlier too great emphasis on the teaching
process, was too closely associated, at least in its early adoption in this country, with kindergarten situations to create
as much interest and discussion among those associated
with Herbart's teachings. When need and time had directed
the attention of investigators to a new scrutiny of human
nature, the solution was a result more of an entirely new
attitude and approach than of Froebelian principles, though
they have much in common at bottom. With Froebel, as
with Herbart, it is difficult to separate philosophy from
psychology. In addition, in the case of Froebel, the nature
and career of specifically native elements is more difficult
to trace because of the very general nature of his educational system as well as its modification by other and later
developments. Froebel exerts his influence rather through
his disciples than through his unmodified system. To some
of these streams of thought, in part inspired by Froebel,
in part independent, and in part implied by Herbart's system, we will now turn our attention.

G. Stanley Hall

With the name of G. Stanley Hall is associated a type of
approach and a wealth of material that have meant and still
mean much for educational psychology. Often colored
by metaphysical attitudes, often too Herbartian in assumptions and intellectualization, Hall's concrete work has nevertheless yielded a rich return in knowledge of children's
habits, feelings, hobbies, games, and, in general, their
evolution into mature individuals from their relatively in-
coherent beginnings of original nature. His studies, extending over twenty years, and supplemented by those of
his students, and conducted in part through the dubious

method of questionnaires, have afforded both tentative conclusions and new points of departure for more adequate results. The major interest, at least in the mind of Hall himself, has undoubtedly been that which interested both Herbart and James — what, namely, is the original nature, what are the unlearned abilities, of the child? Unfortunately, direct observation and experiment were not always the basis of evidence; opinion, hearsay, introspection, and memory often too brightly color the reports. Further, the fields covered often represented a selected group of children; moreover, the topics investigated often proved too complex — division was needed. In particular, as Thorndike later showed, Hall's interpretation of the meaning of the order and dates of original tendencies, as well as his application of that doctrine to teaching and to the hygiene of childhood and adolescence, is based rather on speculation than fact. The Culture Epoch Theory, a typical Herbartian product, falls before the later more objective investigations. All this in no carping spirit; the genius, the industry, the stimulation of the man are factors of incalculable power in the development of our subject; but it is undeniable that many of his conclusions, as well as much of his method, have had to give way before the newer approach. Yet, at bottom, all Hall's studies are inspired by the evolutionary point of view, and are, in spirit at least, genetic. His studies, however much biased by presuppositions, are still real "child-studies," developing as time goes on into more and more objective problems. In particular, Hall's studies in adolescence deserve appreciation; they opened up a new field, and emphasized a new aspect of human life. Thus, as with Herbart, Hall lives and moves in those he has inspired and trained; much of his actual work requires amending; his interests and his problems were carried over into the latter developments.

William James

In the writings of William James we find a distinctly new approach to the problems of educational psychology; an approach that later, in the hands of Thorndike, is to yield the specifically modern point of view. The publication, in 1890, of the *Principles of Psychology*, as well as the series of lectures given in 1891, entitled *Talks on Psychology of Interest to Teachers*, mark the beginning of an earnest and direct and scientific attack on the scholastic psychology of the period we have been discussing. The contribution of even the *Principles* is as great in the field of education as in the larger field of psychology in general. Instead of "faculties," a mysterious soul or will, interest of dubious meaning, there is an objective discussion of such things as instinct and its pedagogical significance, play, habit, methods of arousing interest, the significance of imitation and suggestion, a careful treatment of the problem of discipline and the transfer of training, the meaning of marks, individual differences, and a host of other things that bear all the hall-marks of a modern point of view. In the introduction to the published version of the *Talks to Teachers* (1899) James claims that knowledge of psychology will aid the teacher by narrowing the paths of experiment and trial, by making clear what the teacher is trying to do, by re-animating interest through a knowledge of *how* children learn. This is the objective point of view; but in another respect, also, James is in advance of the older speculative schools, — he sought no closed system, — the facts not the theories were to him always of primary importance. In James, the biological, not the metaphysical, is the basis; intelligence is not a "thing-in-itself," but a tool for use in adaptation; instincts, which he was one of the first to mention in connection with education, are of primary importance;

the organism always reacts, is never passive; experiments, rather than *a priori* reasoning, must settle the question of transfer of training; the emotions are of vast importance, but far from being intellectual matters, are at bottom visceral and biological disturbances; he criticized Herbartian concepts, in particular, apperception; everywhere he emphasized the importance of studying the actual responses of the child.

Edward L. Thorndike

It is, however, in the work of Thorndike that educational psychology first takes form as a consistent and relatively well-rounded body of knowledge, based on experiment and observation, and having always as its final basis of reference the actual behavior of a human being undergoing the stimulus of a definite situation. Deriving, in part from James and the point of view of the *Principles*, and in part inspired by the personality of one of the great translators of Herbartian principles into classroom technique — Hall — yet differing from the latter's actual doctrines, Thorndike's is, in every sense, the outstanding name in modern educational psychology. His concept of "original nature," though not unique, was given more richness and accuracy of meaning through his researches; the laws of learning, as derived from a concrete study of "how animals do learn," are in every sense as fundamental to a satisfactory technique of teaching as the laws of motion to the science of physics; his approach to the study of individual differences has resulted in innumerable concrete changes both in theory and practice. The total product is the result of science, in the exact sense of that word, applied to the tremendously complicated mass of details of human nature. In Thorndike's psychology Herbart's threefold foundation takes on flesh and lives; the mathematical elements lead ultimately to the measurement of abilities, differences, rates, and standards; the assimilative character of the soul becomes translated into sensitivity of the nervous system; the soul itself becomes a group of native traits and characters.

Begun in 1903, and completed in 1913, the three volumes of *Educational Psychology* brought together a "systematic account of present knowledge of human nature and behavior. . . . These volumes represent a selection from, and organization of, recent work in experimental, statistical, and comparative psychology. . . ." A somewhat detailed summary of the main points of these volumes will be necessary in order to do full justice to the significance of the new point of view. To repeat, the absence of purely or even relatively speculative premises and conclusions is conspicuous; the almost universal effort to show useful applications of each generalization about human nature makes the book not only a collection of principles but also a handbook of practice. Some extracts from his essay in the first volume of *The Journal of Educational Psychology* (1910), entitled "The Contributions of Psychology to Education," will bear out this statement.

Psychology is the science of the intellects, characters, and behavior of animals, including man. . . . Psychology makes ideas of educational aims clearer. Psychology helps to measure the probability that an aim is attainable. Psychology enlarges and refines the aim of education. Psychology contributes to understanding of the means of education. . . . Psychology contributes to knowledge of the methods of teaching. . . . The modification of instincts and capacities into habits and powers . . . are the subjects of research. . . False infant psychology or false child psychology is harmful, not because it is infant psychology, but because it is false. Schoolroom life is a vast laboratory. . . .

Nothing could be less Herbartian in method and approach than this.

The three volumes of the *Educational Psychology* are the expansion and the justification of the above more general statements. Volume I, with the subtitle *The Original Nature of Man*, collects and discusses that group of "numerous well-defined tendencies to future behavior. Between the situations which he will meet and the responses which he will make to them, pre-formed bonds exist. His intellect and his morals, as well as his bodily organs and movements, are in part the consequences of the nature of the embryo in the first moment of its life. What a man is and does throughout life is a result of whatever constitution he has at the start and of all the forces that act upon it before and after birth. I shall use the term 'original nature' for the former and 'environment' for the latter." This is, of course, frankly biological and as frankly "materialistic" in the scientific (not philosophical) sense of that term, and dismisses at once, as incompatible with rigorous procedure, any speculative *a priori* concepts. Psychology has become an inductive study; education is a process of action and reaction between man and nature, "original nature" and "environment." Still further :

A man's nature and the changes that take place in it may be described in terms of the responses — of thought, feeling, action, and attitude — which he makes, and of the bonds by which these are connected with the situations which life offers. Any fact of intellect, character, or skill means a tendency to respond in a certain way to a certain situation — involves a *situation* or state of affairs influencing the man, a *response* or state of affairs in the man, and a *connection* or bond whereby the latter is the result of the former.

From this point of view, it becomes apparent what is the purpose or aim of education in terms of educational psychology; naturally, social and philosophical considerations, such as the fabric of the social life, institutional powers, economic conditions, and so on, also determine the direction and goal of the educational process. But whatever modification of the curriculum, whatever determination of hours and place of school, and so on, such latter considerations involve, still, in an irrevocable sense, and having in mind the nature of the human nature described above, educational psychology aims to "perpetuate some of them (tendencies), eliminate some, and to modify or redirect others." This is the first adequately supported system of psychology in which it is shown to be necessary to think of the ends of education in terms of the beginnings of that which is being educated. There is neither a "blank mind" on which education can write anything that philosophy dictates, nor yet is there a "free nature" (will) which, because of some transcendental element, not observable to sense, will inevitably choose the right, the good, the true, the beautiful. The ends of education are circumscribed to begin with. Philosophy is still powerful, but it must come to terms with psychology; philosophy may still choose, but it must choose within the definite limits of original nature. And original nature is limited not only in the general sense, but in each particular instance also; for all individuals differ to some ascertainable extent. To quote still further, the task and province of educational psychology is "1. The description and classification of original tendencies; 2. their anatomy and physiology; 3. their source or origin; 4. the order and dates of their appearance and disappearance; and, 5. their control in the service of human ideals."

Volume II, with the subtitle *The Psychology of the Laws of Learning*, is, like its predecessor, as complete a divergence from accepted and theoretical attitudes and beliefs as it is possible to conceive. Quite as frankly biological, quite as openly and consistently objective and experimental, it offers a body of doctrine and practice that again contradicts, irrevocably, the insinuations of a metaphysics of learning. Such terms as interest, apperception, learning, habit, improvement, ability, rate, durability, and so on receive adequate definition. The discussion is, consistently, joined on to that of original nature. To quote: "These original human tendencies include also certain ones whereby modifiability or learning itself is possible." That is, learning is not independent of structure but a function of it. Learning is as natural a function as is the expression of original nature before learning or modification takes place. To act is to become modified; all activity is learning. Nor are the laws of learning applicable merely to human nature; all animals learn in the same way.

The laws of learning — Readiness, Exercise (*i.e.* Use and Disuse), and Effect — are intimately connected with that conception of "satisfying" and "annoying" which is the result of an investigation of the life processes of the neurons of the nervous system. "By an 'annoying' state of affairs is meant roughly one which the animal avoids or changes. By a 'satisfying' state of affairs is meant roughly one which the animal does nothing to avoid. . . ." Ultimately, such satisfaction and annoyance are properties of the constituent elements of the nervous system, considered from the point of view that "in my opinion they retain the modes of behavior common to unicellular animals so far as is consistent with the special conditions of their life as elements in man's nervous system." This is an interesting contrast with the Herbartian concept of learning and the ideas of "self-preservation" of the soul and the "furtherance and arrest of thought." To quote again,

Capacity to learn and remember could find its physiological basis in the movement-process of neurons. The acquired connections of man's intellect and character would be the results of the unlearned tendencies of his neurons to do nothing different when all was well with them and to perform whatever different acts were in their repertories when their life processes were disturbed. The learning of an animal would be the unlearned response of its neurons.

Certain pseudo-scientific concepts of the learning process are disposed of; "the laws of readiness, exercise, and effect, uncomplicated by any pseudo-aid from imitation, ideo-motor action, or superior faculties of inference," are sufficient. Also, several characteristics of learning, subsidiary to the three main laws, are stated. They are of concrete use in the technique of teaching and go to reëmphasize the fact that all learning is animal learning, that

> He (man) is first of all an associative mechanism working to avoid what disturbs the life processes of certain neurons. If we begin by fabricating imaginary powers and faculties, or if we avoid thought by loose and empty terms, or if we stay lost in wonder at the extraordinary versatility and inventiveness of the higher forms of learning, we shall never understand man's progress or control his education.

Further discussion in the second volume is concerned with the improvement of mental functions, the amount, rate, and limit of such improvement, the conditions under which it takes place, changes in rate and its permanence, and, finally, the effect which improvement in one function has upon improvement in another.

Volume III treats of two additional main topics: mental work and fatigue, and individual differences and their causes. Of the two perhaps the second, to date, has had more actual effect on schoolroom practice; though the first, with the implied corollaries concerning the greater efficiency of self-motivated activity, has been somewhat applied. The question of the relative influence of heredity and environment, heretofore largely a speculative question and settled largely in terms of mere words, is, in accordance with the general point of view of the whole volume, attacked objectively. Yet, unfortunately, there are still so-called educational psychologies used both as texts and as foundations for schoolroom practice that ignore all of this, and which imply more or less definitely that teaching can compensate for any and all germinal deficiencies. It is perhaps particularly in the domain of measurement, which is, of course, implied in the conception of heredity, structure, and learning which we have described, that the greatest difference of opinion has manifested itself. Several attacks have recently been made on the propriety of attempting to measure intelligence and particularly of basing the treatment of the pupil upon findings in this field. William C. Bagley, in his article in *School and Society* for April, 1922, seems to revert in part to the old tradition that mental ability may be created by good conditions of teaching as well as of the general environment. This is, of course, a denial of psychological determinism and a return to the Herbartian free-will controversies. That the question is entangled with the philosophical implications of a democratic theory of education is true; but, as we have already seen, philosophical considerations, no matter how noble, are limited by the psychological nature of the individual and the process of learning. Such a denial of the truth of the principles of measuring intelligence contradicts, also, the phenomena of individual differences, and would seem to run counter to that concept of original nature embodied in the laws of learning.

New Relations between Psychology, Philosophy, and Methods

There is another aspect of the recent educational psychology that deserves mention, namely, its more complete agreement, in spirit and method, with philosophy. Philosophy itself, during the period we have been considering, went through a change and development not unlike that which psychology in general and educational psychology in particular, experienced. Again the names of James, Dewey, and Thorndike deserve major mention from our point of view. All of them, whether dealing with concrete questions of human nature or larger generalizations, reflect that newer philosophical attitude that is, in a sense, the reflection into the field of philosophy of the method and the technique of science. As we have seen, Dewey, in his earlier papers in the Herbart club, was already expressing this newer point of view; James emphatically preached it; and Thorndike in his *Educational Psychology* as well as Dewey in his later *Democracy and Education* have continued it. This more complete agreement between educational philosophy and educational psychology contrasts decidedly with the situation at the beginning of the period we are considering. It is to be expected that this agreement will lead to better and further development in both fields. Both are pragmatic, both interested in fact and induction, both aiming at concrete betterment of social life and individual expression, both are in the service of human values.

Of actual changes in classroom method during the period we are discussing little need be said here. Schoolroom practice is always a reflection, partly of current theory and partly of the native endowment of the teacher. Unfortunately, the theory which affects practice is too often the theory of a school which is passing out. We may, however, briefly note some present tendencies; briefly, since other papers in this volume treat the subject in detail. Such changes as are tending to occur, and which are, here and there, more definitely adopted, reflect roughly that conception which we have seen in our examination of Thorndike. From this point of view interest is now interpreted as part of the biological readiness for a given situation instead of something subsequent to uninterested effort. The curriculum as a whole, and separate subjects within the curriculum, tend now also to be presented from the point of view of readiness and to be continued from the point of view of effect more than was true earlier in the period. The creative self-expression of the pupil, limited by a broad social conception, is now more central in the teaching-learning situation, where once teacher or subject matter (or both) was central. Once association, predominantly intellectual in character, was both process and aim; now, particularly in the project work, both activities and aims are seen in terms of larger psychological reactions, involving attitude, motor expression, and habits as well as mere associative knowledge of a purely intellectual character. Once the school was almost universally thought of as a special environment differing abruptly from that outside; now, we tend to eliminate differences. "Formal steps" have become relatively obsolete; we have realized at last that, if there is no royal road to learning, so also there is none to "imparting" knowledge.

The Present Position

The present period, then, represents a compromise, speaking particularly of practice, between the theories of twenty-five years ago and those which have grown since then as a reaction to them. If we were roughly to forecast the development of the immediate future, we suspect that it will show first a gradually increasing application of all the implications of original nature, a far more deliberate use of the laws of learning in connection with it, a much freer field for the expression of native abilities and individual interests, an increasing realization that, since education in the broadest sense of the word actually does begin at birth, we should therefore control it earlier, and finally not only an increased use of measurement of a more accurate kind than we have now but measurement in fields which, at the moment, have been barely touched on. This last leads us to remark that as far back as 1910, and again in 1912, in the *Journal of Educational Psychology*, Dr. E. Jones of London called attention not only to the importance of emotional conditionings but also to the additional fact that they occur very early in life and that they are very often the basis of later large interests and nervous readinesses of the individual. Whether we call it Freudian, or whether we merely think of it as that branch of psychology which concerns itself with the early emotional experiences and conditionings of infant and child life, is not a matter of importance. It is, however, very important to realize that later interests, even such broad fields of interest as the choice of a profession, are involved. The whole concept of repression bears important relation to the later development of disinterested and refractory children; the process of sublimation is akin to that of socialization. Again the many nervous traits of school children as well as some sense-organ deficiencies and the so-called "nervous breakdowns" of adolescence are intimately related to the early pre-school years. All this is thoroughly in accord with the educational psychology which we have considered in our discussion of Thorndike; it merely emphasizes, because of its contrast with the earlier point of view, the unity of the organism and the fact that neither education nor life is merely intellectual. It is to be hoped that with the further growth of those principles of educational psychology to which Thorndike has given most definite expression, we will see also an adequate extension of social interest and control to the very earliest experiences of the growing and learning child. That we have, in any sense or in any direction, achieved either absolute truth or complete knowledge is doubtful; it is to be hoped also that the immediate future will see a tremendous growth of further research and experiment along those lines which have already been so tremendously productive of satisfactory results.

CHAPTER V

Development of Tests and Measurements

BY

Jesse B. Sears

STANFORD UNIVERSITY

CHAPTER V

DEVELOPMENT OF TESTS AND MEASUREMENTS

The measurement movement in education lies well within the last quarter-century of our educational history. Yet, within the space available here it is not possible to present more than a meager outline of its development, so completely has the idea of measurement permeated every aspect of educational theory and practice. In its broader conception the movement represents virtually a new philosophy of education; in its narrower sense, a new technique, a new set of devices, for use in the study of education.

The movement is not unrelated to the past, however distinctive it may seem in its methods and its accomplishments. The practical collections of quantitative facts about education and about various aspects of the mind reach back some decades. So although the idea of quantity in education and psychology is not entirely new, yet the mere study of how many children and of how much was spent, the studies of sensation and of time reaction, stopped short of our needs. Out of these, however, came a more careful and a wider use of the comparative method of studying educational statistics, and a new approach to the study of the mind by studying individual differences; and from these came the idea of educational measurement as we now think of it. All this time our need has been the same. We needed to know not only how much instruction cost, but also how much instruction we got for what was spent? Not only is the child bright or dull, but how bright or how dull, and what does brightness or dullness mean in terms of achievement in school work? These were the questions for which answers were needed.

Yet, however like efforts of the past in its main purposes, and in the general objects of study, the measurement movement offers a substantial departure, both in its methods and in the tangible character of its conclusions. It studies, not part by part, but all of the mind, by studying its behavior under certain controlled conditions, its progress in studies, and the results of amounts of study. Finally, it states its findings in exact quantitative terms.

Specifically this movement covers three separate, though by no means unrelated, fields; viz., statistical technique as applied to educational and psychological phenomena, educational measurements, and mental measurements. The development of statistical method, together with its application to educational and mental measurement, gives educational statistics almost the status of a distinct science, or branch of the general science of statistics. Whether statistics is regarded as a mere "handmaiden" to psychology and education in the measurement movement, therefore, or whether almost the reverse relationship is claimed, may depend upon one's interest. The truth is, their development has gone along together, and any complete history of measurement can no more omit the method or technique of measuring than it can omit the results of the application of that technique.

In each of these movements the developments have been along two lines: the one theoretical, the other practical; the one in search of general principles and rules, the other of the application of these principles in the management of intelligence and education. The one has given us tests and scales, or units of measure, which embody a theory and technique for measuring intelligence and the results of the application of intelligence to the study of our school subjects.

The other has given us reorganization, altered our procedure, and done away with much waste of time and energy. More than this, if possible, they have, together, thrown new light upon the meaning of mind and upon the meaning of education, and have given us a new hope and a new confidence that education may yet establish itself upon a highly scientific and professional plane.

Only the barest outline of the achievements to date, and, by no means, of the innumerable technical and philosophical problems that have been solved or met with along the way, can be offered here.

Development of Educational Statistics

The word "statistics" has undergone change, but, according to Meitzen, it has been used in one form or another since 1668. Since very early times, collections of classified facts have been made, particularly in connection with the problems of state. Ancient history abounds in illustrations and we are still collecting, for similar practical purposes, very much the same kinds of facts : facts about extent of land, census, marriages, deaths, number of soldiers, tax lists, products, and the like.

At first statistics seem to have been little more than classified lists of important facts. The method employed was too simple to have attracted attention ; hence it was natural that such studies of facts should be thought of only as studies of facts and not at all as studies of the mathematical treatment of such collections. Accordingly, Achenwall, who reviewed the statistical work of his predecessors, looked upon statistics as a study of the total of all the remarkable facts about a state (*Staatsmerkwürdigkeiten*), the purpose of such study being to gain political wisdom.

Such a view as this would probably have persisted to the present had not the need for statistics increased with the development of the state in western Europe, and had not scientific students begun to study the facts about population, deaths, and taxes, and to apply in these studies such new mathematical developments as the theory of probabilities, which had been worked out by Fermat, Pascal (1654), and Huygens (1657), scientifically determined in 1793 by Jacques Bernoulli, and expanded by many subsequent students of statistics. Halley's mortality tables, Jean de Witt's principles for annuity life insurance, the portrayal in graphic form of important state facts by Acherson in 1741, Malthus's law of diminishing returns in agriculture and his study of population, all tended to show that it is possible, not only to count facts, and to average them and study tendencies, but also that even where the facts are widely varied, certain relationships can be found by applying mathematical principles in their analysis. As early as 1662 John Graunt's studies brought to light the relation of death rate to seasons, the ratio of male to female births, and other similar relationships, and really introduced the idea of statistics as a scientific method of observation.

It took a few centuries of experience with enumerations of facts to learn how to treat and interpret facts in large numbers; e.g., how to increase one's accuracy of observation and how to manipulate collections of facts so that real causes could be distinguished from fortuitous causes. It is easy to see what would happen if a weight were placed upon one end of a beam which is balanced upon a fulcrum. There the number of forces involved is few and the cause is intimately connected with the result. But when social, economic, moral, physical, intellectual, and biological forces are operating together in almost innumerable combinations, as is often true when we are dealing with educational problems, it is not easy to see precisely what constitutes cause. Hence, without studying many similar combinations, we can anticipate effect only by a guess. In other words, ordinary inductive reasoning breaks down and we are forced either to guess or find a way to estimate probability. What chance has an American boy of becoming six feet tall, of being able to recite the multiplication tables, or to enter high school at a given age? If the state could guess intelligently about its chances to win in a battle, if the school could guess intelligently about boys, then administration of state and school might be put upon a scientific basis.

What was needed first was a knowledge of averages or central tendencies in great masses of facts, and of the way and extent to which individual cases varied from that norm. The next need was a knowledge of causal relationships: What are the chances that a boy 72 inches high will weigh 152 pounds? That a boy who makes high marks in algebra will make equally high marks in Latin or English composition?

It is not possible, nor is it the purpose, here to trace the development of the mathematical principles and formulæ necessary to solve these and related questions. It is interesting to point out, however, that these are typical of what came to be practical problems for students in all the sciences. The science of statistics did not grow up as a separate and distinct field. Neither did it branch off from mathematics alone, nor did it grow out of the physical sciences alone. Each of these contributed, as the history of mathematics, astronomy, and physics shows; but, after all, the studies of practical problems of government, and the studies of the natural sciences, owing to the complexity of their phenomena, contributed even more. These sciences could not be carried beyond the simplest inferences without a complicated statistical technique. Accordingly it was in the actual collections of social and biological statistics that the necessity for and the possibilities of statistical science as a method of observation of facts in the aggregate had their beginning.

What is suggested by these few comments on the history of statistics applies also for education. We collected statistics for a very long time before any serious attempt was made to tell what general truths were revealed by our columns of figures. We counted children, income, expenditures, attendance, and passes and failures for a long time, as nations counted population, deaths, and marriages, and we did it for similar practical reasons. Educational statistics were merely one special collection of official statistics.

Our interest here is to see whether and in what way students of education have contributed to the building up of a statistical science. This we may do by pointing to the application of statistical method in the solution of educational problems. These contributions begin with Francis Galton (1822–1911), who was not, in a strict sense, an educator, but whose studies of heredity, eugenics, and psychology went far toward laying educational foundations. One has only to read through a list of titles of Galton's publications to realize that his interest in mathematics and in statistical method was both wide and profound. (See appendix to his *Memories of My Life.*) His studies of nature and nurture, of school statistics, and of a wide variety of anthropometric and psychological problems identify Galton with the beginnings of scientific work in education and the immediately allied fields of biology, psychology, sociology, and eugenics. In all these studies the statistical method was applied.

Leaving aside the uses of mathematics in his early studies of meteorology, Galton attacked the problem of heredity by a statistical method and published his *Hereditary Genius* in 1869. This, according to Galton, was the first attempt to apply statistics to the study of heredity. (See preface to the first edition of *Hereditary Genius*.) In this work Galton applies the law of "deviation from an average" (p. 22) in the study of the leading men of the British Isles. Mathematically the study offered nothing new. It was new, however, in the materials used and in the ends sought. In addition to numerous scientific papers in which he used statistics, his *English Men of Science* appeared in 1874, his *Human Faculty* in 1883, and his *Natural Inheritance* in 1889. It is in this latter study that we find the largest development of his statistical principles. Here he explains graphically how to study distributions of facts, defines median and explains its properties, shows how to compare two distributions that are not equal in numbers of observations, shows how the distributions of his facts about human beings conform to the mathematical curve of frequency of error, explains how to handle the problem of deviation from average, how to construct an entire scheme of the distribution when the median and the amount of variability are known, and gives a graphic demonstration of how to figure correlation, or, as he termed it in this study, regression.

From a purely mathematical standpoint there is not so much that is entirely new in Galton's work. (Galton was undoubtedly familiar with Quetelet's *Sur l'homme et le développement de ses facultés, ou essai de physique sociale* (1835) as well as with Quetelet's earlier studies of population and of the theory of probabilities.) It is a study in probabilities. Yet, statistically speaking, it is quite new. How does the law of error apply to the type of social and biological facts in question? As early as 1879 Galton, referring to Weber's law, pointed out that "the geometric mean appears to be equally applicable to the majority of the influences, which, combined with those of purely vital phenomena, give rise to the events with which sociology deals." The statistical implications of this suggestion for the social and biological data with which he worked were very clearly revealed.

This suggests the foundation upon which educational statistics have been built. To this, Karl Pearson, a co-worker with Galton and in several ways his real successor, has contributed. He has clarified, proved, and expanded Galton's work at many points, and particularly in the technique for studying relationships between sets of facts. In America, Cattell and Thorndike took up the same study of nature and nurture, and utilized the statistical method. It is certainly very near the whole truth to say that, with Thorndike, the study of educational statistics proper had its birth.

There is not space to relate the story which the last paragraph suggests, nor to tell what was happening in other fields. According to Meitzen, statistics had been taught in universities since 1660. At first the subject consisted of little more than lists of political and economic facts, but in due course statistical method began to receive attention. Meitzen's *Geschichte, Theorie und Technik der Statistik* appeared in 1886, M. Block's *Traité théorique et pratique de statistique* in 1886, Mayo Smith's *Statistics and Economics* in 1888, Gabaglio's *Teoria generale della statistica* in 1888, Westergaard's *Theorie der Statistik* in 1890, Dr. George von Mayo's *Theoretische Statistik* in 1895, Dr. Bertillon's *Cours élémentaire de statistique* in 1895, and Bowley's *Elements of Statistics* in 1902. These books are in part historical, in part they deal merely with tables of facts, but all treat statistical method in some measure. Bowley's book is more nearly than any other a full textbook treatment. All were concerned with social and economic facts.

In 1902–03 Thorndike offered a course at Teachers College, Columbia University [Education (or Psychology), 108 – Practicum: the application of psychological and statistical method to education], which appears to have been the first attempt of its kind in this country — and, doubtless, in any country. Courses of a somewhat similar character were first offered at Chicago University in 1908–09, at Stanford University in 1909–10, at Brown University in 1911–12, at Harvard in 1912–13, at Indiana in 1913–14, at Minnesota in 1915–16, and at Missouri in 1919–20. In some of these institutions it is clear that the subject had been touched upon in other courses previous to these dates, and that many actual statistical studies had been directed earlier. In 1903 Thorndike's *Educational Psychology* appeared, and in 1904 his *Theory of Mental and Social Measurements*. Whatever had been accomplished by the statistical studies that had come from Teachers College previous to this, and from the scattering studies from other sources, these books established educational statistics as part of the higher curriculum in education. A list of the titles of statistical studies in education which have appeared subsequent to these dates would include a large percentage of the doctors' dissertations as well as other original contributions in the field.

It is difficult to say in few words what the study of statistics has brought to education. Galton was greatly concerned about the *possibilities* of education. He saw the power of nature as no one before him had seen it, and realized that nurture's only hope of control lay in the possibility of selecting and directing nature; hence, his interest in eugenics. These conceptions he arrived at through the use of statistics. Now we are bringing this same viewpoint and technique to bear upon every aspect of school work. In our physical, mental, and educational tests we have units of measure for various aspects of both nature and nurture, and in many of our city school systems, in a few of our state systems, and in many normal schools, teachers' colleges, and university schools of education there have been established bureaus of research and statistics devoted to the quantitative study of the schools. As early as 1904 the results of a simple statistical study of retardation in the schools of New York City appeared in the superintendent's annual report. The facts revealed were startling. To-day such studies are part of routine work in school administration. The survey movement which began in 1911 began with little understanding of the use of statistics, but as rapidly as a technique was developed it was brought to bear in survey work and the progress made in a dozen years is clearly revealed by survey literature.

Mental Measurements

Very early in his studies of human faculty Galton declared that "one of the most important objects of measurement is to obtain a general knowledge of the capacities of a man by sinking shafts, as it were, at a few critical points. In order to ascertain the best points for the purpose, the sets of measures should be compared with an independent estimate of the man's powers. We thus may learn which of the measures are the most instructive." By "independent estimate" he meant a judgment of the man as "mobile, eager, energetic; well-shaped, successful at games requiring good eye and hand; sensitive; good at music and drawing."

While one could hardly say that Galton gave us mental tests as we know them now, surely the above statement, together with the measurement work which Galton did, stand as a worthy claim to an important place in the history of mental measurements. It is not clear just what Galton's work had meant to Binet, who is properly regarded as the originator of mental tests, but surely the above statement clearly anticipates, both in aim and method, what Binet actually accomplished in 1905. What Galton did accomplish was to establish the idea of individual study and measurement of human traits.

In America Professor J. McK. Cattell took up this line of study and soon won recognition for it as a standard division of the field of psychology. The field has been further exploited by Professor E. L. Thorndike, and through his work the results of such studies have been brought more directly to bear upon the problems of instruction. One can see Galton's early studies of nature and nurture passing through his own laboratory into that of Cattell, where more evidence and finer methods of measurement were added, and thence to Thorndike, from whom they have issued as generalizations upon the technique of instruction and as effectual means of measuring the results of instruction, and later, of the capacity to receive instruction. Whatever Galton's work had suggested to Binet, however, it is clear that Binet's own training and work must have brought him naturally step by step to the idea of intelligence and to the idea of tests for intelligence that are embodied in his mental tests. Like Galton and Cattell he saw the importance of exact measurements of individual traits. Like them, too, he tried to "sink shafts" into human capacities. In point of emphasis, however, Binet laid stress upon the total general power or capacity for which his sample soundings seemed to stand and worked for a test that would characterize the whole of mental capacity rather than a single part of it.

In his approach to the task of measuring human intelligence, Binet was not so much a free lance as Galton had been. Appointed in 1904 by the Minister of Public Instruction to membership on a commission charged with the study of measures to be taken for insuring the benefits of instruction to defective children, he found himself face to face with the problem of deciding who among the children are defective. Stimulated by this practical demand, and by what a solution to the question might mean to future commissions, as well as by a genuine scientific interest, Binet, together with Dr. Simon, set to work upon the necessary tests. By their writings it is now easy to trace the careful and patient steps by which they moved steadily on toward their goal. They carefully reviewed the studies upon which medical practice based its diagnosis of mental defects, and proceeded to the detailed study and examination of individual cases. In due course they published the *1905 Tests*, and finally, in 1908, their scale for the measurement of intelligence.

It would not be true to say that this new line of study owed nothing to the past or to the work of contemporaries. Acknowledgment is made by the authors of suggestions received from the work of Preyer, Perez, Sully, and Shinn, and from scattered notes published in the *Pedagogical Seminary*, and especially to the work with retarded children going on at Brussels under the direction of Dr. Demoor. From these sources, however, could not have come the essential contribution, the conception of the practical value of an exact measurement of native intelligence apart from accomplishment, and the development of a means of making such measurements.

That the authors of these tests must have done a considerable amount of careful analytical thinking, or plain theorizing, at the outset, is clear from their publications of 1905 and earlier. The point that stands out in their work, however, is their painstaking study of almost numberless more or less isolated facts about individual children, all as a part of their search for a promising hypothesis as to what native intelligence might prove to be.

In presenting their 1908 *Measuring Scale of Intelligence* the authors state their program as being: "first, to determine the law of intellectual development of children and to devise a method of measuring their intelligence; and, second, to study the diversity of their intellectual aptitudes." This is virtually the program that has been followed by all students of this field as well as by Binet and Simon. From the outset they sought to make their tests "simple, rapid, convenient, precise, heterogeneous." They sought "to evaluate a level of intelligence" and to disregard the results of instruction, and considered it unnecessary to test all of a child's psychological processes. Their tests were based upon the assumption that native intelligence would be adequately revealed by tests of the "faculty of judgment, otherwise called good sense, practical sense, initiative, the faculty of adapting one's self to circumstances." Although the Ebbinghaus Completion Test, devised in 1905, deserves special mention, even in this brief review of intelligence tests, yet, in view of the studies of memory, sensation, and time reaction that were in process in psychological laboratories elsewhere, this program of Binet seems a rather bold departure.

It is not necessary to describe here the tests as originally formulated or as later revised. They were made up of actual responses of children to a very large number of tests and so embodied only such elements as were found to be within the common experiences and common interests of children, age by age. The individual tests were in some cases quite similar to tests previously used by Cattell, and earlier still by Galton, for testing sensory and motor phases of mentality. In addition to this type other tests were concerned with the child's familiarity with common objects, and especially with ability to make comparisons and accurate judgments on higher levels. The 1905 scale included thirty roughly standardized tests, the 1908 scale was more elaborate and included fifty-six tests, arranged by age groups from three to thirteen years. This scale was revised in

1911, providing five tests for each year except one from three to ten and in addition five each for the ages twelve and fifteen.

This idea of mental testing was soon taken up in this country. In the school for subnormal children at Vineland Dr. Henry Goddard introduced the 1905 tests in the latter part of 1908. Later he tested 2000 normal children, and in 1908 prepared a revision of the Binet-Simon scale. A second revision was made by Kuhlman in 1909-12 in connection with his work in the Faribault, Minnesota, school for subnormal children. In 1912 Terman and Childs revised and extended the scale, and in 1916 the Stanford revision appeared. This latter revision by Dr. Terman is also an extension of the scale as well. It includes ninety tests in all, six for each age level from three to ten, eight for the age of twelve, and six for the age of fourteen. It also includes six tests for average adults and six for superior adults, and in a number of cases alternate tests were provided. In 1915 Yerkes, Bridges, and Hardwick published their "Point Scale for Measuring Mental Ability," and Otis worked out a standardization of an absolute point scale on the basis of the Binet tests in 1920.

The Binet tests and their revisions rely very largely upon words and only slightly upon activities, and they appeal largely to abstract intelligence. This naturally places some limitations upon their use. To meet such objections tests of performance have been devised, of which the form board, originating with Seguin, is a common type. The Healy manikin puzzle, picture puzzles, and the maze tests have also proved useful.

All these tests were designed at the outset for use with individuals, persons, or animals. As a consequence their use on a large scale in large school systems was next to impossible. When the United States entered the World War, psychologists were called upon to suggest how psychology might be of service. The result was the development of two types of group tests known as the Alpha and the Beta tests. The former was verbal in character and used to test literates; the latter, of the performance type, was used to test illiterates. The success of these tests gave an added impetus to mental testing and especially to the idea of group tests. Already more than forty group tests have been prepared, many of which are standardized.

From the beginning the questions of what is general intelligence, and how important is general intelligence as a factor in success, have held the center of the stage, even though all the study seemed devoted to the solution of the practical problem of classifying children on the basis of intelligence. Two definitions seem to have been evolved as a result of work to date. One states that general intelligence is a unitary or central inborn factor, while the other conceives it to be a composite of a number of more or less closely related innate capacities to become intelligent in various life activities. More recently attempts have been made to get at the meaning of factors other than intelligence. Professor June E. Downey has devised a tentative scale for measurement of the volitional pattern as the outcome of the "Will-Profile Experiment," Dr. Paul F. Voelker has devised a test for trustworthiness, and S. C. Liao has prepared a moral-judgment scale in the form of a "best reasons" test. These are three quite different approaches to the measurement of character traits other than the intellectual, and though crude and inadequate they indicate lines of exploration that are likely to be fruitful as experiments accumulate.

The work on intelligence tests has been done in part by those engaged in tasks calling for psychological studies, and in part by university and college professors. Binet,

Goddard, Kuhlman, and the very large number of psychologists employed in public school systems and in schools for defectives and delinquents have approached the task with administrative problems to solve, and much of scientific value has come from these sources. The psychologists who were university instructors soon began to offer courses on the subject or to include some discussion of the problem as a topic in more general courses. Brown and Stanford Universities offered work in this line as early as 1911–12, and more recently the work has found a place in all well-staffed departments.

The extent to which mental tests have been employed in a practical way would be difficult fully to define. They were made in the schools and with reference to school standards and school conditions. As a consequence, their practical worth was almost guaranteed from the start. There had long been needed a means for accurate classification of children. These tests were made with reference to just that need. The question was, Could we put this new device to work? As early as 1904 we had begun to make statistical studies of children's progress in school, but, aside from this, there had been little that would provide school people with the experience, to say nothing of the confidence and zeal, necessary to the task of making practical use of mental tests. The truth is, however, that prompt beginnings were made and that the movement has fairly swept across the country. The complete story would doubtless tell of much that is crude and futile — tests half standardized and with little validity, tests badly administered, many tests given but with results inadequately treated, results obtained but no administrative decisions made, tests given without reference to a real program — yet the work went forward. Selection of pupils for special and ungraded classes began to be made on the basis of these tests from the start. Then attempts were made, as under Dr. Dixon at Oakland, to classify all entrants to first-grade work on the basis of mental tests and to follow up with such reclassifications as were necessary for the group as it went forward through the grades. Similarly, rapid advancement and opportunity classes have been formed, doubtful promotions have been determined, and, almost uniformly, the results have shown that mental age is a sound basis of classification when reasonable allowance is made for achievement. In most of the state schools for delinquents mental tests are used in connection with the classification and discipline of children, and as early as 1916 mental tests began to be used in connection with college entrance examinations. The survey movement took up the idea early and most of the city school departments of research are utilizing mental tests in a practical way. In all these capacities the value of the tests has been clearly demonstrated, and the best proof of their practical service is shown by the extent to which they are being used throughout the country.

Educational Measurements

In 1905 Binet and Simon, in their discussion of the necessity of establishing a scientific diagnosis of inferior states of intelligence, declared in favor of three methods: the medical, the pedagogical, and the psychological. By the pedagogical method they meant "making an inventory of the total knowledge of a subject" possessed by a child. After stating that the idea of such a method had been obtained from Dr. Demoor and his colleagues, they add that "these authors do not seem to appreciate the need of precise methods of evaluating . . . the amount of retardation in instruction." So far as carrying out the idea of educational measurement so clearly suggested here their work went no further.

At a much earlier date (1902–03) a Teachers College, Columbia University, bulletin announced a course by Professor Thorndike as follows :

Education (or Psychology) 108 — Practicum. The application of psychological and statistical methods to education. *The course will deal with* means of measurement of physical, mental, and moral qualities, including the abilities involved in the school subjects, and rates of progress in various functions; the treatment of averages; measurement of relationships; *etc.*

It is clear from this announcement that educational measurement, as we now understand it, had at that time become a definite possibility in the mind of Professor Thorndike. In view of the outcome of the work which he thus initiated it seems proper to refer to the year 1902, and to Teachers College, as the time and place of the formal launching of the present movement in educational tests and scales.

Tests, in many respects like the tests of to-day, had been made much earlier than this, though little or nothing came of them. The earliest of these, according to a report only recently discovered by Professor Kandel (*Journal of Educational Psychology*, Vol. IV, p. 551), were devised and used by the Rev. George Fisher, of the Greenwich Hospital school in England, in 1864. This report quotes the following statement :

A book called the "Scale Book" has been established, which contains the numbers assigned to each degree of proficiency in the various subjects of examination : for instance, if it be required to determine the numerical equivalent corresponding to any specimen of "writing," a comparison is made with the various standard specimens, which are arranged in this book in order of merit; the highest being represented by the number 1, and the lowest by 5, and the intermediate values by affixing to these numbers the fractions $\frac{1}{4}$, $\frac{1}{2}$, or $\frac{3}{4}$. So long as these standard specimens are preserved in the institution, so long will instant numerical values for proficiency in "writing" be maintained. And since facsimiles can be multiplied without limit, the same principle might be generally adopted.

This work antedates Galton's development of statistics, and certainly it is noteworthy even though it shows only a partial grasp of the statistical problem involved in devising standards of this sort. It is unfortunate that it was permanently lost so far as any contribution to the present movement is concerned. Another attempt, antedating Thorndike's work by nearly a decade, was far more important in its bearing upon later developments. In 1894, Dr. J. M. Rice conceived the idea of educational tests and soon put such tests to work. The immediate result was striking. At first practically no educator accepted Rice's conclusions. Yet, the general idea would not down and, though his methods were faulty, he at least provoked a discussion which ended some years later, if it is yet ended, in the complete acceptance of the idea of measuring the results of instruction and in the general acceptance of the statistical method in the study of education. This implies, too, the rejection of the traditional disciplinary aim and function of instruction and study. This implication has been accepted for elementary instruction, largely accepted for secondary instruction, and higher education is yielding to it at many points. These far-reaching effects of his experiment Rice probably did not foresee; and, although as a scientific device his fifty-word test in spelling was of little worth, yet the underlying idea was a permanent contribution.

The wide discussion provoked by Rice prepared the way for the more scientific work which was to follow. By the autumn of 1902, Thorndike had learned enough about measurement to give place to the subject in one of his university courses. Whether the idea of measuring the results of arithmetic instruction and handwriting grew out of his study of statistical science or out of his study of psychology of the learning process or, most likely, from both, is not important. At any rate the Stone arithmetic tests were published in 1908, and the Thorndike handwriting scale in 1910. This work not only marks the real beginning of scientific measurement of educational products but also stands as an important final achievement in statistical science. The foundation work of Galton and the equal difference theorem of Cattell had finally issued in an important practical school device.

From this beginning the test movement has gone forward rapidly though the problem did not readily find place in university courses outside of Teachers College. A course dealing with this topic was announced at Stanford University in 1911–12. A course was announced at Chicago University in 1912–13 (Course 72B), but apparently dealt only with the use of test results in connection with the problem of supervision. The University of Minnesota offered a course (No. 126) in 1915–16 which was devoted to the study of "Units and Scales for Measuring Achievement in Reading, Composition, Spelling, Handwriting and Arithmetic," and Indiana University announced a course (No. 23) in 1917–18. According to a survey of catalogs for 233 institutions of higher learning (*Journal of Educational Research*, November, 1920) most of the state universities, half of the state normal schools, nearly half of the non-state universities, and a fair number of other types of schools offered courses in educational measurements in the summer of 1920. Educational measurement has thus become a standard course in most departments, schools, and colleges of education.

Tests or scales have been devised for most of the elementary school subjects and for many of the high school subjects. The reliability of the later tests is comparatively high and the ease with which they may be administered has been greatly increased. More and more attention is being devoted to the question of precisely what is tested by any given test and to the best means of expressing the results of the tests, to the relation of the results to other factors, and to similar practical matters.

According to a recent review of test literature more than fifty separate and distinct functions have been performed by tests (*Journal of Educational Research*, October, 1922) and authors of tests have themselves set forth sixteen different functions. It is obvious that tests cannot become a general panacea for all educational ills, yet they are rendering a large service. As pointed out above in regard to mental tests, practically every city school research department is carrying out an extensive test program and, judging from current literature, from city and state school reports, and from the reports of school surveys, beginning quite early in the survey movement, there are few city schools in which educational tests are not being used and, further, wide use of them is being made in rural schools as well.

From this too brief statement of the origin and development of the measurement movement in education we can see how rapidly it has made contact with every nook and corner of the field. Statistical technique is being perfected, and tests, both mental and educational, are becoming very numerous. We measure cost, teaching efficiency, progress through school, success in studies, mentality, buildings, equipment, textbooks, and attendance by methods and devices almost unknown only a dozen years ago. There are excellent textbooks covering all aspects of measurement, and measurement courses hold a prominent place in higher professional curricula.

Further, changes in school practice are being effected. Active research departments are now organized in some fifty of our city school systems, each devoted to quantitative studies to be used in directing the school policy. The results of mental tests are being widely used as a basis for classifying and grading children, and educational tests are also used extensively in the same connection and as a basis for diagnosing instructional cases.

It would not be correct to say that all this rapid headway has been made without mistakes. A few important controversies have arisen on rather important points; and those who know most about the movement are surest of the tentative character of many of the tests and formulæ that have been used widely and with confidence by many workers; but that the movement represents the largest quarter century of work that has ever been done in education, no intelligent person can doubt. The student of statistics may be going too far with some of his theories to suit the mathematician; psychologists may disagree as to just what intelligence is or as to just what mental tests measure; mistakes may be made in decisions based upon test results; teachers may be frightened and confused at times; teaching may tend to become formal in places because of a narrow interpretation of tests and their functions. Granting all these things, however, we must point to the solid achievements in the way of accomplished reorganization, in the way of available facts about the schools, in the way of a large amount of scientific literature on education, and in the confidence and forward look of the leading men in the field to-day as the real meaning of the measurement movement in education.

REFERENCES

ACHENWALL, GOTTFRIED — *Abriss der neuesten Staatswissenschaft der heutigen vornehmsten Europäischen Reiche und Republiken;* published in 1749.

BINET, ALFRED, and SIMON, TH. — Studies published in *L'Année psychologique* in 1905 and subsequently translated by Elizabeth S. Kite and published as *The Development of Intelligence in Children;* Training School at Vineland, New Jersey, 1916.

BOWLEY, ARTHUR L. — *Elements of Statistics;* Scribner, New York.

GALTON, FRANCIS — *Natural Inheritance;* Macmillan, 1889.

—— *Memories of My Life;* Methuen, London, 1908.

GALTON, FRANCIS — *English Men of Science, Their Nature and Nurture;* Macmillan, 1874.

—— "The Geometric Mean in Vital and Social Statistics"; *Proceedings of the Royal Society,* No. 189, 1879.

HANKINS, FRANK H. — *Adolphe Quetelet as Statistician;* Longmans Green, 1908.

"Intelligence and Its Measurement" (A symposium by leading American students in this field); *Journal of Educational Psychology,* Vol. XII, March, April, May, 1921.

MEITZEN, AUGUST — *Geschichte, Theorie, und Technik der Statistik;* Berlin, 1903.

National Society for the Study of Education —
Seventeenth Yearbook, Part II; "The Measurement of Educational Products."
Twenty-first Yearbook, Part I; "Nature, History and General Principles of Intelligence Testing." *Part II;* "The Administrative Use of Tests."

PEARSON, KARL — *The Grammar of Science;* Macmillan, 1900.

RICE, JOSEPH M. — *Scientific Management in Education;* Hinds, 1913.

TERMAN, LEWIS M. — *The Measurement of Intelligence;* Houghton Mifflin, 1916.

THORNDIKE, EDWARD L. — *An Introduction to the Theory of Mental and Social Measurements;* Teachers College, Columbia University, 1913.

—— "Handwriting"; *Teachers College Record,* Vol. XI, March, 1910.

CHAPTER VI

DEVELOPMENT OF METHOD

BY

WILLIAM A. MADDOX

ROCKFORD COLLEGE

CHAPTER VI

DEVELOPMENT OF METHOD

Traditional Practices and a New Education

It is natural that man in the course of his evolution should first occupy himself with the conquest of physical nature, and that he should only slowly acquire knowledge of human nature and classify and use the principles that he formulates to determine his progress. It is in the effort to discover the fundamental ways in which men act and interact and to apply laws in developing conscious social controls that traditional practices are giving way to a new education. New theories of method and new criteria for judging the worth of subject matter to be taught are rapidly remaking our common schools.

Our state public school systems are themselves new; they came in the main in the decade following our war between the states. They are a product of a long struggle for democratic institutions against social systems transplanted from the Old World. Within the lifetime of our own fathers we have come to look upon these schools as symbols of our faith and hope in democracy, as worth all the burden of tax we bear for them. Our forefathers who fought for the free-school idea before the Civil War did not dream of the industrial and social United States, especially of the modern city, that we have come to know, nor did they realize the limitations since revealed by biology within which these free schools must do the work of social regeneration. They did believe that universal education is a necessary corollary to free government; and gradually there has come the conviction that the perpetuity of our democratic society depends upon a consciously developed means of carrying on our affairs as a group, in short, upon a process of socialization in the schools. If we are to become efficient citizens in a society in which the individual determines the policies of government, we must acquire knowledge socially valuable, gain insight and interest in our common problems, be practiced in thinking out and solving these problems, and be acquainted with the laws of habit-formation; at the same time we must conserve and develop the power of initiative of the individual and the ability to gain our personal desires through teamwork with our fellows for common ends. We must, in short, learn *to live together* before we as individuals can gain a "fullness of life" through formal education. The methods of the New England township can no longer serve as a means in New York or Chicago of carrying on government and training for citizenship. The school must be the socializing force. The implications of this social theory furnish the key to the outstanding experiments in public education during the past twenty-five years. It is Professor John Dewey who epitomizes the new idea in his well-known declaration: "Education is not a preparation for life, but *is* life."

Our early American schools gave a stern, individualistic "preparation for life," for this social philosophy was not reflected in their ideals and methods. The elementary school of even seventy-five years ago was not a significant social institution; problems of specific training for citizenship were not commonly discussed in teachers' meetings. The curriculum of this school was as meager as its furnishings. "Any person," we are told by a contemporary, "who could read tolerably and write sufficiently well 'to set copies' and cypher as far as the rule of three was qualified to become a schoolmaster. . . . The majority of teachers were feeble men who had not the power to perform physical labor, indolent men who had not the will to do, or young men and women who found it convenient to earn, by a few hours in the schoolroom, money and leisure to reach more desired goals." There were indeed some great teachers, such as A. Bronson Alcott; but discipline was usually harsh, for there were no "divine rights of childhood" to be considered, except the other-worldly right to have one's soul saved. There was no group consciousness nor were there common ideals to constitute a profession of teaching. Efficacy of method depended primarily upon the personality of the teacher, his love of learning, and his innate sympathy for childhood. There were none of the many social incentives to improve classroom technique that we feel in this age; the teacher gained his results as seemed best in his own eyes. The pre-Civil War attitude toward method and matter might be expressed in Mr. Dooley's own words: "It doesn't matter what a boy studies so long as he doesn't like it." A fear of spoiling boys was current, for it appears in 1845 that in one Boston school "the average number of floggings reported on the basis of a week's observation was sixty-five floggings a day." And the writer assures us that this was a representative school.

In the early part of the century just passed there were a great many reasons for pedagogical absolutism. First among these was a lack of faith in and knowledge of the original nature or instincts of children. An appeal to interest was to the teachers of that day an appeal to evil, for the theological dogma of original sin was an educational dogma as well. There was much talk of "breaking the will of the child," of discipline, suppression, etc. Children were "to be seen and not heard." All of which is in sharp contrast to our present attitude toward childhood, which at times goes to the other extreme. There is no chance of finding in the newspapers of the period such a notice as recently appeared in the *New York Times* (January, 1923): "The wife of the Governor of Pennsylvania will establish a 'talking school' where the child's individuality will be exercised at will, where children will be permitted to talk as much as they please and a teacher employed to romp with them."

Second, a general belief prevailed that thinking is an activity only of mature life, that childhood is a period in which to store facts and in which to train for later thinking. Minds were "trained," as souls were "purged," by discipline. Third, a general faith existed in what is now called formal discipline with its ancient scholastic sanctions — the belief that mental discipline is inherent in certain selected subjects and in the performance of hard and disagreeable tasks. The Old Testament conception of morality had not been superseded by the teachings of Jesus and Socrates. Fourth, "children being not reasonable can be governed only by fear. To impress this fear is, therefore, one of the first duties of those who have the care of children." In contrast, Horace Mann reported in 1843 that during his visits to the Prussian schools he never saw a "teacher . . . with a book in his hand . . . sitting while hearing a lesson (nor) saw one child undergoing punishment or arraigned for misconduct"; and he saw "tens of thousands of pupils."

Not until toward the close of the past century did the theory of evolution, a consciousness of the interrelation of school and society, the need of conscious control of both nature and human nature for social ends, the conception of education as growth or development, the Hegelian principle of self-activity as the law of growth, finally find expression in a theory of education. The new gospel awaited a new psychology, a new sociology, and the development of the biological sciences. John Dewey and his predecessors in educational theory — Comenius, Rousseau, Pestalozzi, Froebel, Herbart, Col. F. W. Parker; William James, G. Stanley Hall, E. L. Thorndike in psychology; Herbert Spencer, Lester F. Ward, and their successors in sociology; and the many notable biologists of the last forty years, all these have prepared the way for a theory and science of education adapted to contemporary civilization and the problems that are ahead of it.

Pestalozzi: The Oswego Movement, the Beginning of a Revolution in Method

Dr. E. A. Sheldon was a courageous leader in the free-school movement in the decade before the Civil War. As teacher and superintendent of schools at Oswego he threw the weight of his enthusiasm against the traditional school practices of his day. Like Pestalozzi, he had his first teaching experience with the waifs of society, wild Irish boys, sons of sailors in the early Lake Ontario grain trade. Upon examining a set of English Pestalozzian objective materials in an educational museum in Toronto, Canada, he returned to Oswego determined to "psychologize" knowledge for the child and to teach him in a natural way through his senses. The work of Dr. Sheldon and his teachers, Herman Krüsi, I. B. Poucher, Miss Coopers, and others, contains a dramatic story of professional idealism and unselfish service which, perhaps, rises above all their contributions to method. Dr. Sheldon unquestionably inaugurated a far-reaching reform.

Object Teaching: Observation as Method

The textbook was discarded for objects and observation, the memorizing of words without meaning to the pupil was dropped as an objective of the recitation for "clear perceptions" or ideas of things and people. In the attic of the

Oswego State Normal School there are yet to be seen the remains of an elaborate equipment of stuffed animals and birds, minerals, geometrical forms, herbaria, etc., which, with excursions and "conversations," constituted the media of Dr. Sheldon's object teaching and sense training. The beginnings in elementary science made by Oswego mark the beginnings of nature study as a method in teaching.

Unhappily a faulty psychology led the Oswego innovators to follow too simple a prescription. To go "from the simple to the complex" was the logical sequence in building concepts or clear idea-wholes. "A subject was analyzed into its simplest elements." Arithmetic, language, and the newcomer in the course of study — natural history and science — were "developed" orally. "Powers and faculties" of the mind were trained "in a graduated series of exercises," starting "within the (child's) comprehension . . . exercising the child's powers without exhausting them." To the overzealous teacher bent on thoroughness, there was no way for the child to learn to write, read, draw, etc., except to begin in writing and drawing with elemental forms, lines, and curves, in reading with the letters of the alphabet, and practice on these before satisfying a natural desire to express himself.

Mrs. May Howe Smith [1] in *The Proceedings of the National Teachers' Association* for 1866 gives a remarkably clear statement of "The New Education or Plan for Human Development through Instruction":

If subject matter is to contribute to human development, it must be presented in the order of the awakening of the faculties, for man first observes and reads and then analyzes and reflects and finally formulates and applies laws and principles. We believe that in the first years of a child's life the only powers of the mind which are in a high state of development are the *perceptive* or *observing* powers, the physical agents of which

[1] Mrs. Smith, once associated with Guyot in the preparation of his geography, was Oswego's teacher of geography. Geography, so important to Colonel Parker later, was another contribution of the Oswego movement.

are the senses, and they are almost the sole means of acquiring definite knowledge. Place him in touch with the external world, these clear images enter the mind and give rise to ideas. He learns to express those ideas, acquires languages, and thus is able to receive ideas from other minds acting in conjunction with receptive powers through attaining their full development. Later are developed conceptive and retentive powers including memory and imagination. . . . Later still the ability to analyze, reflect upon, compare, contract and otherwise investigate the knowledge we have already acquired and to derive therefrom new ideas which are expressed in the form of abstract propositions. Knowledge becomes really available to us as we have the power to grasp it and make it our own. Last is reached that harmonious action of all the faculties wherein the reasoning power attains its full development and the mind is able to rise to high generalizations, to attain knowledge of general laws and principles. The three stages from infancy to mature age are childhood, characterized by perception and retention; youth, by analysis and reflection; and maturity, the full development and activity of reason.

In the light of modern thought, one follows quite the opposite procedure. We see a new situation first as a vague whole, analyze it, reorganize it into a whole again and use it. As Professor Dewey insists, we learn to swim by swimming in water, not on a bench in practice; to talk by talking to people about things that interest us and them; we think by solving our own problems, not by exercises in logic; we acquire skill as we work, not by preliminary formal exercise.

Under Dr. Sheldon's own direction, however, the tangible results of the Oswego primary methods over old methods and practices were spectacular — at least, they so appeared to examining committees gathered to pass upon the practicability of introducing them into the schools of the county. To these gentlemen there was undoubted interest among the children. They liked the new physical culture, the excursions, and the "objects." "Eyes flashed with delight, each little face was radiant . . . each pupil seemed thoroughly awake." Above all, they "loved" their teachers.

But the teacher, not the child, was the active agent; he, without recourse to a textbook, possessed knowledge, brought an infectious enthusiasm to his task, and was an expert in asking "developing" questions. He, at least, had become active; he no longer "sat" and "heard" lessons. It is true, however, that objective teaching and sense training degenerated in the hands of teachers who did not "clearly comprehend its principles." But, though it had come by way of England, it perhaps never sank with us to the vicious formalism satirized by Charles Dickens's *Hard Times* in the story of Mr. Grandgin, Sissy Jupe, and Bitzer.[1] The movement gave a tremendous impetus to teacher-training and spread the new evangel to newly established normal schools in the Old Northwest and the Mississippi Valley; it did, in fact, inspire their establishment. It is interesting that the Herbartian propaganda for scientific pedagogy began in the Middle-Western normal schools that had early come under the influence of Dr. Sheldon and his disciples.

The Herbartian Contribution

The Five Formal Steps, Apperception, and Interest[2] were the central ideas of Herbartian method that first came to America through Charles De Garmo, Charles A. McMurry, and his brother, Frank M. McMurry, twenty-five years after the Oswego method was introduced. These men had studied the theories of Herbart as they were being interpreted half a century ago by Professor Ziller of Leipzig and later by Professor Rein of Jena. The Oswego movement rose in the East, but it was the Illinois Schoolmasters' Club, the Herbart Club founded in 1893 and expanded into the National Herbart Society for the Scientific Study of Education, with Dr. Charles A. McMurry as its aggressive secretary, that gave us the new doctrines of interest, apperception,

[1] Quoted in Parker's *The History of Elementary Education*, p. 363.
[2] There is no desire to limit the Herbartian influence, particularly as it is seen in, for instance, the Colburn Arithmetics.

correlation, concentration, and coördination. The problem of instruction soon became the metaphysical "problem of reconciling knowledge and will." But Herbartianism was not finally received as a system of metaphysics. "Instruction," according to the first yearbooks of the society, "in the studies of the public schools must be made to reveal to the child the moral order of the world and not only must it furnish this moral insight but it must so touch the heart that a permanent right disposition toward all men, both in their individual and organized capacity, may result." "The demands of civilization took precedence over formal discipline as a guide to selection of studies." The end of education was conceived as social-moral character.

Moral training was to be found in completing Herbart's "cycle of thought." This "cycle" begins in the child's contact with things and with people. These contacts lead to what the theorist believed were dynamic ideas. These ideas, through correct instruction, tend to express themselves in conduct and, if expressed or used, become clearer and lead, in turn, to new ideas. "To know the right is to do the right" is the implication of "the cycle." The five formal steps, preparation, presentation, association, generalization, application, are, as a general method, the heritage from the late nineteenth century. Those of us who began our training as teachers as recently as 1900 were drilled as we, in turn, drilled our students in these important steps.

The case was again stated for the teacher and not for the child. However, of the three principles of teaching stressed in a recent text (Parker's *General Method of Teaching in the Elementary School*, 1919, p. 190), "self-activity, apperception, and preparation," Herbart and Ziller are responsible for the doctrines of apperception and preparation. Instruction began with the subject matter nearest the child, his past experience (preparation). The new knowledge is clearly presented as a second step (presentation). The new knowledge and old are welded, "a veritable reconstruction of experience" (association). New knowledge or concept-making is the result without trial in action or any particular motive on the part of the child except intellectual curiosity. Use was both the test of acquirement and a means of clinching that knowledge (application). There was no assurance that the child would use the result outside the formal exercise of the lesson. Thus we have the inductive-deductive lesson and the principle of use so much emphasized in Dr. Frank M. McMurry's subsequent teaching. A pupil's aim has since been added and the center of gravity placed in the child rather than in the subject. The five formal steps thus remain as an approved "type" lesson when abstract meaning or a generalization is the objective in teaching. Lessons involving the solution of problems (another use of reflective thought), lessons for motor skills (requiring imitation primarily), and lessons for enjoyment (involving neither imitation nor reflective thought) are added in such modern handbooks for the guidance of teachers as G. D. Strayer's *The Teaching Process*, 1911, Earhart's *Types of Teaching*, 1914, Burton's *Supervision and Improvement of Teaching*, 1921.

The Herbartians misled our course of study makers for a generation by the false analogy known as the culture-epoch theory; and this influence has only recently disappeared. We have ceased to think that the child finds inherent interest in recapitulating, as he goes up through the grades, the racial struggle of man from primitive life to modern society just because he likes to play Indian or enjoys stories of Ab. We now think of interest in terms of motive and purpose and of subject matter as a means of satisfying ends set up by the child and society. But self-activity in this sense was not one of the principles discussed by Herbartian enthusiasts. This idea was contributed by Froebel, Parker, and Dewey.

Self-Activity and Motor Expression

The influence of Froebel on our American elementary schools, aside from the kindergarten, was first felt through Col. Francis W. Parker and Professor John Dewey. Froebel, it will be recalled, saw in the flowerlike "unfolding of the innate powers of the child" a principle underlying all instruction. The child became the active agent in the realization of his own powers; the teacher was the guide, not the master. The teacher's first duty was to enter into the lives of his children. The child was not to be molded to adult standards; he was to be allowed to grow. Coercion obstructs growth and learning. As Professor Duggan puts it, "Froebel was in accord with Rousseau in believing the child a behaving not a learning animal." The law of unity and the law of self-activity were to Froebel the laws of development. The Froebelian method of the recitation was, therefore, *motor expression*, or doing the things the child wants to do by reason of his instinctive life and his interests in the activities of community life around him. The kindergarten as an institution was a first step in carrying out this ideal in the entire education of man. Froebel added the emphasis to *expression* that Pestalozzi gave earlier to *impression*, hence impression and expression, learning and doing, thought and conduct were taken together to describe the learning process. Adequate expression must come through words, play, song, the dance, constructive work with clay, paper, sand, drawing, and dramatization. Freedom became mastery of self.

In practice, however, Froebel himself led his disciples astray in attempting to find in his "gifts" mystical symbols that reveal God and His plan to the child; while his "occupations," constructive work with cardboard, paper, sand, clay, etc., were so charged with this mysticism that in the hands of sentimental followers they became the means of expressing only "spiritual yearnings," not the growing ideas of form or color. Even his "games," imitations of neighborhood industrial pursuits that he had seen children enact while playing naturally together, were filled with so much religious meaning that they became highly didactic in the hands of conservatives. His "circle," again a symbol of the law of unity, was nevertheless suggestive of the principles of freedom in action, of social coöperation, living and learning together.

With the advance in psychology and experimental education, American kindergartners have divided themselves naturally into two groups — those who follow Froebel literally with all his vagaries and spiritual interpretations and those of a progressive school who with the aid of Professor Dewey's more recent interpretations accept his doctrine of freedom, self-activity, and social communication as the law of growth, but reject both his science and his theology. Professor Patty S. Hill of Teachers College is representative of the latter school and has made the kindergarten a first grade in a lower-primary group, thus articulating the work between the old kindergarten and the public schools.

John Dewey: Motivation and Problem Solving

Professor John Dewey opened an experimental elementary school at the University of Chicago in 1896 when the influence of Herbartian methods was at its peak. He is a pragmatist or one, so far as we are concerned here, who thinks of knowledge as dynamic, as part of one's actual intellectual resources, a means of interpreting life and an instrument of control. The mind is "a process . . . a growing affair," depending on exercise of its function for development, "requiring continual stimulus from social agencies . . . and finding its nutrition in social supplies." He is, moreover, a student of our experiment in democracy and believes that the problems of our corporate life must be solved in the schools. To him the rapidly changing conditions of society and the growing complexities of our social and industrial life demand an individual who is resourceful and an institution that will train that individual to meet the new obligations in a changing society. He sought, therefore, to escape the implications of current educational theories, especially Herbart's, by applying a thoroughgoing functional viewpoint to method and matter in his new school. This meant that the learning of children must not be, as he puts it, "a process of accommodating the future to the past," but a process of "utilizing the past as a resource in developing the future." He repudiated Herbartian "presentations," based on the belief that the child *is* what he has been taught, as a pedagogue's paradise. To view subject matter in the school from an instrumental or functional point of view is to see it as so much experience gained by the races of man that must be learned by each generation of children as man himself acquired it — through effort in satisfying his wants, in solving his problems, and, in short, in gaining control over the forces of nature and of his own mind. "Learning is an active, personally conducted affair . . . a process of reorganizing, improving, extending," or as it is commonly said among schoolmen, "a reconstruction of experience." As experience implies experiment, trying out, discovery in the face of perplexities, all learning takes place in attempting to remedy inadequacies in our past experience. The function of knowledge is "to make one's experience freely available," when occasion demands, for use in any new situation, however strange. In an autocratic government where the individual plays a small part in controlling the destinies of state he may conform passively to custom, but in a democratic state there is a premium on variations, capacities, and potentialities which must be allowed to develop to the benefit of the nation and of the individual alike. Society is vitally interested in developing the gifts, the initiative and creative genius of the individual. Only a progressive education will allow individual freedom and at the same time socialize the individual as he exercises it.

Professor Dewey, therefore, accepts the two Froebelian principles of method, but purges them of their fanciful religious notions — self-activity and social participation adding a new emphasis. By self-activity he means "opportunity for investigation and experimentation and for trying out one's ideas and things." As the child acquires both knowledge and method of gaining knowledge through self-activity, so democracy originates in and is carried on by self-activity. "The primary business of the school is to train children in coöperative and mutually helpful living. . . . The primary root of all educative activity is in the instinctive and impulsive attitudes and activities of the child and not in the presentation and application of external material." The growth and the well-being of the child and of society are conserved by the same means — a wide diffusion of culture throughout society and a capacity in the individual to think his way out of perplexing situations.

The school must, therefore, reproduce the actual conditions of working, thinking, and feeling that exist in the democratic life outside the school and must give practice in them. The public welfare depends upon coöperative, mutually helpful thinking and living together and upon the ability of the individual to change, meet new situations, and solve his problems. He early found his moral principles in social intelligence or insight and in habits of positive

service. This led him to identify morality with citizenship and service, and immorality with laziness and social
ignorance. Again, from the standpoint of method, "the
school is not a preparation for life, but *is* life." [1] All this
has now become a familiar doctrine in our better schools.

Professor Dewey, in 1896, attacked the Herbartian doctrine of interest in a memorable paper, "Interest in Its Relation to Will," before the National Herbart Society with such
effect that the name "Herbart" was soon afterwards dropped
from it. The concept of motivation developed from the
controversy. The assumed opposition of interest and effort
was rejected by Professor Dewey as a philosophical dualism.
One of the conditions of effective learning is sustained, undivided attention. Divided attention is inevitable when
one is forced to perform tasks that are not satisfying some
conscious need. We "attend," as a rule, just long enough
to find out the attraction's interest for us and straightway
attend to something else if it has no personal meaning.
Ideals of work, and capacity for sustained effort through
devious ways till a task is done — factors so necessary to
individual and social well-being — are not developed by
coercion in the learning of facts or skills which bear no relation to purpose. Undivided attention is given freely only
by the child who sets out to perform a task, the completion
of which will satisfy some more or less immediate interest.
The Spencerian theory of punishment by natural consequences is no guarantee that the child will not willingly
take the consequences to avoid the mental and physical
pain and the struggle involved in superimposed tasks. The
old-fashioned artificial incentives, medals, money, credits,
for success; copying, "being kept in," or floggings and
other painful penalties for failure, are actually immoral

[1] See Dewey's *The Chicago Elementary School Record Monographs*, 1900;
School and Society; Child and Curriculum; How We Think.

in their subsequent effect because they destroy interest and discourage initiative and effort. Interest and effort are *correlative* in the work of the world and only opposed in the school when its method is contrary to life, when the thing to be learned bears no relation to the child or to any social need that he can comprehend. The greater interest we have in the end to be gained in a given task and the greater desire we have for the satisfactions involved in the achievement, the more effort we put forth to secure these satisfying results.

The word "motivation" is used as a factor in effort because it implies a purpose on the part of the child. Genuine educative effort, as opposed to doing blindly what one is told, or mere energetic play must be present when the child is employed in the production or creation of *means* that satisfy *ends* that he himself conceives and *wills* himself to accomplish — whether it be making a rabbit trap or becoming, in the end, a great engineer. Motivation has become the current mode of expressing the need of selecting materials to be taught in terms of their vital relation to the pupils to be taught — of expressing, in other words, in practice the idea that subject matter and method must be interrelated, not isolated, factors in the educative process. "The child's work is motivated whenever he sees a real use in it — when it satisfies some need he feels, provides some value he wants, supplies some control he wishes to possess. . . . So long as the child comprehends more or less clearly the relationship between the *work* he is doing and the *end* sought, his work is motivated." [1]

How to Study as a Generalized Theory of Method

Perhaps Professor Frank M. McMurry of Teachers College has had a more extensive influence on public school

[1] H. B. and G. M. Wilson in *The Motivation of School Work.*

practice than any living leader of educational thought, for he has contributed both as a great teacher of method and as a leader in each of the great method periods, the Herbartian and the functional. He was a pioneer of the American school of Herbart, a ready debater and interpreter of "apperception," "application" (use), "correlation," "concentration," when they were meeting with vigorous opposition in the National Society gatherings. In 1892–96, particularly, he appeared repeatedly on the program of the National Education Association, as well as of the Herbart Club, in defense of them. His *Method of the Recitation*, 1903, written with his brother Charles, was widely used in education classes everywhere; while his special method studies, especially his recent work in geography, are notable contributions. But his name is most generally associated as a contemporary in thought with that of Professor Dewey with his own formulation of the principles of study methods from a functional point of view, as found in *How to Study* and *Teaching How to Study*, 1907, with his numerous treatments of effective study methods which follow this book, and with his work at Columbia University.

In this how-to-study emphasis he sees the fundamental principles of method applied. "How shall one learn alone?" is a more important question than "What shall I teach today?" Study or learning to work alone comes in "the vigorous application of the mind to a subject for the satisfaction of a felt need. . . . Instead of being aimless, every portion of effort put forth is an organic step toward the accomplishment of a specific purpose. Instead of being passive, it requires the reaction of the self upon the ideas presented until they are supplemented, organized, and tentatively judged so that they are held well in memory. The study of a subject has not reached its end till the guiding purpose has been accomplished and the knowledge has been so assimilated that it has been used in a normal way and has become experience . . . until precautions for the preservations of individuality have been included" (p. 283). The factors of study methods are (1) specific purposes; (2) need of supplementing thought; (3) organization of ideas; (4) weighing values; (5) memorizing; (6) application of ideas; (7) a tentative attitude toward truth; (8) self-activity, self-control, self-expression, independence. In 1904, in *What Omissions Are Advisable in the Course of Study* (National Education Association — *Proceedings*, 1904, pp. 194 ff.), a new answer to Spencer's earlier question, "What knowledge is of most worth?" [1] is to be found in his four "propositions for the rejection of useless knowledge":

(1) It must be related to the needs of life in a broad sense.
(2) It must be within the comprehension of the child.
(3) It must appeal to interest.
(4) Details, facts, must be taught in relation to wholes.

These epitomized the current progressive theory of method and of subject-matter values. It should also be added that his well-known criticism of the New York City's teaching methods and courses of study from the standpoint of children's motives, values, and initiatives, has become a valuable handbook in improving practice in the light of our best thought.[2]

Remaking Our Courses of Study

Professor Dewey has had many interpreters. Those who best reflect in practice his spirit and theory of method he has described in *Schools of Tomorrow* (1915). They need not, therefore, be discussed here.

Among the first to apply the functional view to methods of teaching was Professor W. W. Charters, whose *Methods of*

[1] See Herbert Spencer's *Theory of Relative Values.*
[2] See McMurry's *Elementary School Standards*, 1913.

Teaching Developed from a Functional View-Point, was published in 1909, and later, in 1913, popularized as *Teaching the Common Branches*. There were many who attacked the problem of making the curriculum conform to this point of view — attempting to reorganize school knowledge so as to make it less "foreign" to a normal child's interest. "If we seek the kingdom of heaven educationally," as Professor Dewey puts it, or if we "identify ourselves with real instincts and needs of childhood and ask only their fullest assertion and growth . . . all other things will be added unto us." From the standpoint of method, this means that the more closely related the curriculum is to these fundamental interests, the less need there will be for a conscious technique. Dr. F. G. Bonser, in his proposal for courses centered in the industrial arts, may be regarded as the foremost student — with Dr. J. F. Bobbitt of the University of Chicago, perhaps — of curriculum making.[1]

Among the practical efforts to reorganize the curriculum, *The Farmville, Virginia, Training School Course of Study*, finally printed in 1914, and *Guides* to its formulation, deserve notice. This is a product of faculty coöperation under the leadership of Dr. C. W. Stone, now of Washington State College. The present writer was associated in this attempt to incorporate current theory in practice. Professor Dewey's definition of education as reconstruction or cultivation of the child's experience led Dr. Stone and his co-workers to use three stages in learning: *First*, motivation or establishing the pupil's aim — the teacher enabling the pupil to discover inadequacies in his past experience and seeking to arouse consciousness of need for improving it. *Second*, meeting the need — the teacher supplying the

[1] See Bonser's *The Elementary School Curriculum*, Bobbitt's *The Curriculum*, J. L. Meriam's *Child Life and the Curriculum*, Charters's *Curriculum Construction*.

sources in material and suggesting the appropriate procedure for information, problem attack, drill, enjoying, etc. *Third,* merged with the second step, using the newly acquired fact or skill.

On the side of subject matter "centers of interest," providing motive as it operates in each stage of childhood, were sought. Around these "centers" curriculum materials of social value, including the Bible, were selected and organized. These basal and persisting interests were found to be (1) play experience, (2) special days and celebrations, (3) seasonal changes, (4) school needs, (5) story life. The centers of grade-age interest began with "Home Life" and, in a logical expansion, ended in grade VII with "Growth of the State and the Nation."

Professor Charters, in his *Methods of Teaching,* traces the history of such schemes to fill the gap between method and matter from "psychologizing," correlation and concentration, core subjects to the use of central interests. Col. F. W. Parker used the physical sciences — geography, especially — as centers. Miss Katherine Dopp's plan, following Dewey closely, finds interests "in conversation or communication, in inquiry, or finding out things, or construction, and in artistic expression" in the industries. Miss Harriet M. Scott's plan is a modification of the culture-epoch interests. Professor Horn at the University of Missouri in 1908 used a school subject — History. Professor Bonser more recently finds his centers in industrial arts projects and believes they furnish ample motive for drill, enjoyment, and useful knowledge.[1] Mrs. Lois Coffey Mossman, Miss Alice Krackowizer, Miss Margaret E. Wells, and a number of others of his students have more recently worked out practical project programs. Professor J. L. Meriam in his new *Child Life and the Curriculum,* 1920,

[1] See *The Elementary School Curriculum,* 1920, Ch. 9.

gives four activities: observation, play, stories, and hand-work.

The New Psychology

The work of Professors J. McKeen Cattell of Columbia University, E. L. Thorndike of Teachers College and C. H. Judd of the University of Chicago, and that of their associates and students have made possible in the last decade a scientific reëvaluation of our heritage of theory from Comenius to Dewey. Professor Thorndike is, perhaps, more responsible than anyone for the growing use of statistical method in dealing with the problems of both school materials and classroom technique. He published his *Contributions to Mental and Social Measurement* in 1904. Subsequently he published *Principles of Teaching*, 1916, and three volumes of *Educational Psychology*, 1913–14, containing studies in the original nature of man, in individual differences, instincts and capacities, laws of learning and in the factors and conditions involved in improving them. These studies have directed the current of our discussion of method into new channels; the problems of educators have since been attacked from an entirely new angle. "Child-study," so enthusiastically pursued by "neighborhood clubs" of thirty years ago or more, has become a more or less exact body of fact subject to constant verification through laboratory methods common to other sciences. A science of education may be said to have had its beginnings in this generation. Under the direction of Professor Thorndike, Dr. C. W. Stone made the first elaborate investigation of school achievements and reasoning in *Arithmetical Abilities*, 1908. Since that time have come numerous investigations of school subjects, learning and practice curves, mental fatigue, etc. S. A. Courtis's *Arithmetic Tests*, the Ayres *Spelling Scales*, the Hillegas *Scale in Composition*, and several *Silent Reading*

Tests are examples of what has come in the attempt to measure the quantitative results in both skills and content subjects.

These tests and scales have revealed wide variations in ability, the causes of success and failure among children, and the apparent need for as many specific methods in teaching as there are subjects and parts of subjects to be learned or made over into habits. There are differences in capacities and differences in temperaments. There are rapid learners and slow learners, and there are those who by reason of genius or subnormality are not subjects for ordinary methods at all. Perhaps the most significant movement in education that has yet arisen is this attempt to know the facts about how we learn, think, and feel and to base a pedagogy upon them. An illustration of this development is seen in such new titles of educational courses as "Diagnostic Measuring and Remedial Teaching," offered in one of our Schools of Education. The movement is, perhaps, the most encouraging evidence to scientists in other fields that education is itself a science and in the near future will base its procedure on rational grounds, on facts discovered, verified under control, and continually refined in practice. They see the end of faddist and ephemeral theories which last long enough to spoil at least a generation of "handwriters" or "thinkers."

A new pedagogy of the elementary school subjects has appeared to augment the more general laws of learning, and its emphasis is, of course, on special methods or techniques appropriate to the nature of the specific subject or difficulty. A number of excellent "special method" textbooks have recently appeared: Thorndike's *Arithmetic*, Smith's *The Reading Process*, Horn and Ashbaugh's *Spelling Book*. Important studies of Gray, Freeman, Judd, and many others to be found in the *Supplementary Educational Monographs* of the University of Chicago, and the recent publications of the National Society for the Study of Education, especially its *Eighteenth* and *Twentieth Yearbooks*, reflect this trend. The first fruits of the Institute for Educational Research, established at Teachers College, Columbia University, under the direction of Professor Thorndike, to conduct investigations in the field of economy of learning are appearing in our journals and even in our newspapers.

Can There Be a Concept of General Method?

The countless investigations of the abilities of children and their difficulties in learning, and the alleged low-test scores in the drill subjects in some schools where "incidental learning" is the rule, have led some schoolmen to believe that "there is no hidden unified principle lying back of all method." At the same time a great enthusiasm is being shown for what is spoken of as the project method, project-problem method, or project teaching.

Project Teaching — A Method or an Attitude?

With our new knowledge of human behavior and the development of modern psychology and its attack on unverified theory there have arisen two sets of method problems — those rising out of the work of such men as Thorndike, Judd, Freeman, and Gray, and those raised by the followers of Dewey, McMurry, and Kilpatrick, who believe that a consciousness of need, purpose, and motive underlies procedure in all the varied activities of children in learning, and, therefore, supplies a general method. Both groups of investigators rest their case on the laws and conditions of learning. In reality there is no conflict. In fact, two important aspects are being opposed. The future of good teaching seems to depend upon a unification of the contributions made by these groups.

Professor Horn of the University of Iowa, himself an experimental student of method, believes that method depends essentially on the subject matter in a particular subject, that general method is a philosophical fantasy. He has said in a personal letter :

It is my judgment that in the last ten years great advances in educational method have been made along the line of developing superior techniques of learning for each of the prominent subjects. We now know how to teach spelling and writing as accurately as physicians know the diagnosis and treatment of most of their diseases. We are making great strides in the improvement of reading. There has also been some improvement in our methods of teaching other prominent elementary school subjects. Most of these improvements can be ascribed to the application of scientific method, to the making of the course of study, to the determination of economic methods, and to the discovery of the proper tests. As a result of these experimentations, we have made real strides in spite of the confusion created by those who are pushing the project method, and in spite of the inadequacy of this method. It is my judgment that any move in the direction of the establishment of a general method is necessarily fallacious. The way to learn to spell a word is not the way to learn to play on the piano. Even the motivation is not the same in any but a rhetorical sense of the word.

On the other hand, Professor William H. Kilpatrick of Teachers College is finding a place for a new ideal of method and has identified his name with a studied definition of project teaching. He acknowledges his indebtedness for his scientific or philosophical position to both Thorndike and Dewey, and has, through his classroom chiefly, aroused enthusiasm for a new conception of general method.

Distinction is made between "narrow" methods and a "wider" or general method. By "narrow" he means methods or devices necessary to teach special or parts of special subjects, acknowledging the rapid development in scientific measurements. In defining the "wider" method, he makes his fundamental contribution to educational thought. To him an act of learning is always a complex affair ; one never learns one thing alone at a time. We may learn long division, to read, or to make a box or dress, but at the same time we do acquire a number of things, not necessary to proficiency or performance but associated with it, that the teacher does not count in as results. Then, too, not only a new body of associated knowledge and permanent interests may be there to determine the quality of our learning — but ideals and attitudes are also built up that will determine whether the thing we are doing or acquiring will "lead on" to other like activities or cease when the lesson is over. He justifies his use of "wider" in describing method on the ground that it takes into fuller account what any type of instruction actually does for the child and for society.

There are, then, three aspects in any act of learning: (1) *the primary objective* — getting the particular fact or the skill required by the course of study; (2) *associate suggestions* — accessory ideas from collateral fields of knowledge which may be placed at the disposal of the child as a result of vital contacts in the learning, numerous associations of ideas that may "lead on" to later fruitful activities and create abiding interests in these fields; (3) *concomitants* or certain emotional reactions, the disgusts or enthusiasms that come with satisfying or annoying experiences or tasks, affective states which may determine one's future progress in learning, one's ideals and attitudes, one's very character.

To Professor Kilpatrick to "learn" a lesson and be through with it is one thing; to "love" the subject as a result of the learning and to desire to learn outside the class when coercion is withheld is quite another. Society is concerned with our attitudes and ideals, our permanent, dynamic interests, our habits of work and thought, quite as much as it is with the results of primary learning. Tests and scales so far have attempted to measure only the results of this primary learning, but the "simultaneous" learnings incident to drill or recitation are at least as important as the habit formation in the three R's. If the former are difficult to chart and control, there is no reason why in our effort to be practical we should not attempt to control them by method and a careful administration and use of tests. But a great danger in this very testing movement is that teachers will select methods that may bring satisfactory results in primary learning and defeat the purposes of democratic society in not guaranteeing these wider "social outcomes." Another danger in the overemphasis of tests, Professor Kilpatrick points out, lies in the fact that we do not learn in life by any such simple method as scales imply nor are we tested for proficiency in any such practical way. He, however, sees no conflict in the right diagnosis of children's abilities and difficulties and a method or methods that will take in the whole act of learning. Again, this theory of "simultaneous" learnings is Professor Kilpatrick's chief contribution to method and he means something far more comprehensive, as we have seen, than "intuitive" or incidental learning described by earlier theorists. It is the control of these very "attendant" learnings that determines moral instruction and training for citizenship.

Students of Professor Kilpatrick are familiar with his use of the laws and conditions of efficient learning as laid down by Thorndike,[1] and the latter's definition of learning as "acquiring new bonds or changing old bonds" in our nervous system. These new laws are:

I. *Readiness*, or the degree of strength of our desire to respond to a demand for action, depending upon our interest, physical state, and preoccupation. Good teaching requires that a child must be ready for response with a mind "set" to achieve his purpose, hence motive and the correlative place of interest and effort.

[1] See *Educational Psychology*, Vol. III, pp. 327–452.

II. *Exercise: Use and Disuse,* or the old "ever learn to do by doing," vice versa (*i.e.,* habit is determined by exercise or broken by the lack of it), stated in terms of nerve structure or bond connections.

III. *Effect: Satisfaction and Annoyance — Success and Failure:* We learn best that which gives satisfaction or pleasure; annoyance weakens learning or connections between the neurones. We remember a fact when given as a successful answer to a question; we tend to forget it when as a wrong answer the "effect" is unpleasurable.

It follows that the conditions of learning are found best when children are engaged wholeheartedly in work they want to do (ready for it), and have definite purpose in completing (mind-set), and which satisfies a need in achieving that purpose (effort with success). Without purpose the child must be coerced to action with consequent loss in time and effort through divided attention, with loss in "associate suggestions" and a probable unwelcome gain in hatred for all that has to do with the unpleasant task, subject, teacher, and school.

The Project as a Fundamental Concept of Method

The project attitude is a natural outcome of these laws and our discussion of interests, motivation, and problem method. No one recognizes it as a discovery; but only the enthusiast thinks this new word an open sesame to successful application of all our highest ideals of method. No matter how near it is to the common practice of our schools of to-morrow, it is recognized that successful project teaching to-day demands extraordinary ability on the part of the teacher and taxes his resources to the utmost. It is very much easier to teach in "the old-fashioned way" when examinations on subject matter or even efficiency tests are the proofs of effective instruction. Project teaching when it leaves concrete, practical subjects like agriculture or home economics, and is extended to "content" subjects, is difficult and at times impossible. When it is clearly impracticable to teach certain information and habits demanded by the assigned course of study, the project idea should give way to well-motivated recitation and drill, the ideal of yesterday. But much that appears as "impossible" may be accomplished when, with renewed attack on the organization of the curriculum, we establish "centers of interests" or "life topics" by which we may guide and test our results. All teachers are inspired by stories of boys and girls reclaimed by a life-motive project. A boy of fourteen in a one-room school in Virginia is recalled, who had taken seven years to reach the fourth grade. He was learning nothing, the teacher insisted, and was too inert to leave school and follow his father into the cornfield. But the corn-club idea aroused him. He was given a quarter-acre on his father's farm and told that according to the rules of the club contest he must do all the work — he must measure, compute, keep books, select and buy his own seed and fertilizer, make frequent reports to his superintendent and to the state and national departments of agriculture. The boy came to see the relation of school and social need, that arithmetic had social utility and was closely related to his purposes. To get information it was necessary to read; to be understood, to compose and write accurately. As a result of that contest he later graduated from an agricultural high school and finally went to the state college. That corn club, we recall, supplied a project involving half of the course of study and a motive that carried him into scientific farming. As a semester project it contained all the spirit and character of those proposed fifteen years after. It is easy to grasp the vision of the "new" education if we keep in mind all the primary and attendant learnings this country boy acquired. No artificial motivation was necessary for purpose and the high motive was there.

By projects here is meant "purposeful activities" initiated by the children under the guidance of a teacher for the accomplishing of ends immediately satisfying to them and fundamentally valuable to society. It is an idea of the way to go about learning, whatever the subject matter or aim of the lesson. No rigid procedure or technique such as in the Herbartian steps is suggested by the more responsible advocates of the method. All that is demanded is the presence of *purpose, purposeful effort,* the setting up of and achievement of ends by the *children* and, as far as the teacher is concerned, a careful *arrangement* of the *subject matter* involved and intelligent guidance. To resolve it into a method is to formalize it. With the editor of the new *Journal of Educational Method* it is perhaps wise to think that the project is not a method at all, but "a synthesis of current educational ideas and a focus for the original contributions of Dewey, Thorndike, Kilpatrick, and others to the problem of coöperative learning, thinking, and living." Professor Hosic in this connection believes that "so central an idea of method" has not occurred to American educators since Herbart. The formal steps were just steps in a procedure that glorified the teacher at the expense of the pupil, but *this* "is a philosophy at once of life and learning as well as of teaching, capable of infinite variety of applications and rather the basis for a technique than technique itself."

It is with this implication that Professor Kilpatrick champions the project concept. He thinks any "unit of purposeful experience, any instance of purposeful activity where dominating purpose, as an inner urge, (1) fixes the aim (or end) of the action, (2) guides its process, (3) furnishes its 'drive,' its inner motivation for its vigorous prosecution," is a project. Four types of projects are provided: those involving the achieving of ideas, those involving appreciation or enjoying, those involving problem solving, and those involving knowledge or skills and requiring practice or drill. These projects or methods of the child's attack upon his own problems are effective means of acquiring rich "content," and the three R's as well. Though it suggests nature's way, and therefore permits the teacher little activity in the lesson itself, we know that nature's method will not lead the child unaided to as rich experiences as modern life demands. The teacher remains, not on her throne where she may put the fear of God into the child's soul, but as a final social arbiter and manipulator — to a purpose — of method and matter. The *laissez-faire* or do-as-you-please school, however, is as out of harmony with our best thought as is the lockstep. No one proposes that children be allowed to do as they like, to make their own decisions without counting the cost and paying the bill. "Cumulative progress," from generation to generation, Professor Kilpatrick reminds us, "will not be possible without the mediation of adults in the learning process," but "the *sure* inheritance of this race experience tends to be ruled out where the child's experience finds no place." As effort and interest are correlative in nature, so there is no natural isolation of school materials and school method.

Limitations and Defects of Projects by Overemphasis of Purpose and Function

Professor William C. Bagley has in times past questioned the validity of much of the philosophy associated with Professor Dewey's name. He sees dangers in carrying projects too far. He accepts "the economy of purposeful learning without further test and experiment," but, "recognizing the dynamic effect of a strongly felt desire in releasing the energy essential to learning," he "doubts the wisdom of the tenet that all learning should take its cue from purpose." Consciousness of purpose is of late development, biologically, he feels, ripening late in the life of the individual. The child must depend on the adult for control and guidance and we must know when we can safely substitute his purposes for the adult's. Purposes are effective as far as they may be used and hence the limitations of the project method are in the limitations of purposes themselves. After all, the imposition of adult purposes has, as a matter of fact, been one of the most important factors in human evolution. On psychological grounds, he believes that information gained *incidental* to problem solving is not so easily retained or recalled as that mastered for the sake of its own mastery, *i.e.*, through drill, or study for the sake of its results in knowledge and skill.

Still further, he questions the chances of "transfer" unless "we lift procedures and principles out of the matrix of application and their relation to specific and immediate purposes" and drill for proficiency upon them alone. He believes that the functional or instrumental value of knowledge applied alone as a basis of method will prevent the child, engaged only in his own necessarily narrow pursuits, from getting "the full heritage of skill, knowledge, standards, ideals, that represent the gains the race has made." Race experience or selected subject matter furnishes "the foundation, background, perspective, point of view, attitudes. . . . These are likely to defy analysis and to escape the scrutiny of one who is looking only for direct and visible application." Projects should, therefore, never be depended upon alone. Organized and systematic treatment of the same material should follow it, especially in the subjects, history and literature, "where the interpretative and inspirational are greater than the instrumental." [1]

Professor F. G. Bonser, an early disciple of Dewey at Teachers College, sees no reason why the project should be limited to merely practical or constructive activities alone, but thinks it should include "important, purposeful intellectual inquiries and appreciative experiences." Good teaching and a right application of the project idea implies a full recognition of the wealth of spiritual inheritances available to the child. "To interest children only in the immediately stimulating and obvious is little short of criminal," as project teaching is "an attempt at socialization." There is danger of overemphasis of individual projects. There should be much sharing in each other's purposes and problems as it offers the best means of developing coöperative interests and capacities and weeding out selfishness, unwholesome egotism, and interests of narrow range.

Professor Ernest Horn in an article in *The Education Review*, January, 1922, allies himself with those who see the project method as an obstacle to the growth of scientific investigation for more adequate special techniques. He views method only as it may be used to reach tangible objectives of the public schools. He is willing to go back to the shop, kitchen, and farm projects, whence came the name, but objects to the term as including all learning. The older practical projects were directly organized around activities outside the school and efficiency in performance was sought and easily measured and their "transfer" value determined. He would, with Professor Charters, limit the definition of "project" in project-teaching literature by adding the phrase

[1] In this connection, it may be well to examine the claims made for project teaching involving "The Essential Success of Historical Movements" by R. W. Hatch of the Horace Mann School. See *Teachers College Record*, 1918; *Historical Outlook*, February, 1922.

"carried to completion in its natural setting." The fine arts, literature, must be taught by techniques peculiar to them. The mechanical or drill subjects cannot be taught effectively by the "problem attack." He is greatly afraid that teachers will be led to base methods on transitory interests. "For no theory of interest can be accepted that does not include as a part of it a feeling of social obligation."

The influence of the project in teaching has been widespread. It has, no doubt, been made to answer the craving for panacea and may cause "soft-mannered" schools to rise. But it is an impressive fact that teachers in many places are whole-heartedly at work making inventory of children's purposes and filling journals of experiences which will make possible the extension of this idea into new fields of subject matter. A National Conference on Educational Method was organized in 1917 and in September, 1921, the first number of *The Journal of Educational Method* under the editorship of Professor James F. Hosic appeared. A notable series of articles by Professor Kilpatrick on the principles underlying effective project teaching, articles and summaries by the editor, reports on classroom experiments and trials, make this journal the authorized source of information on the development of this new approach. The first considered treatment of the project method in textbook form, however, is M. E. Branom's *The Project Method in Education*, 1919; Professors Stevenson and Stockton and Miss Wells have more recently contributed others. Among special-subject textbooks that are based on the project attack are S. A. Leonard's *Teaching English Composition in the Grades*, Miller's *Practical English Composition*, Guitteau's *Preparing for Citizenship*, Van Buskirk and Smith's *The Science of Everyday Life*, Hoyt and Peet's *Everyday Arithmetic*, and Bolenius's *Boys' and Girls' Readers*. There is also a growing number of textbooks on special method that are largely influenced by this trend in current thought.

REFERENCES

HERRING, J. P. — "Bibliography of the Project Method"; *Teachers College Record*, March, 1920.

Journal of Educational Method.

National Education Association — *Proceedings.*

National Herbart Society (later the National Society for the Study of Education) — *Yearbooks.*

CHAPTER VII
PUBLIC SCHOOL ADMINISTRATION
BY

ELLWOOD P. CUBBERLEY
STANFORD UNIVERSITY

CHAPTER VII

PUBLIC SCHOOL ADMINISTRATION

A Résumé

Twenty-five years ago Professor Monroe and the writer both began work as university professors of education, — the former at Teachers College as professor of the history of education, and the latter at Stanford University as acting-head of a small two-man and wholly undergraduate department of education and in charge of the courses in both the history and the administration of education. In the institutions in which we began our university work we have remained during the quarter-century that has passed. Though the time seems short, as one looks back over it now, it has nevertheless been a great creative period in all lines of educational work, and both the work and the institutions with which we early threw in our lot have expanded greatly as the years have rolled by. During the twenty-five years that measure our respective university services the minor subject, pedagogy, based largely on the recollections and the past practical experiences of a few successful teachers, has been transformed into the new and rapidly expanding professional subject, education, taught in specially organized schools, and based on scientific methods of work and a scientific organization of established principles. The subject was still in the successful-practitioner stage of its development when we began work; it has now evolved, as did medicine and law and engineering before it, into the scientifically organized and taught stage.

When we began our work we each faced situations in

which we had practically no tools with which to work, and during the quarter-century of our service we have both been busy creating the tools which we and others with us are to use. In the history of education the only textbooks available, in 1898, were Painter's *A History of Education*, a little volume of 325 pages, published in 1886; Williams's *The History of Modern Education*, a volume of 444 pages, published in 1892; and Compayré's *History of Pedagogy*, a volume of 570 pages, first published in English translation in 1886. The first two of these were histories of educational theory, and were based largely on material published earlier by the German, Von Raumer, and translated into English by Barnard; while the third, though more a history of practice than the other two, had been written with the needs of French teachers in mind and gave undue emphasis to the history of educational development in France. While Compayré's text was the most usable of the three, all were so markedly inferior to the very able and very scholarly *Text-Book in the History of Education* (759 pages), produced by Professor Monroe, in 1905, that they seem to us of to-day to have been but crude and rudimentary tools with which to try to work.

Through his students, too, Professor Monroe has contributed, during the quarter-century of his work as a teacher, a long list of scholarly researches in the history of education which have not only added much to our knowledge of the subject, but have also contributed materially to the effectiveness of the instruction of other teachers of the subject. In a published list of Doctor of Philosophy degrees granted at Teachers College, from 1899 to 1921, the theses for forty-six of the one hundred and ninety-one degrees have been in the field represented by the work of Professor Monroe. The writer's *Syllabus of Lectures on the History of Education* (1902), while not included in the list, was, however, in part worked out while a student at Teachers College in 1901–02, and owed something of its value to the teaching of Monroe.

The Literature of School Administration

It is, however, with the developments in the field of school administration during the quarter-century under review that this chapter is concerned.   In this field, as in the history of education, there were almost no tools with which to work at the beginning of the period.   If anything, there were fewer tools than in the other subject.   There was no text of any value for use with college students.   Payne, of the University of Michigan, had published, in 1875, a little book of 207 pages, which he called *School Supervision*, and in which he had dealt in a very general way with the superintendent's powers, the grading of schools, and records and reports; and Pickard, then at the University of Iowa, had in 1890 "summarized the experience of twenty years as a teacher and school superintendent" in a little volume of 148 pages, which he called *School Supervision*, and in which he had dealt with the superintendency in general and, more specifically, with the city superintendent in his various official and public relationships.   Both these books were of the personal experience and opinion type, and neither of them gave any comprehensive view of the field of school administration, nor did they try to formulate in principles what ought to be done and why.

The first document to lay down principles of action and to treat, somewhat broadly, the field of city school administration, appeared in 1899, as the *Report of the Educational Commission of the City of Chicago*, a commission appointed the preceding year by Mayor Harrison to formulate some principles for the organization and management of the schools of Chicago.   The secretary of this commission, Professor George F. James, was largely responsible for the character of the report.   As this appeared as a public document and was printed at first in small quantities and for local use only, it was little used by teachers of administration until some years later, when a reprint for the use of students was issued by the University of Chicago Press. This document, while dealing specifically with the work and problems of a single large city school system, nevertheless did formulate fundamental principles in a way that made it for a decade a very useful teaching volume.

In 1904 appeared Chancellor's *Our Schools: Their Administration and Supervision* (426 pages), and in 1908 the same author published a supplemental volume under the title of *Our Schools: Their Direction and Management* (333 pages). These two volumes, taken together, represent our first attempt to formulate, in textbook form, the subject matter of a course in public school administration, and they found extensive teaching use until displaced by the much better organized textbook (*Administration of Public Education in the United States*) by Dutton and Snedden, published in 1908. Both of the Chancellor books contained much concrete illustrative material, based on actual experiences, and both were somewhat less of the reminiscent and somewhat more of the organization type than any books that had before appeared. The Chicago Report, the two books by Chancellor, and the increasing use of the annual reports and courses of study issued by city superintendents of schools, and the rules and regulations printed by city boards of education, all alike tended to provide new instructional material and to give organization to the courses in public school administration being offered in our American colleges and universities.

The courses in school administration offered for the first ten years of the period under discussion continued, however, to be largely a summary of the concrete practical experience of some former successful school superintendent, now turned

teacher in some newly established college chair or department of education. The work of Payne and Hinsdale at
Michigan, of Pickard at Iowa, of Boone at Indiana, and of
Dutton at Teachers College form good examples of such
practical-experience and reminiscent type of instruction;
while the following descriptions of the courses in school
administration, as offered at that time in one of our American
universities, are perhaps typical of much of the early instruction offered:

1. *The Organization and Supervision of Schools.* Lectures and assigned
readings, embracing the organization and supervision of schools in towns
and cities; the relation of these school systems to the State; elementary
schools; high schools and polytechnic schools; the arrangement of courses
of study; plans for grading and promotion; inspection and management;
employment and dismissal of teachers; duties of principals and superintendent, and their relations to the public and to intellectual and moral
training; disciplinary problems; agencies for helping teachers; the school
board and its problems; business management; defects to be remedied;
and problems to be solved.

2. *Seminary in the Study of School Systems.* A study of present conditions and tendencies, based on the study of school reports, as these
relate to enrollment and attendance, comparative expenditure and cost,
public and private schools, city and rural schools, secondary and higher
education, normal schools, and similar topics.

The work in school administration, as in other divisions
of the subject of education, and as in other new subjects of
instruction, had to pass through a formative period. The
decade from 1898 to 1908 covers the important part of this
period. When it is remembered that the first permanent
chair of education was established as late as 1873 (Iowa), and
that when Stanford University opened in 1891, the department of education created there was the tenth such chair or
department established in this country, the reason for the
early formative period's extending over into the first decade
of the present century will be better understood.

At the time Professor Monroe began his work at Teachers
College in 1898, there were perhaps not more than fifty or

sixty institutions in the whole United States that had organized chairs or departments in this new subject, and the instruction then offered by them was quite elementary in nature and almost entirely undergraduate in character. Even Teachers College was then but a small, undergraduate institution. To fill these new chairs it was necessary to draw as professors men from among the most successful practitioners of the time, and these almost of necessity were the older superintendents in our city school systems. Only in a very few instances were young men — as in the case of Professor Monroe himself — who after some teaching experience had obtained the doctorate in history, or psychology, or some similar subject, selected for the new professorships in education and put to work to see what they could find out and could do. To-day the approximately four hundred and fifty American institutions of higher learning and a rapidly growing number of state teachers' colleges offering instruction in education bear witness to the rapid development and organization and expansion of the subject of education, which has taken place during the last twenty-five years. Many of these institutions, following the model set by Teachers College when it affiliated with Columbia University in 1890, have recently reorganized their work in education into teachers' colleges or schools of education, to enable them to care properly for the work in the various phases and divisions of this rapidly developing new subject.

Professional Study of Administration

About 1904 we note the beginnings of a change from the successful-practitioner type of generalized administrative courses toward a more scientifically organized type of instruction, and also the beginnings of a specialization in the work of instruction in school administration. Of this specialization, the separation of state and county school administration from city school administration, and the application of statistical procedure to the study of educational problems, are perhaps the most important of the new developments of that period.

In 1903 the writer expanded his course in school administration from a semester to a year, and devoted the first semester to a study of problems of state and county educational organization, and the second semester to strictly city problems. While some reference to state organization had commonly been included in the earlier general courses, this is the first definite organization, as far as the writer is aware, of a separate course on the problems of state school organization and administration. Elliott began a similar differentiation at Wisconsin in 1905, and Strayer, soon afterward, at Teachers College.

In 1906 the writer published his *School Funds and Their Apportionment* and his *Certification of Teachers*, both being studies which attempted to create teaching material and to establish standards for legislation in this new field of school administration. In 1907 Snedden published his study of the *Administration and Educational Work of American Juvenile Reform Schools*. In 1908 appeared Dutton and Snedden's *Administration of Public Education in the United States*, the first real textbook for college courses on school administration to be published in this country. A volume of approximately six hundred pages, it dealt with state, county, and city administrative problems in a new way, and for the next decade served as the standard textbook in American colleges and universities. In 1911 Swift published his monumental *History of Permanent Public School Funds in the United States, 1705–1905*, a study on which he had been engaged for half a dozen years, and one which opened for him a field of state school finance which he has worked very fruitfully ever since. In 1913 Sies published his study of *Teachers' Pensions and Pension Systems*, this being followed by Furst and Kandel's study of *Pensions for Public School Teachers* in 1918.

In 1914 the writer's *State and County Educational Reorganization* appeared, and in 1915 Professor Elliott and the writer collaborated on a *Source Book in State and County School Administration*. These two volumes, together with the general textbook by Dutton and Snedden, have been much used as texts in the courses in state educational administration which have since been developed in our American colleges and universities. A textbook on the same subject, which would furnish ample teaching material for a separate course in state and county school administration, is now under way, after many delays, and the writer hopes to finish it within the present year. In 1916 the writer's *Public School Administration* appeared, this being a textbook primarily on city school administration, but applying the lessons of city administrative experience to both county and state educational organization.

Of the other new and early specialization in administration mentioned, that of the application of statistical procedure to the study of educational problems, we find its first beginnings in 1902–03, when Professor Thorndike began to teach the elements of the method to his class in educational psychology. In 1904 he published his *Introduction to the Theory of Mental and Social Measurements*. This work marked the beginning of a new era in the study of educational problems, as with the possibility of applying statistical procedure to them an entirely new method of study was now opened up. The first fruits of this method, as applied to school administration, came in 1905, with the publication of two Teachers College doctor's dissertations, one by Elliott on *Some Fiscal Aspects of Public Education in American Cities*, and the other by Strayer on *City School Expenses: The Variability and*

Interrelation of the Principal Items. In 1908 appeared Snedden and Allen's *School Reports and School Efficiency,* an attempt to apply statistical methods to school reporting; in 1909 appeared Ayres's very important statistical study of retardation in and elimination from school, under the title of *Laggards in the School;* in 1912 Holmes published his extensive study of promotional procedure under the title of *School Organization and the Individual Child;* in 1913 Bobbitt's monograph on *The Supervision of City Schools* appeared, giving an excellent discussion of standards and of efficiency methods in administration; in 1913, too, Strayer and Thorndike published their *Educational Administration,* a series of quantitative studies relating to pupils, the teaching staff, curricula, finance, and the measurement of educational output. In 1917 Rugg's *Statistical Methods Applied to Education* came out and at once took its place as the standard textbook in educational statistics, serving to introduce this new type of administrative course into all our leading schools and departments of education. Numbers of articles and volumes applying statistical procedure to pedagogical and mental testing have also appeared, particularly within the past decade, but these lie outside the limits of this chapter, and are left to be treated in the chapters by Professors Leary and Sears.

The titles enumerated above represent perhaps the more important volumes which mark the creative decade from about 1905 to about 1915. Since that time numerous studies, dealing with problems of state and city administrative procedure, have appeared in print. These have come from the pens of students in many educational institutions, and the limits of space preclude their enumeration here. They have dealt with such questions as school funds, school finance, school building programs, state aid, administrative organization, publicity, budget making, teacher training, compulsory education, health work organization, size of classes, rating of teachers, salaries and pensions, textbooks, supervision, economy of time, curriculum studies, and many other similar administrative problems.

Since 1915 three new educational magazines have been started which have carried many articles of an administrative and statistical nature, and the files of which are regarded to-day as part of the necessary equipment of every educational library. These three are *School and Society*, an *Educational Administration and Supervision*, both of which began publication in January, 1915, and the *Journal of Educational Research*, which began publication in January, 1920. The result is that to-day the teacher of school administration finds a growing literature with which it requires much time to keep in touch, his instructional work differentiated into a dozen or more administrative courses, and a constantly increasing number of eager students continually calling for more and more information and guidance.

School Surveys

A little more than a decade ago another important development in administrative procedure, that has added much new instructional material for courses in school administration, was begun in the work of the school survey. The practical results of the survey work have deeply influenced the type of material incorporated into courses and textbooks on school administration. The survey movement has rapidly developed into an important form of educational engineering, by means of which the administrative problems of a school system may be determined, a more intelligent procedure in the organization and administration and supervision of school systems may be formulated, and the returns on the investment of time and money and human effort in education may be increased. With the aid of the new standardized tests

and measures, which the past fifteen years have also seen
evolved, the school survey has now become our most important means for educational administrative diagnosis.

The first type of the city school system survey was the
small "once-over" personal estimate type of survey report
represented by the *Montclair School Survey*, as made by
Hanus in 1911 (28 pages), the first of the city survey reports,
and the *Expert Survey of the Public School System of Boise,
Idaho* (31 pages), as made by Elliott, Judd, and Strayer in
1912. In the *Report of the Baltimore Survey Commission*
(112 pages) in 1911, the second of the survey reports in
point of time, made by a commission composed of Brown,
Cubberley, and Kendall, assisted by Hillegas and Updegraff,
we first find the descriptive and comparative type of school
survey. In the extensive statistical study of a school system
made in the *New York City School Inquiry*, directed by
Hanus, assisted by a staff of experts, in 1911–12, we find a
report consisting of a series of specialized volumes which
represent still another type of survey. This type of school
survey was exemplified later in its best form in the *Cleveland
School Survey*, as directed by Ayres, and the *Gary School
Survey*, as directed by Flexner, both made in 1915–16.

The four early survey reports mentioned — Montclair,
Baltimore, Boise, and New York City — were clearly experimental in character. Each was useful at the time, and
each served to mark out lines to follow and to avoid, and thus
helped to shape later school survey procedure.

In the *Report of the Examination of the School System of
East Orange, New Jersey* (68 pages), made by Moore in the
autumn of 1911; in the *Bridgeport, Connecticut, School
Survey* (129 pages), made by a staff of experts under the
direction of Van Sickle, in 1913; and in the *Portland, Oregon,
School Survey* (317 pages), made similarly by a staff under the
direction of Cubberley in the same year, new lines in city

school surveying were marked out which have been followed in nearly all subsequent city school surveys. While these three reports were still descriptive and statistical and comparative, and were based, with the exception of the East Orange Report, which was done by Moore alone, on a careful examination of the schools by a specialized staff, as had been done in the New York City Inquiry, the strength as well as the weakness of the school systems was pointed out, the different phases of the organization and administration and instruction were evaluated in a series of separate chapters, and in particular the reports were directed toward the constructive development of the school system along good lines in the future, criticisms made being used constantly as a basis for constructive suggestions as to improvement. Quite similar lines were followed in the *Springfield, Illinois, Survey* (150 pages), made by Ayres early in 1914.

Bobbitt, in a survey of the schools of South Bend, Indiana, in the spring of 1914, and still more so in his survey of the schools of San Antonio, Texas, in 1915, developed another type of technique in which he placed the chief emphasis of each report on the proper organization of the courses of instruction in the schools, devoting the report largely to an extended discussion of what the schools ought to teach, and why. In *A Review of the Rockford, Illinois, Public Schools,* 1915–16, made by R. G. Jones, while Superintendent of Schools there, another type of technique was originated in the form of a self-survey, and in the introduction of numerous charts and diagrams, designed to give to the people of Rockford a pictorial presentation of the work of their schools.

In the *Butte School Survey,* made in the spring of 1914 by a staff of experts under the direction of Strayer, the newly developed standard tests were employed for the first time in any extensive way. Courtis had used his arithmetic tests earlier in the New York Inquiry, but the Butte survey

was the first in which the different standardized tests then
available were used to evaluate the instruction given by a
school system. This survey thus developed another new
type of school survey technique, that of a careful measurement of the instruction given, and one that has been followed
in nearly all surveys of city school systems made since 1914.
In the *Salt Lake City School Survey*, made in 1915 by a staff
under the direction of Cubberley, the different types of
technique then developed — descriptive, comparative, statistical, standardized testing, graphic display, and evaluation
by the staff — were all combined in the work of the survey
and its report. This composite type of survey report may
now be said to have become a standard type for a report in a
single volume of readable size ; perhaps the best example of
this type of survey technique which we now have is to be
found in *The Boise Survey* (290 pages), as made by Sears,
assisted by Proctor and Williams, in 1919, and published the
following year by the World Book Company. Perhaps the
best example of the many-volumed, specialized series of
reports type of survey we have, also combining the different
forms of survey technique, is the *Cleveland School Survey*, in
twenty-five volumes, made by a large staff of experts under
the direction of Ayres, in 1915–16.

By 1915–16 it may be said that the city school survey had
become standardized as to type and purpose, and established
as an important part of our administrative technique.
Since that date the school survey has become common, the
number made since then being too large for mention here.
Its successor, the self-survey by local educational authorities,
and the continuous survey by a city department of statistics
and research, have become established as recognized parts
of the administrative procedure of a city school system.
The school survey has also been extended in many new
directions and specialized in character. Cubberley in 1915

applied the technique developed to a study of the school finances of Oakland, Cal.; Hawkins, Strayer, and Trabue, to a study of the educational system of Nassau County, N. Y., in 1917; and numerous school building requirement surveys have been made and published.

To-day we may be said, as a result of the coming of the school survey, to have developed a new technique of fundamental importance in administrative educational diagnosis. Courses for the study of the school surveys as printed have been introduced in many departments and schools of education, and we await now only the production of a satisfactory textbook on the administrative use of the school survey to enable departments of education generally to offer to their students a course that will summarize the results of the best that has been done, and will train students of school administration in the best methods of diagnostic technique.

In 1913 the survey idea and technique were applied to the study of a state school system, in the case of Vermont, in a study undertaken by the Carnegie Foundation at the request of an educational commission, which had been created to inquire into the needs of education in that state. While there had been previous educational commissions which had reported on state educational needs before the Vermont study was made, notably California in 1900 and Illinois in 1909, the work represented in previous reports had been based on hearings and questionnaires and collected statistics, while the Vermont inquiry was made by an expert commission that went into and traveled over the state, basing its report on the results of its examination. The Vermont study, therefore, represents the first real application of the city school survey idea to a study of state educational problems. The chief work on this survey was done by Elliott, Hillegas, and Learned, and the report, a volume of

241 large pages published in 1914, made a careful analysis of the educational needs and resources of the state, and offered a legislative program for the future development of education in the state. This study definitely established a technique for state school surveying.

In 1916 the General Education Board published a study of public education in Maryland, made similarly by Bachman and Flexner for a state educational survey commission. This represented another type of study — that of analyzing and describing existing conditions, and pointing out the more important changes that ought to be made, with a view to securing early legislative action on the recommendations made. The report was, in consequence, more popular in nature and less extensive than the Vermont report had been, though based on approximately as thorough and intensive a study of state educational conditions and needs. This Maryland study has been followed by a somewhat similar study of the state school systems of Delaware (1919), North Carolina (1920), and Kentucky (1921), and one for Indiana is nearly ready for publication. These have all been made by Bachman and Flexner. In 1915 the United States Bureau of Education entered upon the work of state school surveying with a study of the higher educational institutions of Iowa, made by a commission of which Capen was chairman, and soon followed this by state educational surveys of Washington, North Dakota, Wyoming, Arizona, Colorado, South Dakota, and Alabama — all completed by the close of 1919. In 1919 Virginia provided for a survey of education in that state, and a large staff of specialists, collaborators, and advisers, under the direction of Inglis, was selected for the work. In this survey, in addition to the usual general study of the legal and administrative and financial organization of the schools of the state, with recommendations for their future development, an attempt was made for the first time to measure and determine the efficiency of instruction in the schools of a state by means of the use of the standardized tests. By 1920 the technique for the state school survey had been clearly developed, as is shown by the fact that the state school surveys made since and now under way follow the lines laid down in the Vermont, Maryland, Iowa, Washington, and Virginia surveys. The reports of these surveys now provide much valuable material for use with students in courses in state school administration.

Summary of Progress

A review of what has been presented in this chapter will reveal the nature of the period which this memorial volume has under consideration. What has been shown for the subject of school administration holds true for almost all other divisions of the subject of education. The quarter-century just past has been a great creative period in our work. The first six to eight years were an experimental and formative period. New departments were being created to teach a new subject for which there was as yet but little in literature or traditions. The early teachers were largely of the successful experience type, and when young men trained in other lines started work in education, they had to find their work and create their tools.

By about 1905 we clearly note the beginnings of a distinct change. The successful practitioner begins to be replaced by young men who have obtained some little training in education itself, and the beginnings of specialization within the division of administration appear. The study of state and county school administration begins to separate from the study of city administrative problems, or rather from the generalized type of course in administration previously given. The application of the new statistical methods to the study of education also begins, and the mastery of the elements of statistical procedure in time becomes a necessary tool. The new standardized tests and measures are evolved and serve as a means of changing school supervision from guesswork to scientific accuracy.

By the middle of the period under review we find the beginnings of the city school survey, a new administrative instrument of very large importance, and half a dozen years later we find its technique perfected and the city school survey becoming common. This has virtually developed a new field of educational engineering. To-day the local self-survey and the creation of city departments of statistics and research mark the passing over of the survey movement into established administrative procedure, while the results obtained from the different surveys made, both in fact and in technique, now only await organization into textbook form to make them available for teaching purposes. The application of the survey idea to state school organization and problems came soon after, and as a natural consequence of the results obtained from the use of the school survey in the cities. This too has provided the teacher of school administration with much new teaching material, and this too is now passing over into permanent form in the creation of state research divisions to do work for the schools of the state similar to that now done by the research bureaus for the cities.

The twenty-five years under review have witnessed a great expansion of the subject of education along all lines. In administration, the single course of a quarter of a century ago has been expanded into a large division, and sometimes into a department within a school. Instead of the course being but a part of one man's work, a number of instructors are now required to cover the many courses which have been developed in the subject ; and many students who now go to universities for graduate work in education do so to specialize in school administration alone.

CHAPTER VIII

PUBLIC SCHOOL FINANCE

BY

FLETCHER HARPER SWIFT

UNIVERSITY OF MINNESOTA

CHAPTER VIII

PUBLIC SCHOOL FINANCE

A Period of Unparalleled Interest

No period in the history of school finance in the United States is more important or more interesting than that of the last quarter of a century. Before entering upon a detailed consideration of this period, it will be well to call attention to some of the outstanding events and tendencies which give this period a unique significance in the history of American education.

During this period school costs have mounted by leaps and bounds. New policies of school support have been adopted and others are now in the process of early experimentation. New conceptions of what our public schools must endeavor to do for the millions of children who, year after year, pass in and out of their schoolrooms have led to an expansion of the course of study and to the attempt on the part of our public schools not only to furnish new types of instruction, but to provide many types of physical care almost undreamed of by the directors of public education a quarter of a century ago. Some of the projects well-nigh unthought of at that time, but which the public schools of to-day are undertaking, are suggested by the following list : medical inspection, health supervision, dental clinics, psychological clinics, open-air schools, supervised play, special schools and classes for blind, deaf, crippled, and mentally backward or deficient children, care of truancy cases, home visiting, public kindergartens, extensive programs of physical and health education. During the period under consideration a number of states have enacted free textbook laws, and laws providing for continuation classes for minors engaged in industry. The federal government has entered upon a national program for the promotion of vocational education. A number of private foundations, possessing in some cases almost fabulous endowments, have been incorporated and are to-day making generous contributions to the promotion of public education. This period has seen a steady decline in the relative importance of the part played by the state in financing our public schools and a greater and greater tendency to make the locus of responsibility the local school unit and to place the major portion of the burden upon it.

One of the most significant features in the history of school finance during the last twenty-five years is the gradual awakening on the part of the public to a realization that no problem in education is more important than the problem of school support. If one turns to the annual volumes published by the National Education Association, he discovers that in the year 1890 the subject of public school finance was given little, if any, place in the deliberations of this body, either at its general sessions or at the meetings of the Department of Superintendence. The topics under discussion at that time related chiefly to child study, teacher training, discipline, and courses of study. The outstanding topic in 1910 appears to have been individual differences.

In 1911 appeared what proved to be an epoch-making document in the development of city school finance. It was in this year that a committee appointed by the National Education Association presented its preliminary *Report on Uniform Records and Reports*. The final report of this Committee was published in 1912 by the United States Bureau of Education as Bulletin No. 3 of that year. This report is one of the most significant contributions yet made

to the scientific study of city school finance.   In the program
of the National Education Association for the year 1915, the
problem of school finance is given a place, albeit a minor one.
But from 1915 onward, the subject of public school finance
occupies a larger and larger place, not only in the programs
and deliberations of this, our greatest national education
association, but in that of every education organization and
association.   Indeed, at the present writing, there is probably no question related to public education which is en-
gaging a greater amount of thoughtful attention, both on the
part of scientific students and on the part of the general
public.

Scope of Present Chapter

From these preliminary observations, we may now turn
to consider more definitely the course of events in the history
of public school finance in the United States during the last
three decades.   Our account may well begin with a consideration of the increase in costs of public schools and the reasons
for this increase.   Following this, we will direct our attention
to the trend of state policies, the growth of local school
support and its results, the growth of federal aid to public
schools, the present critical situation, and the outlook for
the future.

Growth of School Costs and Causes

In 1870 the United States spent $63,000,000 on public
schools; in 1920 the expenditure was $1,036,000,000, an
increase of considerably over 1500 per cent.

Our approximate total expenditure for public schools
amounted in 1900 to $215,000,000, in 1910 to $426,000,000,
and in 1920 to $1,036,000,000.   These vast increases in
school expenditure are the result of the interaction of many
factors : the rapid increase in school population, the lengthening of the legal school year, the assignment by the com-

munity to the school of a larger and larger number of functions resulting in the introduction of many new types of studies and activities.

The first of the above causes that concerns us is the enormous increase in the number of children for whom the United States is providing public elementary and secondary education, and the great increase in the amount spent for each school child educated at public expense. The fact that the population of the United States increased from approximately 63,000,000 in 1890 to 106,000,000 in 1920 would in itself result in a great increase in the school population and school costs. In 1890 there were approximately 8,000,000 children in average daily attendance upon public schools in the United States; in 1920 there were 16,000,000. In 1890 the average annual expenditure for each child in average daily attendance was $17; in 1920 it was $64. We have seen that the per cent of increase of the total amount expended for public schools from 1870 to 1920 was over 1500. For this same period the number of children in average daily attendance increased 300 per cent, and the average annual expenditure per child 314 per cent. Let us now consider briefly some of the most important reasons contributing to this increase in school attendance and school costs, other than the increase in the total population of the United States.

The number of children attending public school has greatly increased — with a resulting increase in school costs — during the last quarter of a century. This is due not only to increase in population, but also to the enactment of compulsory school laws and the extension of the school age. In 1894–95, according to the Commissioner of Education, there were nineteen states which had no compulsory school law. In 1920 there was not a single state in the Union which did not have such a law. It is scarcely necessary to add that the degree of effectiveness with which these laws have been enforced has steadily increased throughout the last twenty-five years, with the result that a larger and larger percentage of children of school age has been found within the public schools. Not only is this true, but a comparison of the compulsory school age in those states which in the year 1895 had a compulsory school law with the compulsory school age in these same states for the year 1918 shows that, while in New Hampshire the compulsory school age had decreased two years, in New Mexico one year, and in five states had remained unchanged, yet in eighteen states it had increased all the way from one to four years. In this connection, attention should be called to the length of the average school year in the United States, which increased from 135 days in 1890 to 162 days in 1920.

Another factor which has played a large part in the increase of school costs in the United States is the multiplication of high schools and an unprecedented growth of high school attendance. How important these factors are can better be understood by a comparison of what it costs to educate a high school pupil with what it costs to educate an elementary school pupil. In 1918 the average cost in the United States per elementary school pupil enrolled was $31.65; per high school pupil enrolled, $84.48. In 1920 the expenditure per elementary pupil and per high school pupil was approximately double that of the year 1918, being in fact $64.03 per elementary pupil enrolled, and $158.21 per high school pupil enrolled. From these facts we see that it costs approximately two and one half times as much to educate pupils attending high schools as pupils attending elementary schools. These facts become of great significance in attempting to determine the reasons for mounting costs in education when we discover that seven times as large a proportion of our total population was attending high school

in 1920 as was attending high school in 1890. More specifically, in 1890 three tenths of one per cent (.003) of the total
population in the United States was enrolled in high school,
whereas in 1920 two and one tenth per cent (.021) was
enrolled. In the year 1890 approximately three persons out
of every one thousand in the United States were enrolled in
high school; in 1920 twenty-one persons out of every one
thousand. The trend becomes even more impressive when
we turn our consideration from the total population to that
portion of it actually enrolled in school : in 1890 out of every
thousand children enrolled in school only sixteen were in
high school; in 1920 out of every thousand children enrolled
one hundred and two were enrolled in high school. Finally,
we discover that, whereas in 1890 the United States was
spending $4,759,065 for public high schools, in 1920 the ex-
penditure on public high schools, excluding all cities of less
than 10,000 population, and excluding also costs of administration, capital outlay, and debt service, was $66,024,307.

In considering increases in school population and in total
school costs which have marked the last quarter of a century,
the fact must not be overlooked that no less than ten states
have been admitted into the Union since 1888. Four
of these states were admitted in the year 1889, and the
remaining six from 1890 to 1912. The Nation's aggregate
school costs have been greatly augmented by the rapid
development of these new states, their growth in population,
and particularly the fact that they came into the Union
with a marked zeal for public education and possessing vast
federal endowments which stimulated them to establish and
maintain high standards as to the accessibility and quality
of the educational facilities they provided.

It is impossible in the present brief chapter to give the
consideration merited by a number of other causes which,
combined with those already mentioned, have steadily forced

upward expenditures for public schools. Reference was made in an opening paragraph to the expansion of the course of study, to the development of vocational education, to the establishment of continuation classes, and to the fact that a great number of new projects and new responsibilities have been assumed by the public schools during the last quarter of a century. To these must be added three other causes: a steady rise in the educational and professional qualifications demanded of public school teachers, which necessitates a steady increase in the salaries paid; a similar continual rise in building and equipment standards; and a final cause — one which is frequently overlooked by the public — the depreciation of the purchasing power of the dollar. A brief report recently prepared by the Research Division of the National Education Association contains the following significant paragraph:

It is true that there have been some "real" increases in school costs resulting from increased attendance and the broadening of the school's work. Likewise, there have been some "real" increases in the national income in terms of quantity of goods produced, due to the wider use of machinery and general improvement of production methods. But far more important than either of these in bringing about the "rapid increase" in school expenditures and national income is the depreciation of the dollar. The so-called increases in educational expenditures have been largely fictitious. What has really happened since 1913 is that the dollar has depreciated in buying power. As a result, educational expenditures, as well as national income, when measured in dollars, have both shown a rapid increase. (*The Journal of the National Education Association*, Vol. XII, No. 3, p. 118.)

Thus far, attention has been focused chiefly upon the increasing costs of public education during the last quarter of a century and the causes of this increase. Let us now consider the tendencies which have characterized policies in public school finance during this era. The first, and, from some standpoints, perhaps the most important of these tendencies, is the decline in the relative importance of the state as the provider of school revenues.

Decline in Relative Importance of State Funds

During the period under consideration the actual amounts contributed to public education from state funds have steadily increased. But the important question is not whether the state is now giving two dollars or five dollars where formerly she gave one dollar, but rather whether the state is shouldering as large, a larger, or a smaller share of the total school burden than she did twenty-five years ago. The real facts in the case are that, whereas in 1890 the state furnished approximately $23.75 out of every $100 provided for public schools, in 1920 only $16.80 came from state sources. The situation becomes even more impressive when we consider certain individual states, particularly those states which in 1890 derived half or more than half of their revenue from state funds. In 1890 the per cent of total school receipts provided by the state in Alabama was 68; in Georgia, 57; in Kentucky, 59; in North Carolina, 77; in South Carolina, 83; in Tennessee, 82; in Texas, 80. In 1920 the per cent of total school receipts provided by the state in these same commonwealths was as follows: Alabama, 51; Georgia, 44; Kentucky, 37; North Carolina, 30; South Carolina, 16; Tennessee, 18; Texas, 54. Of the above seven states, in 1890, four derived more than 75 per cent of their total receipts from state funds; in 1920, only two, Alabama and Texas, derived more than 50 per cent from the state. It should be noted that in 1890 local zeal for public education was undeveloped in most of these states, and that the decline in the proportion of total school costs borne by the state and the accompanying increase in the proportion borne by local units indicates a desirable and healthy tendency in so far as it indicates more generous support for public schools. However, it is equally evident that in these commonwealths the state has allowed the burden of school support to be shifted to minor constituent school corporations with a degree of rapidity that calls in question the soundness of this tendency.

Declining Importance of State Endowments

In 1890 the public schools of the United States derived 5.45 per cent of their total school receipts from the income of permanent school funds and lands and 18.30 per cent from the proceeds of state taxes and appropriations. In 1920 permanent funds and lands contributed 2.7 per cent and state taxes and appropriations 13.8 per cent. From this we see that the proportion of total school receipts derived from permanent funds in 1920 was only half of what it was in 1890. The significance of this fact cannot be fully appreciated unless we recall that except for the admission of six new states with vast endowments, the per cent of total school receipts derived from permanent funds would have declined much more rapidly than it did.

It should not be overlooked that the actual per cent of total school receipts derived from permanent funds is considerably less than that shown in state and federal official reports. In no less than one third of the states which annually report revenue derived from permanent school funds, these funds exist totally or largely as paper funds, accounts carried on the books of the state, or represented by irredeemable state bonds. In some states, funds once accumulated have been diverted or lost. Other states, such as Michigan, Maine, and Ohio, use for general state purposes all moneys paid into the state treasury to the credit of the state permanent school fund and establish a state debt on which the commonwealth binds itself to pay interest at a fixed rate to the public schools.

A study recently made by the writer, of state permanent school funds, reveals the fact that 15 per cent of the permanent school fund of Nevada, 18 per cent of the perpetual school fund of California, and 32 per cent of Wisconsin's school fund exist only as state debts. All of Louisiana's surplus revenue fund and 58 per cent of her free-school fund are recognized as permanent state debts by her Constitution. The entire principal of the so-called permanent state school fund is practically a state debt in the following eight states: Arkansas, Illinois, Maine, Michigan, Mississippi, New Hampshire, Ohio, and Tennessee.

Many of the debts to state permanent school funds were undoubtedly due to the inexperience of the states at the time they came into possession of these endowments, and to a lack of adequate vision of the possibilities and the purposes of such endowments. Such a defense cannot be made, however, of states which, with generations of experience, continue to mismanage or divert these sacred trusts.

Arkansas is an example of a state pursuing such a policy. A study of the federal grants devoted by Arkansas to her permanent public school fund shows that had this fund been properly managed, Arkansas would to-day possess a permanent endowment of approximately $92,000,000, yielding an annual revenue of $4,600,000, more than one third of the total amount Arkansas expended for public schools in 1920. Instead of any such princely sum, Arkansas has to-day a nonproductive fund whose paltry income of $74,000 is, from the standpoint of a productive endowment, a pure fiction. This fund has been continuously deprived of lands and moneys devoted to it by the Constitution, and defrauded by laws which gave, and still give, title to school lands to persons able to show tax receipts for a certain number of years but who undoubtedly have no just claim to the lands deeded them. A study of the facts in the case, and of present as well as past laws, would seem to show that the citizens of Arkansas have conceived their permanent public

school fund primarily as a fund to be used for the advantage
of individual citizens, or to be employed to rescue the state
from any and every financial crisis. As late as 1921, $180,000
in cash which had accumulated in the state treasury to the
credit of the permanent fund was used to pay the state's
penitentiary debt and was replaced by state paper. One of
the most significant, as well as one of the most disheartening
features of the situation, is the fact that the transactions
involved were entirely lawful, being in fact merely the carrying out of the enactments of the legislature.

Tendencies in State Taxation and Appropriations

It has been shown that state taxes and appropriations
have declined in relative importance as sources of public
school revenue far less rapidly than permanent school funds.
This is due to a number of causes. The increase of permanent school funds is dependent upon additions to these
funds from fixed sources of predetermined value. Appropriations and state tax rates may both be increased by the
legislative bodies of the states. A study made in 1920
showed that twenty-nine states devoted the proceeds of a
state tax to public schools. Twenty of these states employed
a mill general property tax. It is evident that where this
type of tax is employed the revenue produced thereby will
increase as the wealth and population of the state increase.

A further factor which has caused state school taxes and
appropriations to hold their own much better than permanent
school funds is the fact that a number of our states during
the period under consideration have recognized the evils
resulting from the tendency of the state to shoulder a de-
creasing proportion of the school burden, and have adopted
policies definitely designed to increase state school taxes
and appropriations. In 1919 California passed a law which
raised the state grant from $15 to $17.50 per year for each

pupil in average daily attendance in elementary schools. By constitutional amendment adopted November 2, 1920, and by legislation enacted to carry out the same, the grant was raised to $30 per pupil. In like manner, in 1920, California increased her state grant per high school pupil from $15 to $30. Thus we see that in the case of California the state grant was increased approximately 100 per cent in the year 1920.

No less interesting is the action of Massachusetts. This state leads the Union in the antiquity of her practice of supporting schools overwhelmingly by local taxation. In 1915 Massachusetts derived 97.1 per cent of her total school revenues from local taxation. Four years later we find her frankly recognizing the necessity of departing from this policy and passing a law providing for setting aside a portion of the proceeds of the state income tax as an annual current school fund to be known as the general school fund. As the result of this action, whereas in 1905 Massachusetts derived 2.8 per cent of her total public school revenues from the state, and in 1915 only 1.82 per cent, in 1920 the state furnished no less than 12.3 per cent.

New Types of State Taxes

Needless to say among the oldest types of taxes levied for schools are general property taxes and poll taxes. The unsatisfactoriness of the poll tax has led to its abandonment within the past twenty-five years by a number of states. California, which abolished it in 1914, may be taken as an example. In a number of states, poll taxes for school purposes continue to be levied by minor public corporations, such as counties or towns, but in only nine is a state poll tax levied for schools. North Carolina levies the highest state school poll tax, $1.43, and Indiana the lowest, fifty cents. A poll tax of $1 is levied in the seven remaining states; namely, Arkansas, Georgia, Louisiana, Tennessee, Texas, Virginia, and West Virginia.

Although there is a strong tendency to depend less than formerly upon the general property tax, due to a growing recognition within the past decade of the unsoundness of this tax, it still remains the most universally employed of all taxes. No less than twenty states levy a state school mill tax on all taxable real and personal property within the state, rates varying all the way from 0.7 of one mill in Wisconsin to 4.6 mills in Utah.

A recent tendency of great significance is the levying of a state mill tax the rate of which is not specified in the law other than that it shall be sufficient to produce a certain total sum or so much per teacher or per school child. This mode of taxation is employed in at least five states : Arizona, New Hampshire, New Mexico, Washington, and Wisconsin.

The tendency of our national industrial life away from what were once almost exclusively agricultural occupations to an increasingly large proportion of manufacturing and commercial activities has brought about a transformation in the character and in the form of property and wealth. Formerly wealth was represented almost entirely by real and personal property, but within the last twenty-five years wealth and property have tended more and more to become corporate, and many forms of income derived from sources other than tangible property can be reached only by special forms of taxation.

As an outcome of this transformation in industrial life and wealth, states are coming to recognize that frequently the possession of an income, whether derived from an earned salary, from income for professional services, or from intangible property such as stocks and bonds, is a much truer index of ability and of obligation to support public undertakings than is the possession of real or personal property.

According to a recent statement of the Federal Department of Commerce, thirty-three states levy taxes on corporation stock, nine on savings banks, and forty-two on inheritances. Reference has already been made to the use of the income tax by Massachusetts as a source of school revenue. Delaware depends very largely for the support of schools upon her recently created state income tax.

California, after years of experimenting with a state general property tax, abandoned the same in favor of biennial appropriations from the state general fund. But at the time she abandoned the state general property tax she adopted the policy of levying a state tax upon corporations, with the result that approximately 60 per cent of the general fund from which the major portion of all state aid comes is derived at the present time from corporation taxes. The amount provided by the state corporation tax in California is many times as large as the greatest amount ever produced by the state general property school tax. This made it possible for California to increase her pupil grants in 1920, as already noted, approximately 100 per cent. In 1920 the state furnished only 14 per cent of the total receipts for public schools. It is estimated that if the constitutional amendment of 1920 had been in effect in 1921, the state would have furnished no less than 26 per cent of the total receipts for elementary and secondary schools.

An epoch-making event in the history of public finance was the enactment by the state of Louisiana of a law which became effective on July 1, 1920, providing for a severance tax on all natural products severed from the soil, except agricultural products. A number of states, such as Utah and Minnesota, had long levied taxes upon ores, but a severance tax taxes not only ores, but timber, sand, gravel, clay, gas, oil, and all other nonagricultural natural products. The proceeds of this tax in Louisiana are devoted in part to the

State University and Agricultural and Mechanical College, and in part to state institutions for the deaf, blind, and other special classes. None of the proceeds go to public schools. Nevertheless, as a new type of taxation it is of great significance and should prove suggestive to many other states which are looking for new sources of school revenue. It is estimated that the Louisiana State University will receive annually from the severance tax between one and a half and two million dollars. It is interesting to note in this connection that in accordance with the writer's recommendations contained in a survey of public education in Arkansas made under the direction of the United States Bureau of Education, the Arkansas legislature of 1923 enacted laws providing for a state income tax and a state severance tax.

Increasing Importance of Local Support

Parallel with the decline of the relative importance of state funds as sources of school revenue there has been a continuous growth in the proportion of the total school revenue furnished by minor constituent public corporations; namely, counties, towns, school districts, and, in Louisiana, parishes. In 1890, 68 per cent of the total receipts for public schools in the United States were derived from local sources; in 1920 slightly more than 83 per cent. Although there has been an increase in the proportion of the total school revenue furnished by local sources in nearly every state in the Union, with a few striking exceptions, such as Massachusetts already noted, the most striking increase has been in those states in the South Central and South Atlantic groups where, in 1890, 50 per cent or less than 50 per cent of the total receipts were provided by local units. The per cent of total public school receipts derived from local sources in 1890 was, in North Carolina, 2; South Carolina, 13; Tennessee, 13; Texas, 12. In 1920 North

Carolina derived 70 per cent of her total public school revenue from local sources; South Carolina, 84 per cent; Tennessee, 82 per cent; and Texas, 46 per cent. A comparison of the situation in Alabama, Arkansas, Georgia, Kentucky, Louisiana, and Mississippi for these same two years would show increases varying from 15 per cent to 30 per cent.

Whether we view individual states or the United States as a whole, we discover that despite a certain degree of progress in matters of centralization and despite court decisions and the utterances of educational theorists to the effect that public schools are state, not local, institutions, in actual practice, schools in the United States have tended more and more throughout the last quarter of a century to become locally supported institutions.

The results of this tendency are being felt to-day as never before. From almost every state come reports of inadequate funds for the support of public schools and accounts of frantic attempts, in the name of economy, to cut teachers' wages and to reduce school curricula to the narrow and arid state of generations gone by. The majority of our states are to-day financing their schools under the district system. The record of this system wherever found is the same: inequalities in ability to produce school revenue, inequalities in effort and zeal, inequalities in educational opportunity. Generations of local support and local domination of public schools finds the richest nation on the earth denying multitudes of her children any educational opportunity whatsoever, and herding thousands upon thousands of others in dismal and unsanitary hovels, under the tutelage of wretchedly underpaid and proportionately ignorant, untrained, and negative teachers.

It is a realization of the unfairness of existing systems of local support and local control and the disastrous and incurable evils produced by such systems that has led many scientific students of education and several of our states to give serious consideration to the possibilities of deriving a much larger proportion of school revenues from units more capable than school districts of equalizing school revenues, burdens, and opportunities.

Those looking for a solution have turned their attention to the nation, the state, and to larger local units, such as the county. The marked tendency in Massachusetts and California to demand that the state shoulder an increasing share of the school burdens has already been noted. Even more significant is the policy recently adopted by Delaware, which now places practically the entire support of public schools directly upon the state. Other states which have recently made marked advances in this direction are Maryland, Montana, New York, Texas, Pennsylvania, and Washington. This movement has been helped by the work of a number of leading authorities in the field of school finance, who have pointed out that, aside from the nation, the state is the only authority capable of adjusting existing inequalities and that if schools are in the last analysis state institutions, the ultimate responsibility for their maintenance and support belongs to the state.

Increasing Importance of the County

Many of the greatest inequalities produced by the district system are the result of the inequality of these smallest of local units in wealth. It is an inevitable result of great inequalities in wealth that the funds provided by school districts should be very unequal. Another obvious result of inequality in financial ability is inequality in the effort put forth by the various districts to produce school revenue. In general it may be observed that the poorer the district the heavier is the tax. How the county would serve to

equalize school revenues and school burdens may be shown
by a few examples. In Chippewa County, Minnesota, under
the district system the poorest rural district must depend
upon an average wealth of $1600 per child in average daily
attendance at the same time that the richest rural district
may draw upon an average wealth of $34,700 per child.
Were the county to be employed as the unit from which to
derive school revenue there would be available, per child,
an average taxable property worth $5000. In St. Louis
County, Minnesota, the richest rural district has wealth
sufficient to enable it to draw upon $38,500 for each child in
average daily attendance; whereas the poorest rural district
in this same county has $1100 per child. Were the county
depended on instead of the district, there would be for the
support of education for each child approximately $14,900
worth of taxable wealth.

Some of our states, of which Maryland is a notable example,
have depended upon the county as a unit of organization and
school support from the very beginning of their statehood.
Nevertheless, a widespread recognition of the significance of
the county as a source of school revenue is of comparatively
recent development. The truth of this statement is suggested by the fact that the analyses of the public school
revenues prepared by the United States Bureau of Education
for the years prior to 1918 did not report county school
receipts separately, but simply included them under the
general caption, *local receipts*.

Another evidence of the rising importance of the county
in the support of public schools is found in the fact that,
whereas in the year 1918 only 7.9 per cent of the total school
receipts were provided from county sources, in 1920 the
proportion contributed by the county had increased to 11.4
per cent. During this biennial period the increase in certain
states was exceedingly marked. Of seventeen states de-

riving 15 per cent or more than 15 per cent of their school revenues from county funds in 1920, in only three, — Arizona, Maryland, and New Mexico — was the proportion less than in 1918. In all others the proportion remained the same or was greatly increased. The most notable increases were in Kentucky, Oregon, Ohio, North Carolina, Nevada, Louisiana, and Mississippi. Among these states the smallest increase was in Kentucky, where in 1918 the county contributed 17 per cent of the total school revenue and 25 per cent in 1920. The greatest increase was in Ohio, where in 1918 the county contributed only 1.7 per cent and 54 per cent in 1920.

Tendencies in Federal Aid

Of the policies characterizing tendencies in public school finance during the last ten years perhaps none has attracted more widespread attention than that of federal aid. The Smith-Lever Act, approved May 8, 1914, provided federal subventions for extension work in agriculture and home economics. On February 23, 1917, the Smith-Hughes Act was passed, which marks the entrance of the federal government upon a national policy of subsidizing public school vocational education and the training of vocational teachers and supervisors. The Smith-Hughes Law was followed by the Smith-Sears Act, approved June 28, 1918, and the Smith-Bankhead Act, June 2, 1920. The former act provides funds for the vocational rehabilitation of disabled soldiers and sailors; and the latter, funds for the vocational rehabilitation of civilians disabled in industry or otherwise. Of the above acts only two, the Smith-Lever and the Smith-Hughes, benefit children of public school age; consequently, these alone will be considered in the present chapter.

Smith-Lever Fund

Not a dollar of Smith-Lever money reaches public schools; nevertheless, in view of the fact that a portion of this fund is devoted to club work for children of school age, the Smith-Lever fund can hardly be excluded from even a brief account of recent tendencies in federal aid to public schools.

In 1920 there were no less than 442 Smith-Lever agents working exclusively with boys and girls. The expenditure for this club work amounted to $885,000. The Smith-Lever Act provided an initial annual appropriation of $480,000, that is, $10,000 for each state in the Union. In addition to the above initial appropriation, the act provided for an appropriation of $600,000 for the second fiscal year of the operation of the act, and $500,000 additional for each year thereafter throughout a period of seven years, until the annual appropriation shall amount to $4,580,000. Thereafter, this amount constitutes a continuing annual appropriation. The initial appropriation of $480,000 continues to be distributed in flat sums of $10,000 per state, but the additional appropriations are distributed among the states in the proportion that the rural population in each state bears to the total rural population of the United States. These additional appropriations must be matched by moneys coming from within the state, which may be supplied by state appropriations, by districts, counties, or other public corporations, by private institutions, or by individuals. In 1916 the total amount available for Smith-Lever work of all types from federal and all other sources amounted to $1,675,846; in 1922, to $10,680,000. The total amount of Smith-Lever funds available from 1915 to 1922 was approximately $41,900,000.

Smith-Hughes Aid for Vocational Education

As long ago as 1862 the federal government had begun a policy of subsidizing industrial and agricultural education. But prior to 1917 moneys devoted to such work had never been paid to the public schools. The Smith-Hughes Act is significant in that with its passage, "the federal stimulus passed from the colleges to the public schools." The Smith-Hughes Act is significant not only for the aid it grants for industrial and trade training and for teacher training, but for the machinery it has established in every state to organize and direct vocational education. It is impossible here to enter upon a statement of the conditions and of the standards which must be met by the states in order to participate in Smith-Hughes moneys. Two provisions which bear directly on school finance must, nevertheless, be noticed: first, that the states must match the federal moneys dollar for dollar; second, that Smith-Hughes moneys are paid to the states only as reimbursements for moneys previously spent.

The Smith-Hughes Act provides an annual fund, increasing from a total of $1,860,000 in 1918 to $7,367,000 in 1926, which amount thereafter becomes a continuing annual appropriation. What the Smith-Hughes Act accomplished for vocational education during the first four years of its enforcement was summarized in a news-letter of the National Society for Vocational Education, issued in June, 1922. A few of the results set forth in this pamphlet are reproduced here in summary form.

Enrollment in federally aided vocational schools increased from 164,186 in 1917 to 323,028 in 1921.

The enrollment in federally aided teacher training courses increased from 6589 in 1918 to 13,358 in 1921.

In 1916 only two states in the Union, Wisconsin and Pennsylvania, had compulsory part-time or continuation school laws. As the result of the Smith-Hughes Act, 21 states now have compulsory part-time education laws, and every state has a definite state board for the administration of vocational education.

Extension of Federal Aid

The provision of federal aid to foster vocational training in public schools inevitably led to the question: Ought not the federal government to aid the states in other educational fields, notably in the support of elementary education? Out of a strong conviction in the affirmative arose the Smith-Towner Bill, which sought to provide an annual federal fund for $100,000,000 to be distributed among the states for subsidizing education. The Smith-Towner Bill failed of passage, but was succeeded by the Towner-Sterling Bill.

Those advocating federal aid on any such scale as that contemplated by the Smith-Towner and Towner-Sterling bills point out the great inequalities among our states, both as to the educational facilities provided and more particularly as to ability to finance schools. In 1920 the average school term in the United States varied from approximately nine months in Connecticut, Delaware, New Jersey, New York, and Rhode Island to five months and two weeks in South Carolina. The annual salary of teachers varied from over $1200 in Arizona, California, Massachusetts, New Jersey, New York, and Washington, to less than $500 in Arkansas, Georgia, North Carolina, South Carolina, and Tennessee. Variation in ability to provide school revenues, as measured by wealth per child six to twenty years of age, extends all the way from $27,000 in Nevada to $2000 in North Carolina and Mississippi.

It is urged that conditions such as these, together with existing illiteracy and the well-established fact that thousands of school children are now growing up in the United States without any chance whatsoever of receiving an education, present a situation not to be found in any other leading nation in the world. The advocates of federal aid assert that education can no longer be regarded even as a state problem, but that as the states have failed to fulfill the responsibility which up to the present time has been intrusted to them, the federal government must come to the rescue and at least play a minor part in removing educational inequalities for which, to a large extent, the states are not responsible.

One of the interesting factors in the situation produced by the effort to pass the Smith-Towner and the Towner-Sterling bills is the organized opposition which these measures met. The United States Chamber of Commerce appointed a committee to study the subject of federal aid. This committee did not agree and consequently prepared two reports — a *Majority Report* and a *Minority Report*. The *Majority Report* pronounced federal aid unwarranted; declared the states had achieved as much success in providing public education as could reasonably be expected of them, and branded federal aid as a menace to democratic institutions. The *Minority Report* took an entirely contrary view.

Undoubtedly the most bitter opposition came from Catholic organizations whose attitude is expressed in a resolution offered by the Louisiana Federation of Catholic Societies : [1]

Resolved that, we the representatives of the Catholic Federated Societies of Louisiana, are unanimously opposed to such measures as both un-American and un-Christian, and earnestly urge our people to support our Christian schools with increased unanimity and loyalty and to combine in opposing the advocacy, adoption, and advocates of these subversive and destructive educational schemes, thus erecting an impregnable barrier against this sinister menace to religion and constitutional menace to family and nation.

Conclusion

Many important events and tendencies which have marked the history of public school finance in the last twenty-five years must be omitted from the present summary account. Mention, however brief, must be made of the establishment of a number of private foundations which have made important contributions both through subsidizing important

[1] For a more complete account of ecclesiastical opposition see F. H. Swift's "Clerical Issues in the American Educational Crisis" in *The Journal of Education and School World* (London), Vol. LIV, pp. 562–566.

public school projects and by subsidizing scientific studies bearing upon problems of school support. The General Education Board (incorporated 1903), the Carnegie Foundation (created 1905), the Russell Sage Foundation (incorporated 1907), the Anna T. Jeanes Fund (created 1907), the John F. Slater Fund (established 1882), the Julius Rosenwald Fund (created 1915), and the Commonwealth Fund (created 1921), are among the most important of these private foundations.

From funds provided by the above private foundations, school buildings, libraries, teachers' homes in rural districts, salaries of state school inspectors, and model and experimental schools have been made possible. More than this, these foundations have provided funds to subsidize scientific studies in education. In 1917 the Carnegie Foundation published an outline of curricula designed for the professional preparation of American public school teachers. A publication which perhaps more than any other has stimulated a great number of states in the Union to increase support of education is one prepared by Leonard P. Ayres, under the auspices of the Russell Sage Foundation.

Space does not permit an account of the multitude of activities of the General Education Board, directly affecting not only the general problem of public school education but the problems of school finance. This board has subsidized multitudes of educational projects both private and public, has directed and in part financed state public school surveys. A study of the public school finance of Arkansas, made by the writer, showed that the General Education Board provided 52 per cent of the cost of the State Department of Education of Arkansas in 1921. Everything that bears upon the question of the establishment of new types of institutions and the extension of increased educational opportunities has important significance to problems of support. One of the most recent and most notable projects subsidized by private foundations is the Educational Finance Inquiry, a commission established in 1921 under the direction of Professor George D. Strayer of Columbia University, and receiving grants amounting to no less than $170,000 from the General Education Board, the Carnegie Corporation, the Milbank Foundation, and the Commonwealth Fund. This commission is of special interest in the present case, owing to the fact that it was definitely created to make a nation-wide study of public school finance.

In the production of scientific studies in the field of public school finance, as in nearly every other field, Teachers College, Columbia University, was one of the earliest and most productive pioneers. Elliott's *Fiscal Aspects of Public Education*, Cubberley's *School Funds and Their Apportionment*, Hutchinson's *School Costs and School Accounting*, Strayer's *City School Expenditures*, Swift's *History of Public Permanent Common School Funds in the United States*, were among the earliest notable studies in this field and still remain outstanding classics.

That public institutions are rapidly becoming as alert as private institutions to the surpassing importance of building up a body of scientific knowledge in the field of public school finance is evident from the character of a number of publications now being put forth by the United States Bureau of Education and by the research publications of such universities as the University of California, of Iowa, and of Minnesota. In 1914 the University of Iowa published Stewart's *Coöperative Methods of School Support in the United States*. The University of California in Volume III of its *Publications* includes a treatment of "State Aid to Public Schools" by David R. Jones. Probably no one of our state universities, however, has contributed as much to the literature of public school finance as has the University of Minnesota. The most important of the Minnesota publications up to the present time are Orfield's *Federal Land Grants to the States* (1915), Kent's *State Aid to Public Schools in Minnesota* (1918), Kelley's *History of Public School Support in Minnesota* (1920), and a series of studies now in process of publication prepared under the direction of the author of the present chapter, the first volume of which, dealing with public school finance in California and Colorado, was published in October, 1922; and the second volume, dealing with Massachusetts, New York, and New Jersey, appeared in December, 1923.

The science of school finance is still in its early infancy. Only recently has the importance of this field and the fact that it is fundamental to all educational progress and to the realization of our nation's supreme social and spiritual ideals begun to be appreciated. Throughout the United States to-day, city, state, and national organizations and commissions are working with a zeal and a devotion unsurpassed. On one hand the extreme individualist or the self-seeking opportunist declares that public education has exceeded all legitimate bounds and demands retrenchment. This cry is met on every hand by the carefully worked out and intelligent findings of scientific students who are at one in declaring that school facilities must not be lessened but immeasurably increased, that the increases in school costs have been accompanied all along the line by vast increases in national income, and that the present situation is not one which should arouse fear but rather one which should urge us to the working out and adoption of scientific policies of taxation, and of the distribution of school funds and school burdens. From the utterances of these careful, painstaking, and able experts, America derives hope, courage, and the promise of success in the greatest educational experiment that has ever been undertaken by a free people.

CHAPTER IX

ELEMENTARY EDUCATION

BY

CHARLES L. ROBBINS
UNIVERSITY OF IOWA

CHAPTER IX

ELEMENTARY EDUCATION

Introduction

A striking index of the status of elementary education a quarter-century ago is found in the fact that in the *Report of the United States Commissioner of Education* of that time there was practically no attention given to this field. Colleges, secondary schools, institutions for defectives, education in foreign countries, all were treated quite fully; but, with the exception of a brief discussion in connection with some statistics presented, one might get the impression that elementary education had a place of slight importance or that elementary schools were in a static condition with no problems and no need of special attention.

It is not true, however, that the system was without critics or without friends with suggestions for improvement. In the nineties the American disciples of Herbart began a campaign which was directed at both content and method of education, especially elementary education. *The Report of the Committee of Fifteen* of the Department of Superintendence of the National Education Association was an attempt to outline for the elementary schools of the country an organization of subject matter designed to accomplish through correlation those ends which the Herbartians set up in education. In this report, especially in the remarks of some of the dissenting members of the committee, are to be found a few lightning flashes indicating the storm of criticism which every aspect of elementary education was to face within the next quarter-century.

Conditions in 1897

Described in terms of the average pupil (a method perhaps a little better than no description at all) the elementary school of a quarter-century ago was a rather pitiful institution. The average pupil, whether boy or girl, attended a one-room school, and was taught by a young woman who had little if any training beyond the elementary subjects. During the term of about 140 days he spent 70 per cent of his time on the formal subjects, which were taught in a very mechanical manner. In all the subjects which he pursued, the idea of discipline was predominant. His spelling list had no close connection with the words he actually needed or would later need; nor did much of the arithmetic (mental or written), by which his mind was supposed to be trained, bear a vital relation to the kind of arithmetic which was characteristic of the society in which he lived. The reading which he studied was at best made up of fragments from the writings of the great, at worst of selections from the intellectual scrapheap of the ages. His practice in the art of penmanship was mostly futile because inadequately or wrongly directed. His study of the science of grammar did little to improve his use of his mother tongue or to increase his ability to understand the literature which he read, but did much to prevent him from developing an appreciation of that literature. His knowledge of geography and history was chiefly in the form of a skeleton from which some of the more important bones were missing. The school that he attended was supported almost entirely by local taxation, with a little aid from state taxes and the income of the public school fund. His teacher was probably as good as could be expected in view of the facts that her total income from her vocation was less than three hundred dollars a year, her tenure short, and her life ambition outside the field of teaching.

This picture may be supplemented by a study of extremes. If the child lived in a community where the best type of school was provided, he might enjoy a school year of approximately two hundred days, while his young fellow-citizen in a community of the poorest type could have the privilege for only three months. Teachers at the top of the scale had training that included not only elementary and secondary studies but higher and professional as well; while those at the other extreme could not boast of completing even the eight years of the elementary school. The richest type of curriculum included such studies as geography, history, literature, music, drawing, physical training, natural science, and even a foreign language. The poorest type, however, offered the mere rudiments of reading, writing, spelling, and arithmetic. In the better schools spelling was already under a process of adaptation to real needs; but in the poorer it was a hodgepodge of bizarre combinations of letters selected for their recognized difficulty. On the one hand, reading meant first-hand familiarity with classics suited to children; on the other, it was a formal study of the fragmentary and the futile. In many of the cities, school buildings and equipment showed intelligent attention to health, convenience, and usefulness; but in the poorest rural districts and in many small towns the buildings were but little better than cattle sheds, while the equipment was practically nothing. The teachers in even the most progressive communities had little security of tenure, while in the worst they were at the mercy of local politicians. A hundred dollars a month for nine or ten months of the year was within the reach of a few teachers. The same amount often represented the yearly income of others.

Attendance

The number of pupils attending elementary schools rose from slightly more than 15,000,000 in 1897 to about

20,000,000 in 1917. The average daily attendance increased from a little more than 10,000,000 to more than 15,000,000. The average length of school term expanded from 143 days to about 161 days.

In 1897 there were compulsory attendance laws in 30 states, one territory, and in the District of Columbia. The usual age of compulsory attendance was from 8 to 14; but the beginning age was 7 in several states, and the age of leaving 15 or 16 in a few. According to a study made by H. R. Bonner, Statistician of the United States Bureau of Education, there were in 1917–18 compulsory attendance laws of some kind in all the states. In some cases the enactments amounted to little because children were unnecessarily exempt or because there was no minimum school year, or because consecutive attendance was not required. Eighteen states required seven years' attendance; twelve required six; two required five; eight, including the District of Columbia, required four. The nine other states made such liberal provisions for authorizing excuses that no definite term of years can be stated. In twenty-eight states attendance for the full term was required. This period varied from nine months in five states and the District of Columbia to three months in three states, and no minimum in six states. In twenty-five states an absence of one day or less constituted an infraction of the compulsory attendance laws. Two, three, four, and five days, respectively, constituted an infraction in other states. In nine, however, no provision was made in this matter.

An important question in the enforcement of the compulsory laws is whether to base the requirements upon age or upon educational attainments. It is customary in a few states to exempt pupils from attendance if they have completed a certain amount of school work. In twenty-four states there is no exemption for educational attainment.

In twenty-two states, however, children who have completed the work of the elementary school may be exempt even though they have not reached the legal age. In two states pupils who have finished the fourth grade may be exempt. The strongest pressure for exemption comes because of the needs of industry. In sixteen states there is no requirement whatever for the granting of working papers. In fourteen these documents are issued to children who are able to read and write, while in only five are they denied to all who have not completed the elementary school course. In some cases, the applicant for working papers is required to show that he has attended school regularly either during the current year or during the preceding year. Eleven states make such requirements. Poverty as a cause of exemption from school attendance is recognized in several states; there are, however, thirty-one which do not exempt children because of poverty or need of supporting themselves or dependents.

Bonner gives a very effective presentation of the actual scope of compulsory attendance by showing the percentage of children who are affected by the application of the various phases of compulsory school laws. Five per cent of the children live in states having local option in regard to compulsory attendance; 22 per cent are in states which do not have truancy officers in all districts. Ten per cent are in states providing unnecessary exemptions. In the matter of the period of attendance, 65 per cent are in states not requiring seven years; 55 per cent, in states not requiring a full school term; 85 per cent, in states not requiring the nine-month minimum; 14 per cent, in states not requiring consecutive attendance; 38 per cent, in states which make exemptions because of reaching educational standards; 86 per cent are in states which issue permits to children who have not completed the elementary school; 53 per cent live in states where the law is not enforced by the truant officer; 34

per cent are in states in which it is not the function of the chief executive of the school to decide on permits to leave school to go to work.

Selection and Organization of Subject Matter

The twentieth century began with the influence of Pestalozzian ideas still strong not only in matters of method but also in many details of the organization, if not the selection, of subject matter. The psychological element in education stressed by the Pestalozzians received further emphasis from the advocates of certain ideas of Herbart and his followers; but the *Report of the Committee of Fifteen* did much to shift attention from the psychological to the sociological. As a result of differing points of view on the part of those who have worked at the readjustment of the subject matter of elementary education, together with the force of custom, the exigencies of school administration, the pressure of public opinion or of certain groups, and the general development and application of scientific methods, the past quarter-century has been a period of considerable confusion. The subject matter of the elementary school has been modified more or less by the application of principles which have not always mingled harmoniously. On the one hand, we see ideas which are chiefly psychological; on the other, theories and forces essentially social. The complete harmonization of the two points of view is still a matter for the administrator of the future. For the sake of simplicity of treatment, the two groups of ideas, although not mutually exclusive, will be treated separately, the psychological first.

Although Pestalozzi finished his career in the early part of the nineteenth century and both Herbert Spencer's advocacy of Pestalozzian ideas and the Oswego (Pestalozzian) movement came shortly after the middle of that century, the period covered in this study has been characterized by the attempted application of much that the great Swiss educator taught. Among the ideas which have been more or less influential in the selection or the organization of subject matter are the following : 1. From the simple to the complex ; 2. From the concrete to the abstract ; 3. From the empirical to the rational ; 4. From experience to expression ; 5. From particular experiences to general powers ; 6. From the psychological to the logical.

During the past two decades these ideas and their rather crude applications in the making of textbooks have been subjected to such criticism by psychologists and such pressure from various social conceptions of education that they have been reduced to a place of secondary importance. The simple has been interpreted not as the elements derived by logical analysis but rather as the familiar ; or the process of individual development has been shown to involve going from a situation of complexity to one of simplicity through educative direction. The concrete and the abstract have been shown to be correlative rather than antipodal. The attempt to select subject matter for the purpose of developing general powers has been given up or is held in abeyance until the psychologist can provide a more satisfactory basis for the application of the idea than is now possible. The idea of organizing subject matter according to the psychological development of the learner is still of importance ; but its force is lessened by social demands, by the fact that many pupils are lost to the school through elimination before they have reached the stage of development most favorable to the assimilation of certain materials of social value, and by the needs of school administration.

The emphasis of certain poetic aspects of the idea of evolution, interpreted chiefly by the disciples of Herbart, led to a wide vogue of the culture-epoch theory — the assumption that the mental growth of the individual child parallels the cultural evolution of the race just as his physical development is supposed to follow the lines of organic evolution. Although neither anthropologist nor ethnologist has been able to give a very definite picture of the evolution of culture nor the psychologist to agree with his fellow-workers in regard to the stages of child development, the culture-epoch theory has been used as a basis for the selection and organization of the materials of elementary education. Since the results have not been satisfactory enough to command general approval, the theory is now held only by those who seek in poetry or mysticism the foundations of education.

Closely connected with the culture-epoch theory is another principle of organization which, although difficult of application, has found general acceptance — correlation. This principle is both psychological and sociological in its interpretation. From the one point of view, it demands that all kinds of learning experience shall be woven together by the establishment of vital connections; from the other, it calls for a close relationship between school work and the social life of the time. The attempt to apply the doctrine of correlation in school led to a more or less systematic search for those branches or "centers" which could most profitably be used as the bases around which to group those elements that are vital in the development of the individual and in making him the kind of social being which society demands (concentration). Francis W. Parker, Charles De Garmo, Charles and Frank McMurry, and John Dewey were the leading American interpreters of the principles of correlation and concentration.

Another Herbartian idea that has had and must have general application is that of apperception. Applied to the selection and organization of subject matter, it means that new ideas must be presented and built up through experiences already gained. Although apperception has no essential connection with the practice of advancing more or less gradually from the easy to the difficult, general practice seems to have approved a combination of the two ideas. It seems clear, however, that as long as a large percentage of pupils drop out of school at an early age, social necessity may demand the mastery of certain materials regardless of difficulty. Such mastery cannot be secured, however, without the previous development of the necessary apperceptive masses. Geography, history, and civics have been the chief fields in which this conflict of ideas has appeared.

In spite of the fact that the school is designed to be an institution for fitting the rising generation to live in the social environment of the present and future, the force which has been most powerful in determining subject matter is custom. New materials are introduced by current social pressure exercised by groups outside the school, as shown in Jessup's study of *Social Factors Affecting Special Supervision;* but once these materials are in they are likely to persist through the force of custom. Although it is probably true that the pressure of social groups is a crude indication of the demands of society, there is no likelihood that such a random presentation of demands will result in the proper selection or balance of the materials of instruction. Even though music, drawing, domestic science, manual training, and physical training have found their way into the elementary school through the determined efforts of special groups of people, there is no reason for believing that such an introduction of subjects means the proper selection of the most useful elements nor of their efficient organization for teaching and learning.

Under the unorganized pressure of social forces, school students have recently been making systematic efforts to determine exactly what the school must do in order to meet the needs of social and individual life in the complex society of the present. The course of study in spelling is determined by a study of the words actually used in correspondence. The amount and nature of the work in arithmetic is coming to depend upon the mathematical needs of the ordinary citizen of the present rather than upon the idea of using the subject as a "whetstone of the wits." Both history and civics are now in process of being determined by a careful study of the needs of the present.

The content of elementary education is continually being remade — not in the old fashion of introducing new subjects, bag and baggage, but rather in the newer mode of careful study of essential elements. Spelling offers the best example. We now inquire not concerning the subject as a whole, but rather concerning each word. We have even gone so far as to ask if this particular word shall be taught to this particular individual. The future will undoubtedly see much more of this careful analysis of subjects, judgment of social value, and study of individual needs. What has been done in the field of spelling by Thorndike, Ayres, Horn, Ashbaugh, Cook, Jones, and others will be attempted in other elementary school subjects.

The general result of the attention recently given the subject matter of elementary education is the wide acceptance of the idea that such content shall be provided as will afford a basis for mutual intercourse, mutual understanding, and mutual sympathy. As expressed in the first *Report of the Committee on Minimum Essentials of Elementary School Subjects* the fundamental basis for the selection of materials is the conception that "the function of the elementary school is to provide those educational opportunities necessary to insure, with the assistance of the other institutions of society, the acquisition on the part of elementary school children of those habits, skills, knowledges, ideals, and prejudices which must be made the common property of all, that each may be an efficient member of a progressive democratic society, possessing the power of self-support and self-direction, the capacity and disposition for coöperative effort, and, if possible, the ability to direct others in positions of responsibility requiring administrative ability."

A noteworthy attempt to weave into the program of the elementary school a wide variety of vital activities is that of Superintendent Wirt of Gary, Indiana. Although the mechanical aspect of his plan (that of having two schools in one building) has attracted most attention and has led to much discussion and imitation, it is probably true that the more important contribution of the Gary system is the development of a scheme of activities including work, study, and play. Dewey's emphasis on occupational interests, the traditional stress of the literary and linguistic element, and the rapidly growing recognition of the importance of the recreational aspect of life, all find an attempted embodiment in the Gary plan.

Methods of Instruction

Although American elementary education has been and still is dominated by the textbook method of instruction, various attempts have been made to keep the use of books from degenerating into a mere memorization of words. Among such efforts may be mentioned the Pestalozzian object lesson; the Herbartian five formal steps; the development lesson (inductive or deductive); methods analytical, synthetical, rational, topical, logical, natural, experimental, and visual; the excursion; the problem; and the project. The Herbartian movement that was strong in the last decade of the nineteenth century did much to guide teachers toward the actual use of such important ideas as comprehension of subject matter; organization through comparison, contrast, and generalization; building up of units of knowledge rather than the collection of isolated facts; and the application of ideas. The recent attention given to method of teaching through use of problems and projects can be traced back directly to the Herbartians. The project is but the evolution of the type study; the problem, but the present outgrowth of the Herbartian use of induction and deduction. Progress has thus been made through the finer application or practical modification of details inherent or implied in the five formal steps.

In contrast with the general methods of instruction mentioned in the preceding paragraph is the attempt to discover the best technique of teaching each specific subject. The *Eighteenth Yearbook* of the National Society for the Study of Education (of which Part II embodies the *Fourth Report of the Committee on Economy of Time in Education*) marks a very definite stage in the process of adding to knowledge of best general methods that specific knowledge that is essential to the best teaching of a given subject. Writing, reading, spelling, and drawing are the special subjects treated in this report.

A method of class management which demands special mention because of its obvious relation to the present interest in preparation for group life is the socialized recitation. Pupils are encouraged to use freedom and initiative, while the teacher remains in the background instead of dominating obviously as in the ordinary class. In addition to the attention given the mastery of subject matter, much stress is laid upon the cultivation of right social attitudes and conduct. When combined with the use of problems or projects, the socialized recitation gives pupils a great opportunity to think independently, to execute their own plans, to judge the results of their work, and to work with and for one another.

An essential accompaniment of the efforts to improve methods of instruction is the development of standards of achievement and instruments of measurement. One of the most striking developments of recent years is the invention of various tests and scales by which it is possible to measure the accomplishment of pupils and to a certain extent determine both the quality of instruction and the extent to which the pupil is working up to his capacity as determined by intelligence tests. Tests or scales are now available in the following fields : reading (rate and comprehension), writing, spelling, arithmetic, grammar, drawing, English composition, sewing, history, and geography. Although these instruments of measurement are still in various degrees of crudeness and their refinement demands many years of work, they mark a stage of educational progress of greatest importance. Through their application both the method and the content of elementary education will be subjected to continual adjustment and improvement.

Grading and Promotion

The efforts to make improvements in the selection and organization of the subject matter of elementary education have had a parallel in the work of grading and promotion. Within the past few years a great amount of attention has been given to the fact that, although the work of the ordinary elementary school is arranged on the apparent supposition that the average pupil can proceed quite regularly in the consecutive completion of eight one-year units or sixteen half-year units, the actual distribution of pupils through the grades shows a great deal of maladjustment, that is, failure of pupils to progress according to the outlined arrangement of subject matter. Studies by Ayres, Thorndike, and Strayer showed that pupils were not only retarded but also eliminated in tremendous numbers. Strayer, for example, discovered that in 133 cities of 25,000 or over, 38 per cent of boys and 32 per cent of girls were over age ; that in 186 cities of less than 25,000 the figures for boys were 38 per cent and for girls 36 per cent; while only about 4 per cent of the pupils in either group were under age. It was also revealed that the schools held pupils quite well until the age of eleven or twelve, but that after that there was a very large amount of elimination. Strayer estimated that about 90 per cent of pupils "have done the work indicated by being found in the fourth grade, 80 per cent of them have reached the fifth grade, 70 per cent the sixth grade, 55 per cent the seventh grade, 40 per cent the eighth grade, 35 per cent the first year of high school."

Obviously the situation called for some plan for better adjustment. Several schemes tried in various places will here be mentioned, not because they have had wide use — we are still in the stage of rigid grading with annual or semi-annual promotion — but because they indicate a realization of the weaknesses of our present system and display definite efforts to overcome them.

Early in the last decade of the nineteenth century, P. W. Search, Superintendent of Schools in Pueblo, made an effort to adjust progress through school to the capacities of the pupil by an arrangement which made it possible for each child to proceed at his own rate, regardless of the speed of others. In some places this plan was modified by adjusting progress to the capacity of several groups in a class, each group being composed of pupils of about the same capacity. In the San Francisco Normal School, Jesse D. Burks improved the Pueblo plan by a division of subject matter into units. Superintendent Washburne of Winnetka, Illinois, proceeded to a higher stage by the establishment of achievement units.

In contrast with the Pueblo plan of breaking up a class into individual units is the Batavia system. Under the direction of Superintendent Kennedy, a scheme was here evolved by which special attention was given to the slower pupils, by the regular teacher if the class was small, by a second teacher when the class exceeded fifty in number. The reverse of this system is found in the North Denver plan, according to which special attention is given the brighter pupils.

The new Cambridge plan consists of such an arrangement as will provide a basal course of eight years with a parallel course of six years. Promotions are made three times a year. It is thus possible for the gifted pupil to proceed rapidly, while the mediocre or dull pupils advance at a slower pace. Failure of promotion means the loss of only a third of a year instead of a longer period, necessary when promotions are made annually or semi-annually. The Portland, Oregon, plan is much the same as that of Cambridge, but has the advantage of readjustment without loss every year and a half.

The differentiated-course plan is still another attempt to adjust the school to the capacities of its pupils. The fundamental idea is to have all normal pupils advance evenly through the first six grades. Then differentiation of courses and promotion by subjects are introduced with the idea of such adjustment as will retain pupils and advance them regularly. As this plan was worked out in Santa Barbara, California, it provided for the first six grades three parallel courses with varying amounts of work. Each was adapted to the capacities of a group — the slow, the average, or the gifted. In Baltimore, under Superintendent Van Sickle, the differentiated-course plan was modified in such a way as to provide a number of central schools in which gifted pupils, with the consent of their parents, were given a greatly enriched course for grades seven to ten inclusive, and in which they completed the work of these four grades in three years.

The attention which has been given nonpromotion, elimination, and rapid advancement has resulted in a reduction of retardation and an increase of acceleration. The results may be due to better selection and organization of subject matter, to improved methods of teaching, to greater conscientiousness on the part of teachers, to better systems of grading and promotion, or to advancement from grade to grade regardless of accomplishment. Whatever the cause or causes, improvement seems to be shown by the figures presented in recent statistical reports.

The Teaching Staff

The most certain method of improving the quality of elementary education is through selection and training of teachers. A recognition of this principle is shown in the tendency toward centralization of the certificating authority in state departments of education. In 1898 there were only three state systems which issued all certificates; there were twenty-six in 1919. Further evidence of recognition of the principle is found in the fact that in 1898 there were but twenty-nine states that recognized professional training for the granting of one or more certificates while there were forty-seven in 1919. These facts, however, are subject to some discount because of the practice of many states in issuing lowest grade certificates to persons who have only to pass examinations, no definite academic or professional training being prescribed. In 1919 there were twenty-nine such states. Seven others prescribed some professional course; five required graduation from high school; three demanded graduation from high school and professional training with or in addition to high school courses; and four set a standard of graduation from high school and professional courses of higher grade varying from six weeks to a year. Although the examination method of certification generally makes it possible for persons of very low attainments to enter the field of teaching, there has been, according to information secured by the United States Bureau of Education, "a growing importance of professional subjects and the addition of such subjects as agriculture, music, and physical education."

The most striking phenomenon in the recent development of the training of elementary teachers is the rapid rise of teacher training in high schools.   Twenty-one states (1919) have established teacher-training classes or normal training work in high schools or in connection with high schools and recognize this training in their certification laws or regulations as fulfilling the requirements for some grade of certificate. Most commonly such courses are a part of the regular four-year course ; occasionally an additional year is required.

In spite of the growth of the normal training work of high schools, and all that normal schools and teachers' colleges have been able to do, the elementary teachers of the country are still on a very low level of training.   An accurate statement is not possible, but probably two thirds are altogether without the development which is to be secured through professional courses in normal school, college, or even high school.   Teachers with the best preparation are to be found in the cities ; with the poorest in the country.

From three rather comprehensive studies,[1] it is possible to give a fair picture of some of the facts concerning teachers in country schools.   Conditions in three widely separated states (Alabama, Nebraska, and Pennsylvania) are similar in regard to the unsatisfactory training, experience, and tenure of rural teachers.   The number of teachers who have had only an elementary school education is 16 per cent in Alabama, 4 per cent in Nebraska, and 25 per cent in Pennsylvania.   The lack of professional training is indicated by

[1] Bulletins of U. S. Bureau of Education: 1919, No. 41, *An Educational Study of Alabama;* 1919, No. 20, *The Rural Teacher of Nebraska;* and 1921, No. 34, *Status of the Rural Teacher in Pennsylvania.*

the following figures, which show the percentage of teachers who entered upon their work without any such preparation: 63.6 per cent in Alabama, 70 per cent in Nebraska, and 76 per cent in Pennsylvania. The dolefulness of these figures is mitigated somewhat by the fact that there seems to be an increasing number of beginners who enter teaching after at least a little professional training. So long as many states permit entrance by way of the examination route with only academic subjects prescribed, it is not likely that the evil conditions now existent will be changed. The spread of the practice of consolidating rural schools promises such a demand for teachers of superior training that the future of the untrained teacher seems to be limited to those schools that are small, poverty-stricken, and lacking in ideals of excellence.

Past Progress and Present Problems

Within the past twenty-five years much has been done to enrich the conception of the aims of elementary education. It is now coming to be generally accepted that the function of the elementary school is not merely to give pupils possession of the tools of learning — the three R's — but to provide the content necessary to a common basis of national life. Consequently, great enrichment of materials is offered in the elementary school. Much has been done also in the selection and organization of content, and better textbooks have been provided. In the methods of instruction, an increasing desire for improvement has led to many changes by making the processes of instruction better adapted to the capacity of the pupils. In general, it may be said also that a milder discipline has been characteristic of the period. Although no very great general changes have come in grading and promotion, it is true that many attempts to break up the lockstep and to provide a kind of organization that will be adapted to all kinds of pupils have been made. It may be safely said that although the quality of teachers still leaves much to be desired, there has been considerable improvement. The average length of school year has increased. Attendance is vastly larger than a quarter-century ago. Compulsory attendance laws are as a rule better, although it cannot be said that we have yet reached a very high level of law enforcement in this particular. Great progress has been made in rural education through consolidation of districts and the consequent possibilities of giving richer content, having better buildings and equipment, and securing better teachers. The most striking phase of improvement of the past quarter-century is that of securing objective measures of results of instruction. The development of standard tests and scales will undoubtedly be considered one of the greatest achievements of this period.

The greatest problem of national education at the present time is the equalization of opportunity. Present inequalities demand the solution of a complex problem that involves at least the following elements: an increase in the average length of the school term; the improvement of compulsory attendance laws to decrease considerably the percentage of school term lost through absence or nonattendance; better training of teachers; great increases in the salaries of elementary teachers; finding bases of taxation which will provide more money for the support of schools with a resulting increase in the amount of money available for each pupil enrolled; the elimination of all child labor that interferes with school work.

The problems of the content of elementary education involve the discovery of more adequate methods of determining what ought to be taught, the further elimination of useless or relatively useless subject matter, and the improved organization of the courses of study. A particularly inviting field is that of study of the methods of instruction. Although considerable progress has been made in developing the technique of investigation, much still remains to be done before we can adequately measure various practices and proposed innovations. The solution of the problem of adapting instruction to individual needs and capacities is still to be found, and with it the elimination of the evil effects of systems of organization essential in handling large numbers of pupils.

The promise of development in the field of elementary education is great. The growth of courses in elementary education and supervision in universities and the increasing number of experimental schools furnish evidence that the future will see no lack of attempts to apply scientific methods to the study of this field. The present insistent demand for national attention to education is based largely upon a realization of the need of such an equalization of opportunities for elementary education as will provide throughout the nation a citizenry trained in the elementary tools of learning and socialized by training in the elements of good citizenship. The work of the future is tremendous, but present interest and enthusiasm indicate that it will surely be accomplished.

REFERENCES

BONNER, H. R. — "Compulsory Attendance Laws"; *American School Board Journal*, 59 : 37–39, 103 ; 60 : 39–40.

CUBBERLEY, ELLWOOD P. — *Public Education in the United States;* Houghton Mifflin, 1919.

DEWEY, JOHN — *School and Society;* University of Chicago, 1900.

Elementary School Journal (formerly *Elementary School Teacher*), 1900 —.

HARRIS, W. T. — *Elementary Education.* One of a series of monographs on education edited by N. M. Butler, 1904.

MCMURRY, FRANK — *Elementary School Standards;* World Book, 1913.

National Education Association — *Proceedings*, 1897.

National Society for the Study of Education —

    Fourteenth Yearbook, Part I; "Minimum Essentials in Elementary School Subjects."

    Fifteenth Yearbook, Part I; "Standards and Tests for the Measurement of the Efficiency of Schools and School Systems."

    Sixteenth Yearbook, Part I; "Second Report of the Committee on Minimum Essentials in Elementary School Subjects."

    Seventeenth Yearbook, Part I; "Third Report of the Committee on Economy of Time in Education," Section 1.

    Eighteenth Yearbook, Part II; "Report on Economy of Time in Learning."

    Nineteenth Yearbook, Part I; "New Materials of Instruction." *Part II;* "Classroom Problems in the Education of Gifted Children."

    Twentieth Yearbook, Part I; "New Materials of Instruction." *Part II;* "Factors Affecting Results in Silent Reading."

PAYNE, BRUCE R. — *Public Elementary School Curricula;* Silver, Burdett, 1905.

RICE, JOSEPH M. — *Scientific Management in Education;* Houghton Mifflin, 1913.

Teachers College Record, 1900—.

United States Bureau of Education — *Reports* and *Bulletins.*

CHAPTER X

SECONDARY EDUCATION

BY

ALEXANDER J. INGLIS

HARVARD UNIVERSITY

CHAPTER X

Introduction

An outstanding feature in the educational history of recent years is the development of the American secondary school. Within the past three decades, and especially within the past ten or fifteen years, secondary education in America has undergone changes of great significance, involving in their quantitative aspects a remarkable increase in the facilities afforded and in the number of persons brought within the influence of the secondary school, and in their qualitative aspects important modifications in the character of the education provided. It is the purpose of this chapter briefly to consider the more significant phases of development in secondary education within the past three decades.

Schools and Enrollments

The most significant fact in the development of education in America during the past quarter of a century is the remarkable growth of secondary schools and the great increase of attendance thereat. Complete and wholly reliable statistics are lacking and probably never will be available. Nevertheless, a general idea of the development of secondary schools since 1890 may be gained from figures for schools reporting to the United States Bureau of Education. Such figures are presented in the table on page 252.

From 1890 to 1918 (the latest year for which comparable figures are available) the number of public high schools reporting to the Bureau of Education increased from 2771 to

TABLE

Showing the Growth of Secondary Schools and of Secondary School
Enrollments 1889–90 to 1917–18

Items	Schools	1890	1900	1910	1918
Number of Schools	Public	2526	6005	10,203	13,951
	Private	1632	1978	1,781	2,058
	Total	4158	7983	11,984	16,009
Number of Pupils	Public	202,963	519,251	915,061	1,645,171
	Private	94,931	110,797	117,400	158,745
	Total	297,894	630,048	1,032,461	1,803,916
Pupils per 1000 of Population	Public	3.2	6.8	10.0	15.6
	Private	1.5	1.5	1.3	1.5
	Total	4.7	8.3	11.3	17.1
Number of Graduates	Public	21,882	61,737	111,363	224,367
	Private	8,070	12,216	14,409	23,832
	Total	29,952	73,953	125,772	248,199

This table was derived from data given in the Biennial Survey of Education, 1916–18, Bureau of Education Bulletin, 1919, No. 91, pp. 127–128, 310; and the Report of the Commissioner of Education, 1917, Vol. II, p. 511. Public high school figures for the earlier years are less complete and less reliable than those for later years. Figures for private high schools are less complete and less reliable than those for public high schools. Figures for grades corresponding to the four upper grades of the high schools only are considered in this table.

13,951, and the total number of secondary schools (public and private) increased from 4485 to 16,009. Within that period one public high school was established for every day in the calendar years included — a gain of over 450 per cent from 1890 to 1918. Reliable evidence indicates that to-day there are more than 16,500 secondary schools in the United States.

Even more striking and significant is the great increase in enrollments at secondary schools from 1890 to 1918. In 1890 the enrollment in public high schools reporting to the Bureau of Education was 202,963, and the combined enrollment of public and private secondary schools was 297,894. In 1918 the figures for enrollments were, in public high schools, 1,645,171 and in public and private secondary schools 1,803,916. This means that the number of pupils reported in attendance at public high schools increased more than 700 per cent from 1890 to 1918, and that the total number of secondary school pupils increased more than 500 per cent. With allowance for increase in population, it means that for each thousand of the total population the number of secondary school pupils increased from 4.7 in 1890 to 17.1 in 1918—*i.e.*, secondary school enrollments increased more than two and one half times as fast as the population increased. Doubtless by this time (1923 — five years later) the total enrollment in secondary schools has passed the 2,000,000 mark.

This is certainly a very remarkable development. Its meaning should in some respects be clear. First of all, it means that a much larger proportion of our citizenry is receiving some amount and some kind of secondary education, and presumably that the average level of trained intelligence has been raised measurably within the past quarter of a century. Second, it means that the group of pupils now attending the secondary school constitutes a far more heterogeneous body in capacities, economic or social status, and educational needs than was the secondary school clientele of 1890 or 1900. Third, it means that new and diversified demands have been made on the secondary school. Fourth, it means that problems of financial support have become increasingly important and difficult. Fifth, it means that within a very short space of time the secondary school has had to make many important and difficult adjustments — demands which could not be met adequately within the brief period of such an extraordinary development. It may safely be prophesied that it will take at least a generation to meet at all adequately adjustments already demanded by the changed character of the secondary school clientele.

Of some special interest and importance is the status of nonpublic secondary schools and their relation to public education within the past three decades. Until well into the later half of the nineteenth century nonpublic schools were dominant in the field of secondary education in the United States and their influence was very strong even to the end of the century. In 1890 reports to the Bureau of Education indicated that more than one third of all secondary schools were nonpublic and that those schools enrolled nearly one third of all secondary school pupils. In 1918 the proportion of nonpublic secondary schools had decreased to about one eighth (12.9 per cent) and their enrollments had decreased to about one twelfth (8.8 per cent) of the total secondary school enrollment. Clearly, developments of the past three decades have established the dominance of the public high school in the field of secondary education. Clearly, too, its favorable status in this respect is due to the fact that in recent years, with all its youthful defects and shortcomings, the public secondary school is more and more nearly meeting the demands of American society.

Programs and Curricula

No less significant than the quantitative development above outlined is the qualitative development of secondary education during the past quarter of a century, especially as far as the public high school is concerned. In 1890, and for the most part until well beyond 1900, the American secondary school was an institution almost wholly academic in character; its program in most cases being limited to English, foreign languages, mathematics, natural sciences, and history, and its curricula being organized almost wholly on the basis of differing combinations of these studies. This is clearly shown in the *Report of the Committee (of Ten) on Secondary School Studies* in 1893, and is reflected in the *Report of the Committee on College Entrance Requirements* in 1899.

At various times during the nineteenth century (in part as inheritances from the omnibus academy movement) various nonacademic studies had found a somewhat precarious place in some secondary schools, and during the last quarter of the century "commercial" (clerical) education, manual training, and some technical studies had established themselves in a few of the larger schools. Prior to 1900, however, clerical studies were the only nonacademic subjects that were at all common in public high schools.

The extension of secondary school programs to include nonacademic studies and other significant changes in the program were largely developments of the twentieth century. Most of the characteristics of programs and curricula of the modern secondary school have manifested themselves generally within the past ten or fifteen years, significant changes following four somewhat different, though somewhat related, lines : (1) the introduction of new fields of study, *e.g.*, agriculture, home economics, and vocational studies in general ; (2) the introduction of new subjects in fields already represented in the program, *e.g.*, community civics, music other than general chorus work ; (3) the introduction of subjects new in the sense that they represent a reorganization or realignment of subject matter and method, *e.g.*, general science, introductory mathematics ; (4) the modifications of certain subjects with reference to their application in special fields, *e.g.*, household chemistry, economic geography. In addition, it should be mentioned that several studies, formerly common in secondary school programs, have practically disappeared, *e.g.*, Greek, astronomy, geology. And finally, it should be noted that many of the older subjects have undergone such changes in content or method that they constitute educational instruments noticeably different from subjects bearing the same titles a decade or two ago.

Particular importance attaches to the development of practical arts and vocational education during the later part of the period under consideration. While its beginnings can be traced well back in the history of the American secondary school, it was not until the twentieth century that practical arts education began to make general progress in the public secondary school, and it was not until after 1910 that real vocational education established itself at all generally in the public high school. Before 1915 several states had entered on a comprehensive program for the development of vocational education, but the most significant step was taken in 1917 when by the Smith-Hughes Act the Federal Board for Vocational Education was established and federal funds were provided for the encouragement and support of vocational education in trade, agricultural, and home economics subjects. That act marked the beginning of federal participation in the support and control of secondary education. What its final results will be only time can tell, but there can be no doubt that it has already afforded a powerful stimulus for the development of vocational education.

Along with changes in the program of studies in the secondary school have gone changes in curricula and in the policies of curriculum organization. The curricula recommended by the Committee of Ten in 1893 are typical of secondary school curricula and illustrate the policies of curriculum organization which obtained during the last part of the nineteenth century and, for the most part, during the first decade of the twentieth century. They comprised (1) the Classical Course, (2) the Latin-Scientific Course, (3) the

Modern Language Course, and (4) the English Course — curricula which included academic studies only and which were differentiated solely on the basis of varying combinations or proportions of those subjects, as implied by the titles given the "courses."

In the light of our revised conceptions of the functions to be performed by the public secondary schools, the defects of such curricula are obvious; particularly the limitation of the curricula to academic studies, their evident dominance by the college preparatory function, the failure to recognize the factor of elimination, and their differentiation on the basis of predominant academic subjects rather than on the basis of the different activities of life to which various groups of pupils will apply their education. But, in spite of their numerous defects, the curricula recommended by the Committee of Ten were accepted generally throughout the country. Until well after 1900 the Committee's recommendations practically determined high school curricula in most communities, and it was not until well into the second decade of the present century that newer policies of curriculum organization gained any general acceptance. Even now the older organization is to be found in many high schools, perhaps in a majority of high schools.

What are these new policies of curriculum organization? Among others they involve the following significant features: (1) curricula based on as wide a variety of studies as is justified by the capacities and needs of the pupils concerned and the ability of the community to provide them, with proper regard for reasonable economy in support and for efficient instruction; (2) curricula in each of which adequate attention is paid to the proper balance of aims and functions in secondary education; (3) curricula so organized that as far as possible each pupil may secure the maximum of benefit according to the amount and character of his study, with due recognition of the fact that most pupils will not complete the full secondary school course; (4) curricula organized with as much flexibility as possible so that necessary readjustments can be made by the pupil with a minimum of loss; (5) curriculum differentiation based on significant differences in the careers for which various groups of pupils are preparing themselves.

While all the above-mentioned changes in programs and curricula are observable in the history of secondary education in the past quarter of a century, it would be a serious mistake to assume that they are complete. Such is far from being the case. Rather we may confidently expect that those changes will be in progress for many years to come.

Teachers

Among the serious problems in part created by the rapid increase of secondary schools and of secondary school enrollments during the past three decades was and still is the problem of an adequate number of teachers properly equipped. At the highest reasonable estimate the number of secondary school teachers in 1890 did not exceed 25,000. In 1922 the number was probably not less than 100,000. At present the annual increase in new teaching positions and the requirements for replacements demand about 15,000 new secondary school teachers each year.

At no time during the past quarter of a century has there been available for secondary schools an adequate supply of *well-educated* teachers; and the available supply of *well-trained* secondary school teachers was and is relatively insignificant. As a matter of fact, professional preparation for secondary school teachers was all but unknown before 1900 and represents one of the important developments of the past decade or two. Since 1900, and more noticeably since 1910, professional training for secondary school teachers has been provided in most collegiate institutions and has received definite recognition in the certificating laws of most states. It is possible that increased facilities for the training of secondary school teachers and the development of professional consciousness can soon overcome the instability of the teaching staff. Whether this is true or not, the future alone can determine. For some time certainly the problem of supplying an adequate number of well-trained secondary school teachers must be a vital one. Until it is solved, secondary education in America must be of inferior quality. At present it must be recognized that the average level of classroom instruction in the American secondary school is relatively low.

Instruction

During the past two or three decades many factors created the need for changes in the organization of subject matter and in methods of instruction. Among the most important of these were the following: (1) changes in the character of the secondary school clientele; (2) the introduction of new subjects of study; (3) reorganization in grades seven to nine; (4) developments in the field of educational psychology, especially with respect to the laws of learning, the psychology of individual differences, the nature and measurement of intelligence; (5) the disclosure of prevailing defects by means of objective measurement; (6) changes in our conception of the functions to be performed by the secondary school.

How far and in what ways have these and other factors resulted in real changes in secondary school instruction? Far more than appears on the surface and far less than might appear to be the case to one judging on the basis of educational literature. Far more than one might expect from the recent development of controlling factors, but far less than must be the case eventually if instruction is to meet the demands created within recent years. Here the limitations of space do not permit any extended analysis of changing instruction. It must suffice to point out some of the more significant tendencies observable.

(1) The most noticeable changes in instruction are those which involve better recognition of the factor of individual differences. In 1900 secondary school instruction in any given subject was practically the same for all pupils regardless of their capacities and needs. A uniform and stereotyped methodology prevailed, for the most part determined by the needs of college preparation. Since that time there has been a growing tendency to organize content and method as far as possible in terms of the varying capacities and needs of the particular group of pupils concerned in any given class.

(2) Not less significant is the tendency to reduce the emphasis on formal values and to emphasize the functional in content and method. This tendency is observable to a greater or less extent in almost every field of secondary school instruction. Examples of it are found in the substitution of functional for formal English grammar, in the direct method of teaching a foreign language, in general science and in the applied sciences, in introductory mathematics and applied mathematics, in community civics and modern methods of teaching history, and, of course, in all practical and vocational studies.

(3) Closely related to the tendency to emphasize functional values, if not really a part of it, is the tendency to emphasize social values in secondary school instruction — "to socialize" secondary education. On the side of content this means emphasis on materials according to their social importance. On the side of method it means emphasis on coöperative activity and the creation of classroom situations

which as far as possible stimulate actual situations in life and provide social experience.

(4) A fourth tendency observable is that which involves a reorganization of subject matter and method in terms of the laws of learning, instead of in terms of the scientific arrangement as viewed by the specialist. This is especially noticeable in community civics, general science, and introductory mathematics, but it may be observed more or less in most fields of secondary school instruction.

(5) Closely related to this is the tendency to reorganize subject matter and method so as to subordinate deferred values and make each unit of study of value to the pupil in terms of the amount and quality of his study. Formerly, for example, the pupil's first year of study in a foreign language was devoted primarily and almost exclusively to forms, syntax, and vocabulary; his use of the language for reading, writing, or speaking being deferred to later years, so that if he proceeded no further, he had acquired little except some knowledge of the anatomy of the language. Modern methods aim to provide him with a use of the language proportionate to the amount and quality of its study.

(6) Motivation has always been and always must be an important element in instruction. Nevertheless, its importance has been emphasized further in recent years by the fact that in increasing numbers pupils without special interests or ambitions have entered the secondary schools. Hence there is observable in recent years a tendency further to recognize the factor of motivation. This is evidenced by increased emphasis on diagnosis and guidance in and through the organization of instruction, as well as by the development of certain somewhat special methods, *e.g.*, the project method.

These rather general tendencies have been incorporated more or less in some special methods of instruction. Thus "supervised study" emphasizes the factor of individual differences and laws of learning. Thus the "project method" emphasizes the factor of individual differences, the laws of problem-solving, functional values, motivation, and social values. Thus the "socialized recitation" stresses individual differences and social values. And finally, many of these tendencies are involved in such comprehensive schemes of reorganization as are represented in the Dalton Plan.

While all these tendencies in instruction are observable in modern practice, it is not to be supposed that they are universally, or even generally, present. It is not to be expected that new theories can at once find their way into general practice, and it would be absurd to expect that the rapid developments of the past ten or fifteen years would be represented generally in secondary school practice at this early date. The translation of general theory into special practice in the classroom is a difficult and time-requiring process. New textbooks must be prepared, teachers must become acquainted with the new ideas, and, not least in some cases, the public must gradually be educated to accept new doctrines. It will take many years for classroom instruction to catch up with the demands of the present.

Extension Downward and Upward

Since 1910 the scope of secondary education has been extended downward by the junior high school movement and (less generally) has been extended upward by the junior college movement.

Before 1900 several proposals (notably those of the Committee of Ten in 1893) had been made to reorganize the school system so as to provide six grades of elementary education and six grades of secondary education. Prior to 1910 some beginnings had been made to put those proposals into practice, but at that date there probably existed less than twenty-five six-grade public high schools in the country and few of those really represented the type which has developed during the past decade. After 1910, however, the development of reorganized systems proceeded rapidly, the reorganization usually taking the form of elementary schools, junior high schools, and senior high schools on a six-three-three, a six-two-four, or a six-six plan. By 1918 the reorganization had developed so rapidly that a somewhat selective estimate by the Bureau of Education indicated five hundred and fifty-seven junior high schools reported. In 1922 probably more than one thousand communities had provided reorganized school systems involving junior high schools. It is impossible to say how many systems have been reorganized otherwise than with respect to administrative divisions and grade combinations, but to an increasing extent in recent years there have been manifest elements of real reorganization in the actual education provided.

The earlier proposals for reorganization were concerned primarily with plans for an earlier beginning and a longer period of secondary education of the sort already represented in the high school, and the proposers were actuated in large part by ideas of a longer period of preparation for college. Later proposals, however, and those which have been effective in developing the junior high schools, were in keeping with our changed conceptions of the functions of secondary education and emphasized a different kind of education rather than a downward extension of the secondary education previously provided. They involved primarily: (1) a broader and richer type of education in grades seven, eight, and nine; (2) earlier and better provision for individual differences; (3) a better articulation between elementary and secondary education; (4) provision for educational diagnosis and guidance; (5) recognition of the factor of elimination; (6) economy of time in education.

In the reorganization, administrative divisions and grade combinations gain their importance because they are necessary in order to carry through the real reorganization of education. The greatest danger at present is that the real reorganization, necessary and intended, may be lost sight of in the reorganization of administrative divisions.

Less general has been the upward extension of the secondary school so as to provide "post-graduate" study of a type generally comparable to or practically paralleling the first two years of college work.[1] For the most part the junior college movement has developed since 1910, though some beginnings were to be found before that date, and the first specific law for junior colleges was passed by the California legislature in 1907. Since 1910 several junior colleges have been established in connection with public high schools, but as yet the movement has gained headway in a few states only.

This upward extension of the public high school has been due to several factors, among which the most important are: (1) a great increase in the number of persons desiring and deserving an education beyond the high school; (2) the consequent overcrowding of many colleges; (3) the demand for facilities of higher education nearer the homes of pupils and not involving the expense of living away from home; (4) a need for better instruction in the earlier college grades; (5) changing conceptions of the functions of secondary and collegiate education. Nevertheless, there are practical reasons for believing that the movement will not become general for junior colleges attached to public high schools, the most important reason being that they are economically

---

[1] Reference here is limited to junior colleges operated in immediate connection with public high schools. Independent junior colleges or those attached to a state university are primarily a college problem, not a secondary school problem.

justifiable in the larger cities only. If organized as regional schools, they become essentially collegiate institutions with quite different relations to secondary education proper. In most communities there is far greater need for the improvement of our present schools than there is for its expansion to include two additional grades.

Changing Conceptions

Along with all the changes previously mentioned and related to them, in part as cause, in part as effect, have come fundamentally important changes in our conceptions of the functions to be performed by the secondary schools. During the past quarter of a century especially, our conceptions of the functions of secondary education have changed from those dominated by selective ideals to those which postulate that the opportunities of secondary education should be made available for each citizen according to his needs, capacities, and willingness to make the necessary efforts. This is a profoundly significant change and deserves some special consideration.

Throughout its history, secondary education in all countries has been dominated by the conception that it is suitable and desirable for those only who, by virtue of social, economic, or intellectual superiority, can be expected to assume positions of leadership in life. The selective ideal still dominates secondary education in almost all countries, certainly in most European countries. In its beginning secondary education in America inherited the prevailing selective functions of Europe, and, in spite of various tendencies of the academy and early high school movements, those selective functions persisted and dominated secondary education in America throughout the nineteenth century. Needless to say, they are still dominant in many parts of the country and still obtain in the minds of many citizens.

Nevertheless, they are manifestly giving ground to broader functions.

In the last decade of the nineteenth century (at the beginning of the period under consideration in this chapter) the American secondary school was organized and administered on the basis of the traditional conception that secondary education was suitable and desirable for those only who, because of social and economic status or by virtue of intellectual superiority and ambition, looked forward to the higher professions and to careers of leadership. At that time it was not expected that the average child should attend the high school, but, for the most part, it was taken as a matter of course that he should leave school after receiving a "common school education." The high school was still considered as something of an educational luxury to be indulged in only by those whose superior social and economic status permitted opportunity for leisure and "culture," or whose capacities and ambitions justified higher training.

As long as the selective conception and the ideal of training for leadership dominated both secondary education and higher education, it was inevitable that the two institutions should be closely related and it was but natural that secondary education should be viewed primarily in terms of college preparation. In any event it is certain that preparation for college dominated the American secondary school throughout the nineteenth century. Nevertheless, it should be noted that the character of both institutions and of the relation between the two was a natural result of the selective conception. As long as the selective ideal dominated the secondary school and the college, preparation for the latter was bound seriously to condition the former. The result was a vicious circle. As long as preparation for college determined the character of the secondary school, the tendency was for those only to attend the secondary school who expected to go to college or who desired the kind of education typified by college preparation. Likewise, as long as those attended the secondary school who needed or desired the college preparation sort of education, that was the sort of education to be provided for them. This is manifest in the *Report of the Committee (of Ten) on Secondary School Studies* in 1893 and in the *Report of the Committee on College Entrance Requirements* in 1899.

No significant movement ever develops overnight, and it is seldom, if ever, possible to set an exact date to mark the beginning of a new movement. Certainly it would be impossible to set any exact dates for changes in our conceptions of the functions of secondary education. Doubtless they began well back in the nineteenth century, or even in the eighteenth century. Probably, indeed, they are to be associated with long-developing changes in the whole theory and organization of American society. Nevertheless, we can rightly say that the last quarter of a century has been marked by an increasing manifestation of changed conceptions of the functions of secondary education.

Within that period the increased patronage of the secondary school shows clearly that people have ceased to look on it as an educational luxury to be reserved for the few. It is clear that at present the secondary school is looked upon as an integral part of the school system, to be attended by children with little reference to social, economic, or intellectual status. Whether we would wish it or not, the fact must be faced that the character of the secondary school clientele at present necessitates the abandonment of the former conception of the selective function of secondary education. Developments of the past quarter-century have necessitated the substitution of selection by differentiation for the former selection by elimination and restricted instruction.

Both in our changing conceptions of secondary education and in changing practice there are to be noted three somewhat separate, yet somewhat overlapping, stages : (1) the change to a conception that education above the elementary school should be provided for pupils other than those going to college; (2) the change from a limited academic education for all to differentiated studies suited to varying social and economic needs; (3) the change from a type of instruction (subject matter and method) geared up to require a relatively high level of intelligence to instruction adapted to varying capacities.

The first of these changes was under way by the close of the nineteenth century. The second received great impetus in the past two decades. The last has barely manifested itself, and as yet is scarcely recognized either by laymen or by educators. It remains as one of the chief problems to be solved in secondary education. Except as the practical arts and vocational studies may be utilized as a sort of educational salvage department, the secondary school of to-day makes little provision for the pupil of average or below average intelligence, the academic studies as at present organized and taught demanding for successful achievement an intelligence quotient probably not lower than 1.05. Secondary education can never adequately perform its functions until subject matter and method are organized in terms of the varying capacities of pupils. This is the most difficult, but probably the most important, problem to be solved.

REFERENCES

Briggs, Thomas H. — *The Junior High School;* Houghton Mifflin, 1920.

Foster, H. H.—*Principles of Teaching in Secondary Schools;* Scribner, 1921.

Inglis, Alexander J. — *Principles of Secondary Education;* Houghton Mifflin, 1918.

JOHNSTON, CHARLES H. — *The Modern High School;* Scribner, 1916.
—— *High School Education;* Scribner, 1912.
Koos, LEONARD V. — *The Junior High School;* Harcourt, Brace & Howe, 1920.
LULL, HERBERT G., and WILSON, H. B. — *The Reduction of High School Instruction;* Lippincott, 1921.
MONROE, PAUL. — *Principles of Secondary Education;* Macmillan, 1913.
National Education Association — *Reports of the Commission on the Reorganization of Secondary Education;* United States Bureau of Education.
PARKER, SAMUEL C. — *Methods of Teaching in High Schools;* Ginn, 1920.

CHAPTER XI

VOCATIONAL EDUCATION

BY

W. THOMAS WOODY

UNIVERSITY OF PENNSYLVANIA

CHAPTER XI

VOCATIONAL EDUCATION

Introduction

Well; when is a man likely to succeed best? When he divides his exertions among many trades, or when he devotes himself exclusively to one? . . . From these considerations it follows, that all things will be produced in superior quantity and quality, and with greater ease, when each man works at a single occupation, in accordance with his natural gifts, and at the right moment, without meddling with anything else. . . .

PLATO.

This vision of an ancient seer and educational statesman implied a democratic education in so far as all individuals should be prepared for the task for which by nature they were best fitted; but until recently few nations exerted themselves to undertake the labor of directing their citizens in this important matter. Germany was exceptional in this regard. With a view to promoting the supreme good of the state she regulated the individual's life and education with Platonic foresight and severity. This attention to vocational preparation of her citizens was both a result of her economic expansion and an effectual factor in the furtherance of it.

In the early literature on the subject of vocational education in the United States the references made to foreign example and leadership, and particularly those relating to Germany's schools, were numerous. English and French practices were also dealt with. In congressional debates on Land Grant colleges and in periodical articles advocates referred in glowing terms, though often inaccurately, to Germany's progressive example. By 1890 the fact was accepted by many that new types of schools — trade, manual training,

273

technical, commercial, apprenticeship, corporation, agricultural, and evening schools — must be developed to provide adequate vocational preparation.

An estimate of the very recent popularity of the idea of vocational education as a necessity in American schools may be gleaned from periodical literature. While there is much chaff in the articles, the fact of extremely rapid increase in their number is sufficient evidence that an interest in special forms of education began to develop in the last twenty years of the nineteenth century, and made a phenomenal advance after 1904.

Economic and Social Changes

The need for vocational education follows the long march of events in our industrial history of the nineteenth century. The shift of interest to manufacturing is seen in the rapid increase of patents from an average of 77 between 1790 and 1811 to 192 from 1812 to 1817 and 544 in 1830. In 1860 there was a total of 4819 patents. Cotton, woolen, and iron industries grew enormously; cotton goods manufactories increased from 4 in 1805 to 795 in 1831, while the volume of raw materials utilized increased sevenfold; the value of the woolen output increased fivefold in the period from 1810 to 1840; the iron industry grew more slowly, but after 1830 received a great impetus from railroad building and from the fact that anthracite was used for smelting purposes after 1837. Though these steps were remarkable for a nation just emerging into a consciousness of its industrial greatness, they were but a harbinger of the increase in the value of manufactures which came in the last half of the century. In 1850 the value of manufactures was over one billion dollars; in 1880, over five billion; in 1909, over twenty billion; and over twenty-four billion in 1914. In the period from 1850 to 1900 the national wealth increased from over seven billion to more than eighty-eight billion dollars.

The importance of the United States in world trade has increased by leaps and bounds since 1860. In 1880 the value of exports exceeded that of imports and has so continued to the present. In 1900 the United States ranked first among the nations of the world as an exporter. In these exports the value of manufactured goods has increased rapidly. In 1860 manufactured goods constituted 12.76; in 1890, 17.87; in 1910, 45.32; and in 1920, 51.52 per cent of the total value of exports. The total value of exports rose from approximately $333,000,000 in 1860 to $857,000,000 in 1890, $1,745,000,000 in 1910, and $8,228,000,000 in 1920. The total value of imports increased from approximately $353,000,000 in 1860 to $789,000,000 in 1890, $1,557,000,000 in 1910, and $5,278,000,000 in 1920.

In this world trade agricultural products were a large factor. In 1860 over 51,000,000 bushels of wheat and over 54,000,000 bushels of corn were exported; twenty years later the export figures for these two commodities were 550,767,121 and 439,656,935 bushels respectively. The total value of our agricultural products in 1870 was almost two billion dollars; in 1890 two and a half billion; in 1900 a little less than five billion; in 1910 nearly eight and a half billion; and in 1919 almost twelve and a half billion. The great increase of agricultural products depended to a large extent on improved machinery.

With the spread of manufacturing, a novel characteristic appeared in the population of the United States. In 1810 but 4.9 per cent of the total population, or 356,920, dwelt in cities of over 8000, and in 1860, only 16.1 per cent. But by 1900 this figure had doubled and the total urban population was reckoned at 40 per cent. In 1910 the urban population constituted 45.8, and 51.4 per cent of the whole in 1920.

Another important factor at work in bringing forward the problem of industrial education is the change in the tendency of immigration. Since 1880 immigration from Northern and Western Europe has declined markedly, while the proportion from the south and east has increased. This influx of unskilled labor from countries having a high percentage of illiteracy in place of a group that was somewhat skilled, the passing of the small shop as a training place, and the policy of unions in limiting the number of apprentices, have precipitated the problem of industrial education upon the schools.

Types of Schools and Courses

The actual expansion of American education to include vocational preparation has, until recent years, made but slow progress. Important forerunners of this expansion were the manual labor institutions which sprang up after 1825, largely inspired by the labors of Fellenberg, and the manual training schools of the last quarter of the century. Both of these movements, however, sought after a more perfect discipline and were not distinctly vocational. Each attempted to combine the work of the hands with that of the head. Disciplinary value lay in manual occupations because they exercised the powers of observation, reasoning, and will. Some, doubtless, felt that this introduction of manual work was the basis of industrial education; but the utilitarian, vocational aim was seldom mentioned and never emphasized by teachers. Nevertheless, by their very character, the manual training schools of the eighties prepared the way for acceptance of the idea of industrial education. Being realistic in curriculum, they furnished an antidote for the dominant literary education of the high school.

A school was established by the Ethical Culture Society of New York in 1878, and two years later the St. Louis Manual

Training School was opened. The first was an elementary school, the second a high school. In the field of secondary education, the manual training idea began to spread rapidly. Private manual training schools were established in the next few years at Cleveland, Cincinnati, Chicago, and Toledo; and public institutions were provided in Philadelphia, Baltimore, and Omaha by 1886. The early work of these schools consisted of set exercises in joinery, turning, forging, and so forth, according to the "Russian System." At Toledo a beginning was made in instructing girls in household arts.

At the same time efforts were made to bring manual training into the public elementary schools. In 1888, after a few years of private experimentation, manual training became a part of the course in the elementary schools of Boston and New York; and a state law was passed by New Jersey in 1885 providing subsidies to encourage cities to offer manual training in their courses.

During the early part of the last century a definite indication of the growing need for specific preparation was registered in the establishment of a number of evening schools to give instruction of practical utility in mathematics, science, and drawing. Cooper Union was established in New York in 1854 and a day technical school was combined with it in 1900; but its greatest service has been accomplished through evening classes. Another school, the Mechanics Institute, opened evening courses in 1859, supported by the General Society of Mechanics and Tradesmen of the City of New York, which had been created in 1785. The Ohio Mechanics Institute in 1828 offered a definitely realistic curriculum — botany, chemistry, mechanics, geometry, and arithmetic. A similar tendency is to be noted in the instruction offered in such schools as the Gardiner Lyceum of Maine, established about 1823, designed for the education

of "farmers, mechanics, navigators, and merchants";
Franklin Institute of Philadelphia (1824); and the Maryland Institute for the Promotion of Mechanic Arts in Baltimore in 1847.

Other institutions worthy of mention in this connection
are Tuskegee Institute (1881); Drexel Institute, Philadelphia (1891); Lewis Institute (1896); and Armour Institute
of Technology (1893) in Chicago; Pratt Institute in Brooklyn (1887); Spring Garden Institute of Philadelphia (1851);
Philadelphia Textile School and School of Industrial Art
(1876); People's Institute of Boston; the Baron de Hirsch
Trade School of New York; and the Williamson Trade
School — all established in 1888.

Another extension of vocational preparation has developed largely during the last thirty years in the Young
Men's Christian Association of America. In the first twenty
years of its existence but little educational work was done;
and the few classes maintained were not vocational in
character. Gradually, however, arithmetic, drawing, bookkeeping, stenography, and a great array of distinctly vocational subjects were introduced. In 1905–06 sixty-three
courses were offered in the West Side Young Men's Christian
Association of New York City, distributed in industrial,
commercial, and cultural fields. Thirty-six per cent of the
students in 1905 were enrolled in commercial subjects, while
twenty-six per cent were enrolled in industrial and scientific
subjects.

In the past twenty years other provision has been made
for vocational preparation through the establishment of
special courses by educational authorities and by industrial
and commercial concerns. In 1901 the Board of Education
of Chicago made provision for education of apprentices of
the masons' and bricklayers' associations, beginning with
instruction in arithmetic, English, drawing, architecture,

and woodworking. This experiment developed rapidly. The apprentice (in 1904) attended school three months in the year, studying ordinary English branches as well as those relating definitely to his trade. The remainder of the time was spent in his vocation.

In 1903 Illinois passed a law with the following requirement:

In all municipalities where a manual training school is maintained for the technical instruction of apprentices, such indentures shall further provide that it shall be the duty of the master to cause the apprentice to attend such school for at least three consecutive months in each year without expense to the apprentice.

Another variety of industrial preparation developed early in the twentieth century, in factories, and commercial establishments such as those of the National Cash Register Company, General Electric Company of Lynn, Mass., John Wanamaker, Sears Roebuck & Co., and many others. Concerning this establishment of education in the "going concern," Professor Snedden outlines its more perfect development and then asks:

Is not the plan of vocational education here suggested the only one that will assist our workers in modern highly specialized productive enterprises? Is it not the only one adapted to factories for textiles, locomotives, firearms, jewelry, clothing, furniture, packed meats, books, newspapers, automobiles, shoes, stoves, and buttons? Is it not the only one adapted to commercial education for department stores, large banks, commission houses, large offices? May not something analogous to it be the best means of training young men for the successive farming stages of skilled farm hand, tenant farmer on a major and two minor specialties, and finally owning farmer?

With the suggestion that as "good training of physicians benefits all of us, since we are likewise private employers of physicians," so "good training of any sort benefits us or our representatives as employers, and also as employees." Pursuing this line of reasoning, such education should be supported by the public.

Higher Technical Education

Higher technical education, based upon the equivalent of secondary education, is provided in independent schools and colleges, in schools established in connection with older universities, on private foundations, or in state universities. The Rensselaer Polytechnic Institute was founded in 1824, Lawrence Scientific School at Harvard in 1847, Sheffield Scientific School at Yale in 1860, Massachusetts Institute of Technology in 1865, Worcester Polytechnic Institute in 1865, Lehigh University in 1866, Stevens Institute of Technology in 1871, Case School of Applied Science in 1880, Rose Polytechnic Institute in 1883, Georgia School of Technology in 1888, Carnegie Institute in 1895, and the Polytechnic Institute of Brooklyn, reorganized in 1889. Other technical schools have been added to older universities such as the School of Mines at Columbia in 1864, and the Towne Scientific School at the University of Pennsylvania in 1874. A third type of higher technical school developed in the land grant colleges. The *Report of the United States Commissioner of Education* for 1916 gives statistics for 69 institutions established under the land grant and subsequent acts. In 52 of these institutions for white students there were 15,710 pursuing engineering courses, and 23,408 in other courses of technical nature.

A coöperative plan was also introduced in the Engineering Department of the University of Cincinnati, in accordance with which about thirty-five manufacturing companies agreed to send apprentices to the University to pursue an engineering course six years in length, leading to the regular degrees. These apprentices were to be possessed of a high school education or its equivalent. By having the apprentices work in pairs, turn about, at study and factory work, there was no loss to the employer.

Some idea of the important position of higher technical instruction in colleges, universities, and technological schools may be gained from the following number of students] pursuing engineering courses in 1916: general engineering, 6166; chemical, 2383; civil, 7182; electrical, 6637; mechanical, 7751; and mining, 1922. It was not until 1915 that agriculture began to lead mechanic arts in the race for students in the agricultural colleges. In 1911 there were almost twice as many students in the mechanic arts courses, but in 1912, 1913, and 1914 the number pursuing agriculture rose steadily, while mechanic arts remained substantially unchanged. In the agricultural and mechanical colleges in 1915 there were 17,169 students of agriculture, 4431 students of household arts, and 16,554 of mechanic arts.

Commercial Education

Of the many schools for specific vocational preparation that have striven for recognition in the past quarter of a century, the commercial schools have perhaps met with most opposition. The materialistic aim of commercial education was strangely out of place in an atmosphere surcharged with the excitement of pursuit of true culture. Moreover, the charlatan character of many private ventures doubtless threw the movement all the more into disrepute, and made it more difficult for commercial subjects to find a place in the curriculum of the regular schools. But thirty years after Spencer's emphasis on utilitarian values in education, we were beginning to be able to see the problem differently, thanks to the pressure of events.

The whole idea of commercial education began to be better defined after 1880, and particularly after 1890. Leaders were needed. As the old colleges and universities required the preparation of the Latin grammar school, the academy, and the high school, thus completing a system, so the creation of collegiate and secondary schools of commerce was necessary to complete a system of commercial education. The Wharton School, opened in 1881 with a total of thirteen students, contributed an important spokesman : Edmund J. James in 1892 advocated the creation of separate commercial high schools, adducing from Germany, Austria, France, and other countries many proofs of our backwardness. In the present century a number of such schools have been established. Among the most noteworthy of the separate commercial high schools are those at San Francisco, Washington, Louisville, Boston, Brooklyn, New York City, Cleveland, and Springfield.

The striking increase in commercial education may be seen in the following figures :

TABLE I

Year	Private Commercial and Business Colleges	Students	Students in City, Normal, and Secondary Schools and Colleges
1895	398	80,662	51,182
1905	529	146,068	116,712
1915	843	183,286	235,534
1918	890	289,579	278,275 (In high schools only)

As a general rule the courses in commercial education have been from one to four, or recently even five, years in length. They seek to prepare definitely for a business career and also to enable students to enter schools of commerce at universities. At the outset, the distinguishing feature was the omission of classical studies, and some limitation on other academic subjects. Nevertheless, *general* commercial training, rather than technical, was urged, and James maintained that through commercial education was to be realized "another highway to that state of mind and heart known as culture."

It may be of interest here to note the type of curriculum of the early collegiate commercial school. The retention of many purely academic subjects is worthy of notice. The Wharton School curriculum in 1881 was distributed over three years. To be admitted to the sub-junior, one must pass examinations or have completed the freshman and sophomore work of the College or Towne Scientific School. In the sub-junior course were offered social science, mercantile practice, English, German, French, physics, mineralogy, Latin, and drawing, the last two being elective. In the junior year social science, taxation, industry, commerce and transportation, wage questions, mental and moral science, English, geology, physics, Latin, German, and French were offered. The senior studies were law, social science, original research in theory and history of economic questions, history, English, physics, and astronomy.

A similar tendency may be noted almost twenty years later in the courses outlined for commercial high schools and departments. Latin was, for traditional reasons, retained in the preliminary curriculum drawn up for the School of Commerce of the Central High School of Philadelphia; but, in practice, the first-year Latin was made a study of "etymology and fundamental English." The Latin requirement lasted but one year, German being then substituted. The Committee of Nine proposed a requirement of two years of German, French, or Spanish in 1903. The curriculum of the New York High School of Commerce (1903) required four years of German, French, or Spanish. Algebra, plane geometry, ancient, medieval, modern, and United States history also retained a prominent place and gave an air of academic respectability so far as traditional standards were concerned. The retention of many such subjects and the all too general nature of commercial education have in recent years been condemned.

Agricultural Education

An interest in agriculture as an educational proposition may be noted as early as 1775, when a Society for the Promotion of Agriculture was established at Philadelphia. Seven years later a similar society was created in Massachusetts. An agricultural school was established in Maine in 1821 and another in Connecticut in 1824. The New York and Michigan legislatures sought to encourage agricultural instruction in schools in 1823 and 1838 respectively. The earliest publicly supported agricultural high school was established in 1888 in connection with the University of Minnesota. Ten years later ten such schools were reported.

State action was taken by Wisconsin (in 1901) when an act was passed providing free county secondary schools of agriculture and household economy. The course was to consist of two years' work at the beginning; and each school so established was granted $2500 as a state subsidy.

Since 1900 the number of agricultural high schools of various forms has increased rapidly. In Wisconsin there are county agricultural high schools similar to that mentioned above; in the South, Alabama established schools for large areas, and the same type has also found a place in Georgia, Virginia, California, Minnesota, Oklahoma, Massachusetts, and New York; in many states secondary schools have also been established in conjunction with agricultural colleges and state universities. Prominent among recent developments is the Farm Life School of North Carolina. Many other schools offer "courses" in agriculture, but do not specialize in that subject.

In 1913 about 2300 high schools of the United States were reported as teaching agriculture; in 1914, 1553 were reported with 32,021 students; and in 1917–18, 2012 high schools reported 38,728 students. There have been more institutions reported at times; thus in 1915, 4665 schools were mentioned. The smaller figure for the most recent date is said to be due to the fact that "more careful inquiry" is made into "work reported as agriculture."

Vocational Education of Women

Briefly stated, the demands for vocational training of women in the schools depend upon the following: (1) Expansion of the sphere of women's activities in an industrial society now includes many things beyond the home, leaving less opportunity for giving instruction to the young. (2) The application of science to the tasks of the household requires systematic instruction, which cannot be given at home because many mothers are not trained for the purpose, even though they are not employed outside the home in any other occupation. (3) Its teaching constitutes a reform measure. Healthy people are apt to be happy. Healthy, happy people are valuable social assets. Scientifically planned meals, child hygiene, harmonious decoration, scientific regulation of ventilation, heating and plumbing systems, and skillful expenditure of the family funds, it is maintained, conduce to this end. (4) If women are to enter occupations outside the home, there must be preparation for them, and guidance in making the choice.

Some instruction in domestic arts appeared in colonial days when mistresses gave lessons in "all sorts of needle work," "plain work," "marking," and "pattern drawing," but little importance attaches to the movement before 1875. A "private cookery" school was instituted in Boston in 1874 and another three years later. In 1879 the Boston Cooking School was opened, which later united with Simmons College. Private concerns and some classes in public schools stimulated an interest in this branch of domestic art to such an extent that in 1885 it became a part of the work of the school system. Sewing had been introduced successfully about 1865. The importance of instruction in cookery was recognized about the same time in Philadelphia and New York; in the former city classes opened in 1878, and seven years later sewing and cooking entered the public elementary schools; in the latter city a cooking school opened in 1876, and was later incorporated. By 1888 cooking and sewing had become part of the elementary school curriculum.

Extension of instruction to the secondary school in any branch of domestic art was slow and came about only through the newly created types of schools, the manual training, technical, vocational, and cosmopolitan high schools. In 1901 Wisconsin provided by law for county agricultural high schools which were to teach domestic science. The next fifteen years saw great advancement of the idea in secondary schools. In 1917–18 2865 public high schools, or about 20 per cent, offered courses in home economics which were attended by 1316 boys and 100,671 girls. These constituted, however, but 10 per cent of all girls at public high schools and a little less than 6 per cent of all boys and girls so attending. The academic courses still occupy the major part of the field, drawing almost 72 per cent of all students.

Other organizations, such as the Boston Trade School and the Manhattan Trade School, founded just after the beginning of the present century, are important in that they represent an effort to reproduce actual conditions in the school situation. As recognized pioneers in the labor of this movement may also be mentioned the Young Women's Christian Association, the American School of Home Economics of Chicago, the Lake Placid Conference of Home Economics, and the Summer School of Chautauqua, New York.

Home economics in higher institutions of learning was introduced somewhat later, though some attention was given to the practical side in western institutions at an early date. Following the example of Mt. Holyoke College since 1836, the earliest step seems to have been taken at the University of Iowa in 1869, when young women were required to work in dining room and kitchen; but similar opportunities were soon offered at other institutions. As a general rule, however, domestic science instruction at state agricultural colleges and state universities began in the first decade of the present century.

Other higher institutions that deserve a fuller account, if space permitted, are Simmons College, opened in 1902, Drexel Institute, Pratt Institute, and the School of Practical Arts of Teachers College. These have done most for the movement through the preparation of future teachers. In the past ten years the enrollment in the School of Practical Arts has increased from 580 to over 2000 students, of whom 330 are pursuing graduate work. On account of the great increase in numbers, and also because of the fact that many institutions now exist which offer opportunities for training in the first two years of domestic science, entrance to the School of Practical Arts now depends on the completion of the first two years' work elsewhere; thus the school at Teachers College is free to devote its energies to more advanced instruction.

The increase of interest in home economics has been general in colleges, universities, and technological schools during the twentieth century. In 1905 there were but 849 students of household economy in such schools; in 1910 there were 1934; while in 1916 there were, in 195 institutions of the above grade, 17,778 students. In 1917–18 there were 773 degrees in home economics conferred in these institutions.

Federal Legislation

Federal legislation on vocational education had its beginning prior to the Civil War, when in 1857 Justin S. Morrill introduced a bill to establish agricultural colleges. Though opposed by several senators, and criticized variously as "fraud," "delusion," and "cheat," the Morrill Act was passed in 1862. It provided for a gift to the states of 30,000 acres of public land for each senator and representative then in Congress, for "endowment, support, and maintenance of at least one college, whose leading object shall be, without excluding other scientific and classical studies, and including military tactics, to teach such branches as are related to agriculture and the mechanic arts. . . ." Mr. Morrill emphasized in his plea for the bill that he desired to "do something for the farmer," but the purpose and plan were so indefinitely conceived that much of the federal grant was wasted. While professing to do "something for the farmer," the schools, during their early years, turned out more students of classics, sciences, and mechanic arts than of agriculture. Not until 1915 did the number of students in agriculture exceed those in mechanic arts.

Following the first grant for agricultural and mechanical colleges in 1862, came an appropriation for experimental stations in 1887, the authorization of an annual grant in 1890 — increased in 1907 — the Adams Act of 1906, the Smith-Lever Bill of 1914, and the Smith-Hughes enactment of 1917. All of these extended the function of the federal government in the field of education. A further extension is now contemplated by the Towner-Sterling Bill.

The efforts to secure federal assistance for vocational projects from 1862 to the end of the nineteenth century, upon whatever reasons they happened to be based, furnished a fitting prologue to the activities of the twentieth. Besides the bills already mentioned to promote agricultural education, the unsuccessful Davis and Page Bills, of 1907 and 1912 respectively, represent efforts to secure federal support for vocational education. At length a commission was appointed to investigate the situation and make report on the desirability and feasibility of giving federal aid. The Commission presented a long report, urging the extension of federal grants to vocational education, and upon the basis of the following reasons:

(1) There is pressing need of vocational education.
(2) The problem of vocational education is too extensive to be worked out except by a national agency.
(3) The states are too poor to attempt a solution of the problem.
(4) Federal grants would start an interest and stimulate local effort in the direction of vocational education.
(5) Federal grants in this case are constitutional on the basis of promoting general welfare.
(6) The mobility of the population and of labor in particular justifies the application of federal resources to the problem.
(7) The training of teachers of vocational subjects is expensive and teachers are migratory; both reasons justify federal aid for their training.
(8) A bureau should be maintained by federal appropriation to assemble and distribute information on vocational subjects.

The foregoing reasons are quite as interesting to a student of history as is the bill which followed in February, 1917. So far as a basis for federal grants to vocational education is concerned, they are as unsound and irrational as those urged by Mr. Morrill and his colleagues more than sixty years earlier.

The Smith-Hughes law, 1917, provided for the following: a Federal Board of Vocational Education and state boards to coöperate with it in case the state accepted the provisions of the act; aid for salaries of teachers, the amount to be matched by the state; federal supervision of work and expenditures; and investigations connected with the several fields of vocational education. The federal grants for the various purposes are shown in the following table:

TABLE II

Years	Agricultural Education	Trade, Household Economics, and Industrial Education	Teacher Training	Investigations
1917–18	$ 548,000	$ 566,000	$ 546,000	$200,000
1918–19	784,000	796,000	732,000	200,000
1919–20	1,024,000	1,034,000	924,000	200,000
1920–21	1,268,000	1,278,000	1,090,000	200,000
1921–22	1,514,000	1,525,000	1,090,000	200,000
1922–23	1,761,000	1,772,000	1,090,000	200,000
1923–24	2,009,000	2,019,000	1,090,000	200,000
1924–25	2,534,000	2,556,000	1,090,000	200,000
1925–26	3,027,000	3,050,000	1,090,000	200,000
Annually	3,027,000	3,050,000	1,090,000	200,000

The coöperation of the federal government and the states under the Act is said by the Federal Board to rest upon these fundamental ideas :

First, that vocational education being essential to the national welfare, it is a function of the national government to stimulate the states to undertake this new and needed form of service ; *second*, that federal funds are necessary in order to equalize the burden of carrying on the work among the states ; *third*, that since the federal government is vitally interested in the success of vocational education, it should, so to speak, purchase a degree of participation in this work ; and, *fourth*, that only by creating such a relationship between the central and the local governments can proper standards of educational efficiency be set up.

The word " vocational " may be stricken out of the " four fundamental ideas " quoted above and they remain equally defensible. Further extension of federal support to Americanization, teacher training, etc., as proposed by the Towner-Sterling Bill, rests upon the same arguments.

Many, who are convinced of the genuine need for vocational education, are frankly skeptical of the federal provisions for it. Professor Kandel stated certain objections in 1917, and many of them still stand. First, dual control is introduced, which is undesirable. If vocational education is worthy of a place it should be part of a general system, not isolated. Second, it deals with the problem in piece-meal fashion, giving assistance to agricultural, trade, home economics, and industrial subjects and the training of teachers for these groups, and makes no pretense of dealing with vocational education as a whole question. Third, expensive machinery is erected in Washington to draw out of one pocket funds to be placed in another. Fourth, the Federal Board itself is badly constituted. Only three of its members are to give their full time to the task, and into their hands is intrusted the expenditure of millions. Those possessed of decentralizing leanings point out that the state has capitulated to national authority in that state boards must have their plans approved by the Federal Board before aid can be granted; others, however, insist that inadequate safeguards are set over the expenditure of federal funds; finally, that the action of Congress has undertaken to settle in hasty manner a question the solution of which should have depended upon painstaking scientific study by experts.

State Legislation

Recent years have witnessed in the states a marked increase in legislative activity relating to various phases of vocational education. In 1920 and 1921, over one hundred acts were passed in the several states of the Union relating to vocational rehabilitation, continuation, trade, and agricultural schools. Many of these acts were concerned with the acceptance of the provisions of the Smith-Hughes Act.

There are a number of acts on compulsory continuation education. California provided in 1921 for compulsory part-time continuation education for workers from 16 to 18 years of age; Connecticut, in 1921, provided for part-time continuation education for workers between 14 and 16 years of age in case the equivalent of the eight elementary grades has not been completed; Delaware, in 1921, required boards of education in counties and special districts to provide part-time educational opportunities in general, civic, and vocational subjects for all persons under 16, not attending a full-time day school — attendance to be enforced when the part-time classes are established; Florida, in 1921, authorized and required boards of education to organize and maintain part-time schools; the 1919 law of Illinois required part-time education for those between 14 and 16 years, whereas the amended form of 1921 *permits* the authorities to maintain such schools. Where the schools are established, attendance of employed minors, 14 to 18 years of age, who have not finished four years of secondary school work, is required eight hours per week for 36 weeks each year. Indiana, in 1921, charged local authorities to require attendance of lawfully employed minors from 14 to 18 years for not less than four nor more than eight hours per week. Similar acts or amendments have been passed by Kentucky, Michigan, Montana, Nebraska, Nevada, New York, Utah, West Virginia, and Wisconsin.

Next to continuation education, vocational rehabilitation received most attention at the hands of state legislators; approximately one third of the total number of bills related to this subject. In a majority of cases, these bills merely provided for the "acceptance of the benefits of an act passed by the Senate and House of Representatives of the United States of America in Congress assembled to provide for the promotion of vocational rehabilitation of persons disabled in industry or otherwise, and their return to civil employment. . . ."

Vocational Guidance

The development of an industrial society has brought with it many educational problems, but none more difficult and far-reaching than that of vocational guidance. It is true that the problem is an old one, hinted at centuries ago, but it is so urgent now as to be unavoidable. Bloomfield mentions a document from an English source as early as 1747 and Richards published *Vocophy* in 1881, but little was accomplished in the United States before the work begun by Parsons at Boston in 1908. That which went before is interesting to us now, but not of great importance.

Leaders in modern vocational guidance recognize that two things must be known : the capacities, qualities, and desires of the individual; and the nature of occupations themselves and the qualities necessary for success in them. Vast fields of labor are at once opened up when we recognize the need for analysis of these two things, the individual and the occupation. Likewise, in the study of any one of them, and the application of the truth arrived at, to a practical problem, opportunities for disagreement arise. Momentous to-day is the difference of opinion concerning the use and interpretation of the results of various tests that have been devised. The facts are the same — cold, impersonal, unwilling. But they do not mean the same thing to different people. Thus, while there is one set of facts, scientifically arrived at, action based on them may not be united. One theorist believes that there is enough of scientific knowledge to sustain him in giving direct advice to enter a given profession; another may content himself, while knowing the same facts, with merely supplying information about a vocation and allowing the individual to make a choice without hindrance or direction.

But questions broader than individual welfare are involved. Do psychological tests spell disaster for the ideal of American democracy? Denouncing American democracy as a fetish, President Cutten recently emphasized the future possibilities in vocational testing whereby each will find the sphere for which he is fitted by nature. His conclusion is that "it must inevitably destroy universal adult suffrage . . . and we come back again to the rule of the aristocracy — this time the real and total aristocracy."

The above interpretation of the function of tests was attacked by W. C. Bagley, who characterized it as "most unfortunate," maintaining that "far from revealing the need of an 'aristocracy of brains'" the tests point "compellingly towards the need of a much more thoroughgoing *democracy of culture* than our educational system has yet achieved." Whipple, on the other hand, believes that "the real meaning of democracy is properly safeguarded in the notion of 'equity of opportunity'" and that "the existence of fundamental and relatively permanent individual differences in intellectual capacity has been incontrovertibly demonstrated."

Colvin recently summarized the findings concerning the prognostic value of tests:

We must, therefore, conclude that on the whole, psychological tests have justified their use as prognostic of academic achievement. . . . The army tests have indicated the probability at least, that there are certain intelligence levels for various occupations, ranging from below average intelligence for day laborers to decidedly above average for the professions. It is not altogether certain that these results can be taken unreservedly at their face value, but they are at least suggestive and may be employed together with other data in assigning men to occupational groups and in advising pupils in regard to various life callings.

There has been disagreement in the past concerning the variability in degrees of ability; types have been described by all generations since Plato told us of the men of iron, silver, and gold. Modern psychology, however, seems to indicate the non-existence of clear-cut types. Thorndike's interpretation of the facts may be accepted as representing the current view when he concludes that "it is very hard to find any case of a negative correlation between desirable mental functions," and "better adaptation to the world in any respect seems to be positively related to better adaptation in all, or nearly all, respects . . ."

Regarding the permanence of youthful interests, another question of great importance to guidance, the same author found "a correlation of .6 or .7 . . . to be approximately the true degree of resemblance between the relative degree of an interest in a child of from ten to fourteen and in the same person at twenty-one. . . . On the whole the resemblance between interest and ability may safely be placed at about .9 of a perfect resemblance."

It is evident that much has been done, and more is hoped for, in the analysis of the individual. The weight of expert opinion is in favor of accepting the present tests tentatively and perfecting them as instruments for classification.

Meanwhile, the other phase of the guidance problem is receiving more and more attention — the study of the occupations open to men and women, and compilation of information as to where and how suitable training may be obtained to prepare for them. In 1921 the Public Education and Child Labor Association of Pennsylvania published a *Survey of Opportunities for Vocational Education in and about Philadelphia*. The surveys of cities such as Minneapolis, Indianapolis, Evansville, Wilmington, Richmond, and Cleveland, and reports and bulletins of vocational guidance bureaus have also contributed to this end. Boston provides a book giving a description of its high schools, and places this in the hands of each eighth-grade child. Chicago, with similar intent, suggests the proper high schools for elementary school graduates, and describes opportunities in other city institutions that are open to high school graduates. Similar efforts are made in other cities.

From the foregoing facts concerning (1) pyschological investigations and (2) study of occupations and specific preparation for them, it appears that vocational guidance to-day covers a wider range of activities than was earlier thought necessary. A broad conception of the problem to-day is suggested by Brewer, when he says it is concerned with : "(1) Laying a broad foundation of useful experiences, (2) studying occupational opportunities, (3) choosing an occupation, (4) preparing for the occupation, (5) entering upon work, (6) securing promotions and making readjustments."

The six points above represent a broad and sane interpretation of the task of vocational guidance. It may discourage some workers inasmuch as it would accomplish much more than is generally attempted. Often, guidance has meant and means only advice and placement. It must do more, and so far as guidance bureaus are able to become effective in the several functions indicated, they will measure up to the highest conception of their task.

But many difficulties lie in the path, particularly with regard to the individual who has undertaken a job. There must be considered the relation between the employer, the employee, and the guidance bureau. The former and the latter must come to agreement regarding the employee. The former is interested first in profit; the latter in the welfare of the boy and girl and the result to society. There must be coöperation on the part of the employer and the guidance experts. The employer must come to realize that his best interests are served by well-placed, well-paid, and safeguarded employees. Without this justice, there can be no industrial peace.

To this problem, which so closely concerns employer and vocational guide, it was hoped that an answer might be suggested by scientific management which came into great prominence as a result of the work of Taylor, Gantt, and Emerson. If, as stated, "Scientific management" is "devised by industrial engineers for the purpose of subserving the common interests of employers, workmen, and society at large . . .," it would seem that unity of purpose exists already between managers of employment and vocational guides. Theory and practice must be considered, however, in order to appreciate the help or hindrance of scientific management to vocational guidance. In this connection some observations made to the United States Commission on Industrial Relations are significant.

Hoxie reported in his study, *Scientific Management and Labor*, "that the average manager in a scientific management shop is not only quite indifferent to, but profoundly ignorant of, the broader and deeper aspects of the problem of vocational selection and adaptation." According to this judgment, made after careful study, it appears that the contributions of scientific management to vocational education and guidance are of decidedly dubious character.

Schneider, in his *Education for Industrial Workers*, is likewise of the opinion that scientific management tends rather to increase the strength of a capitalist employer class than to offer "any effective guarantee against overspeeding and exhaustion of workers."

Briefly, efficiency will not of itself solve social problems. It is but a narrow phase of a broad problem. It is easy and comfortable to adopt a fetish. Would it be better for our democracy, if, instead of "efficiency" as the password for success, we were to try "mutual aid" — or temper "efficiency" with the Golden Rule?

In this industrial-minded age a mere human being needs a friend. The business man *may* be that, but he is primarily concerned with "returns." To him vocational education is necessary for the sake of industry. As the Federal Commission on National Aid stated: "Vocational Education is therefore needed as a wise business investment for this nation, because our national prosperity and happiness are at stake and our position in the markets of the world cannot otherwise be maintained."

Let the educator be wary lest in educating men vocationally he merely prepare them for the industrial juggernaut. One must agree with Brewer that "the best vocational guidance is that accomplished by means of educational guidance." The best thing that can be accomplished by the guidance movement is to keep children in school longer rather than rush them into jobs — to keep vocational interests broad, rather than sacrifice them early for the sake of narrow efficiency.

The Present Situation

Evidence of the great expansion of opportunities for vocational education, the beginnings of which have been noted in several fields, is to be seen in recent figures. Under the Smith-Hughes Act, a total of $2,307,460.44 was allotted to the states for the fiscal year ending June, 1919, for encouraging instruction in agriculture, trade, home economics, and industrial subjects, and the preparation of vocational teachers. The table on page 299 shows the increase in the number of federally aided vocational schools of the several types since 1918, the number of students teacher training institutions assisted, and the number of students in teacher training courses.

Vocational rehabilitation and return to civil employment of disabled persons discharged from the military or naval forces of the United States was provided for by law, June 27, 1918. The number of training centers of various types in 1921 was 183; in these 12,315 "trainees" were enrolled for agricultural, commercial, and industrial preparation. The total funds appropriated for the purpose up to and including 1922 was $209,078,137, and the actual expenditure of the

TABLE III

FEDERAL AIDED SCHOOLS, STUDENTS, AND TEACHER TRAINING INSTITUTIONS — 1918–1921 [1]

Year	Total Schools	Total Students	Agriculture				Trade — Industrial			
			Schools	Students	Schools Training Teachers	Students	Schools	Students	Schools Training Teachers	Students
1918	1741	164,186	609	15,453	40	1534	809	117,934	45	1101
1919	2039	194,895	863	19,933	60	1334	575	84,765	68	2774
1920	3150	265,058	1375	31,301	64	2310	753	86,737	70	6150
1921	3859	305,224	1721	42,709	61	2936	836 [2]	83,532	68	6384

Year	Home Economics				Part-time Continuation				Total Teacher Training Schools	Total in Teacher Training Courses
	Schools	Students	Schools Training Teachers	Students	Schools	Students	Schools Training Teachers	Students		
1918	323	30,799	60	3319	3 [3]	3 [3]		635	94	6,589
1919	463	39,414	78	3098	138	50,783	11	158	144	7,364
1920	700	48,938	85	3652	322	98,082	5	344	135	12,456
1921	914 [2]	63,806	79	4954	388	115,177	2	481	150 [4]	14,755 [4]

[1] From *Fifth Annual Report of the Federal Board*, pp. 223–307.
[2] No report from Wisconsin.
[3] Not separately classified in 1918.
[4] No report for Pennsylvania.

appropriated sum was nearly $146,000,000. The cost of administration alone, 1920–21, was $9,063,154.75.

Federal aid for vocational rehabilitation of those disabled in industry or otherwise was provided for by law, June 2, 1920. Allotments to the states for this purpose amounted in 1921 to $777,951.44. The total number of cases dealt with during the year was 5619. At the close of the fiscal year 1921, thirteen states had not accepted the federal provision by legislative enactment.

In commercial education advancement has been made, especially in the character of the course of study. The courses in the first few years of the century were singularly academic, and the course favored by the National Education Association in 1903 seems unusually strait-laced, compared with the liberal supply of commercial subjects in the modern cosmopolitan and commercial high schools. There was a time when commercial education was planned to train only bookkeepers and stenographers. More specific ends are now sought after, as retail selling, and special secretarial service, in addition to earlier objectives. Nevertheless there is a demand for more specific objectives. Surveys have shown, almost without exception, that commercial education pursues its own sweet way without much regard to business practice. Specialization is the rule of modern business. If it hopes to meet business needs the school must follow that practice. If business concerns do not ordinarily combine the task of bookkeeper and stenographer, why should the school insist on such a practice?

In 1917–18, 2953 public high schools reported 278,275 students in commercial courses, of which number nearly ten thousand were in junior high schools. In 1918 there were 890 private commercial and business schools with 289,579 students. Is this equality of opportunity? Over a quarter of a million youths must, if interested in a commercial occupation, enter private commercial schools. The number of students in high school commercial departments and courses exceeds by far those in any one of the subjects that are federally subsidized.

The assistance rendered by the federal government to home economics, agriculture, industrial and trade training, has been mentioned in the above table. In 1917–18, 2865 public high schools offered courses in domestic science attended by 101,987 students; 2012 offered work in agriculture to 38,728 students; 1831 offered technical or manual training courses attended by 96,833; and 250 offered trade training courses attended by 16,614.

The changes in the curriculum of secondary schools, involved in the introduction of manual training, domestic science, industrial arts, and agriculture, bear evidence to the fact that successful efforts have been made to restore to secondary education its proper functions in the educational system. It cannot be said to-day, as it was twenty-five years ago, that "The bells of our university leaders jingle, and with pack horse constancy we have blindly followed . . ." The guiding principle to-day is to be found in our study of occupations and in the development of vocational courses that train specifically for them. It is now conceded that general vocational preparation is impossible, albeit some practice seems to belie the statement. The general truth, however, is borne out by the fact that in 1917–18 about thirty per cent of the students in public high schools were pursuing vocational courses.

The recognition of vocational education as a legitimate and very important objective of the secondary school has come about in response to new industrial, commercial, and social needs, incident to our economic expansion. In place of the few callings which formerly demanded specific training, there are now many; and for these adequate training through apprenticeship is no longer practicable. The foremost critics of the old formal education of the secondary school pointed out repeatedly that it did not prepare for life. "We only toil and labor to stuff the memory, . . ." says Montaigne; Penn complains that "we are in pain to make them scholars but not men"; while Milton defines a complete education which shall fit for "all the offices both private and public of peace and war" and bewails the fact that we "spend seven or eight years in scraping together so much miserable Latin and Greek as might be learned otherwise easily and delightfully in one year." The best interpreters of secondary education have had in mind the preparation of men for life situations, whether through classical or modern "real" studies. "It is therefore proposed," says Franklin, "that they learn those things that are likely to be most useful and most ornamental; regard being had to the several professions for which they are intended." On the whole, it appears that the inclusion of specific vocational objectives in modern secondary education is but a fuller realization of an old ideal, in terms of modern social and economic standards and conditions.

Advanced preparation along vocational lines has already been mentioned. In 1916 there were 17,778 students of home economics in 195 colleges, universities, and technical schools; in the same year 32,041 students pursued courses in engineering; 17,145 in agriculture; 795 in forestry; 9223 in commerce; and 1953 in architecture.

Mention should also be made of nurse-training institutions which have experienced great increase in point of numbers since 1880, when but 15 were reported with 323 pupil nurses and 157 graduates. In 1918 there were 1776 such schools having 55,251 pupils and 13,751 graduates. Of 1606 general hospital schools reporting in 1918 there were 1416 which offered a three-year course, and three which offered a four-year course. This lengthening of the course from one or two years has been accomplished by the majority of institutions during the past ten years.

The Place of Vocational Education

The origins touched upon in the foregoing pages represent the groping of a people for a realization of their opportunities through a more elaborate system of education and training. "Remember," said Bacon, "that the learning of the few is despotism, the learning of the many is liberty; and that intelligent and principled liberty is fame, wisdom, and power." Vocational education seeks to offer hitherto unknown opportunities for the many.

This new education is demanded by the individual worker, for without it he is unable to cope with modern industrial conditions; industry makes similar demands in the name of efficiency. Traditional respect for the worth and right of the individual should insure the educator's attention to this project; respect for material success does insure the attention of the leaders in industrial and commercial life. But, traditionally, educators have stood afar off from business, while men in commercial life have scoffed at education. The two must come together, otherwise there can be no satisfactory solution of this problem. Mere efficiency, demanded by business, does not mean complete living, nor good citizenship; on the other hand, general preparation alone cannot now make an economically independent individual. The first necessity is life; the second, abundant life. Abundant life gives to society; mere living has nothing left over. Unless we achieve the second, the first is of small significance for social progress.

A broader purpose must then be conceived, and it seems quite evident that it can come about best through integration of the points of view of educator and industrialist. Coöperation has been heralded at numerous conventions as the only way to a successful conclusion of the matter. Recently a regional conference was held on commercial education for the District of Columbia, Delaware, Maryland, Pennsylvania, and southern New Jersey, designed "to promote better understanding and closer coöperation between business men and teachers of business, economics, and social science subjects." The coöperative tendency may also be noted in the attitude of business towards numerous vocational surveys that have been made. At the recent meeting of the National Society for Vocational Education, held at Detroit, employers appeared to state their needs to the convention.

The welfare of the individual, and so of society, depends on the genuine coöperation of industrialists and educators. Neither one nor the other may be dictator. In coöperation there is compromise. The narrow aim, to secure efficiency alone, often found in the commercial or industrial concern, must be broadened. In times past it was necessary to compel the master to cause his apprentice to be taught to read and write; also to safeguard them against their masters "if they use them rigorously." "Rigorous usage" is not uncommon to-day, and the most efficient individual in the shop may be a loss to society. The following statement, reported in the National Education Association *Proceedings* a few years ago, is descriptive of the attitude of too many concerns : "These boys will work all their lives for our company and we want them to do things our way. We don't want the boys to draw; we want them to read drawings. We don't want them to boss. We want them to be bossed," and he might have added, "and we don't want them to think, but to become automatic machines."

On the other hand, many critics from the field of business object to the lack of initiative in the schools' product. The "follower habit in children is a consequence of the autocratic government of schools when collected into systems. . . . Filled with these motives (developed in schools) when he comes into industry, he naturally watches the clock, is late in coming in the morning, is quick to jump away at the stroke of the bell at the end of the day."

For the responsible jobs in industrial life we shall undoubtedly find that the point of view of modern education, expressed by Dewey, in *Schools of Tomorrow*, Kilpatrick and others in their discussion of the project method, by Miss Parkhurst in *Education on the Dalton Plan,* and by Sanderson of Oundle is the one that promises most. These changes in method and organization seek to stimulate nature-given powers, not to repress them. The tendency of the new school of thought is to venerate those capacities which, allowed to develop, are most prized in actual life situations. Vocational education of the present must divorce itself more completely from the idea of general training, with which it was burdened on its first development in the United States; and in this task there are no more useful auxiliaries than modern psychology and the new philosophy of method.

Occupational education must be based upon more thorough knowledge of the requirements of each occupation. How many persons are engaged in specialized activities? How special is the skill required? Just how long a time is needed to give that skill? There is vast wastage if the student spends four years in a commercial course in order to learn to operate an office machine, act as bill or entry clerk, or in some other very limited capacity. For one who is to serve in such a place would not a broad education be best, with intensive drill in the function to be performed? All who labor, look forward to leisure. How shall those occupy their leisure whose routine job ceases at a given hour and whose education has stimulated no deep interest in literature, history, music, sociology, economics, or politics?

REFERENCES

ALLEN, FREDRICK J. — *Guide to the Study of Occupations;* Harvard University Press, 1921.

BREWER, JOHN M. — *The Vocational-Guidance Movement;* Macmillan, 1922.

Federal Board for Vocational Education — *Reports* and *Bulletins.*

National Society for the Promotion of Industrial Education — *Bulletins.*

National Society for Vocational Education — *Bulletins*.
National Vocational Guidance Association — *Bulletins*.
SNEDDEN, DAVID — *Vocational Education;* Macmillan, 1920.
United States Bureau of Education — *Reports* and *Bulletins*.
——*Library Leaflet*, 1922, No. 15, "References on Vocational Education."

CHAPTER XII

EDUCATION OF EXCEPTIONAL CHILDREN

BY

JOHN F. REIGART

PRINCIPAL, PUBLIC SCHOOL 166, NEW YORK CITY

CHAPTER XII

EDUCATION OF EXCEPTIONAL CHILDREN

A Period of Educational Awakening

However reluctant one may be to acknowledge the fact, it is none the less certain that the task of trying to educate everybody, which our public schools are engaged in, has proved to be far more difficult than the originators of the idea of such a possibility thought it would be when they set out upon the undertaking.

No one to-day would challenge this statement by the author of *The Evolution of Dodd.* The past twenty-five years have seen a period of awakening from complacency regarding our educational system, culminating in the demonstration of the unexpected extent of illiteracy and incapacity among enlisted men. To reach the goal of universal education requires more than compulsory school laws. In the general lack of a permanent census of children of school age, tables of statistics showing percentage of attendance based on school registration have been misleading, and thousands have been overlooked. Children, when found, need to be housed in school buildings and to be taught by skilled teachers with adequate facilities. Campaigns for new buildings and for a larger supply of trained teachers, the very great increase in state aid, and the demand for a national educational program are evidences of the discovery of the need for school extension. The quality, as well as the extent, of public education is no longer a matter for self-complacency. The survey searchlight reveals the shortcomings of city and state systems. From kindergarten to university, forms of administration, courses of study, and methods of instruction are undergoing critical investigation. In the effort to find out where we are, the problem of whither we are going has not been neglected. Academic discussions of the knowledge that is of most worth, of individual or social aims, are no longer satisfying. Such questions are now referred to the laboratory and to tests from practical life.

Neglect of Exceptional Children

During the period in review no movement has been more marked than that of the education of exceptional children in the public schools. It has been a process of the gradual discovery of new problems, and of successive steps of differentiation in school activities. Thus far the movement has been limited mainly to large cities where it is possible to form classes or schools for various types of children. Even here the sense of responsibility was slow in emerging. Attention had been focused on the machinery of the schools, on standardized methods — Lancasterian, Socratic, Herbartian, etc. — and on the introduction of specifics, as physiology, civics, manual training. Those who did not fit the system could shift for themselves. Blind, deaf, and crippled children could market their infirmities; newsboys abounded. Incorrigible children were not compelled to sit interminable years in school.

Enforced School Attendance Led to Segregation of Incorrigible and Mentally Defective Children

With the extension of compulsory school laws and their more effective enforcement, the machinery became cluttered up with intractable material. By necessity, then, came classes and schools, probationary or industrial, for incorrigible children. Children utterly incapable of making progress in school studies were set apart in classes for mental defectives. Day schools and classes in regular public schools were formed for some of the blind, deaf, and otherwise handicapped children who had not been gathered up in institutions.

Influence of the Child Study Movement, the New Psychology, and Mental Measurements

Along with this tendency to extend the scope of the public school and to make special provision for pupils that could not be assimilated, came, as a result of the Child Study Movement, the growing demand for further differentiation to meet the needs of newly recognized types of children. Such pioneer studies as Warner's *Health of London School Children*, Galton's *Heredity*, and Hall's *Contents of Children's Minds* pointed out the significant fact that children differ in physical powers, in native ability, in interests, and in experience. Child study associations and magazines sprang up in all sections of the country. Under the leadership of President Hall and the newly founded Clark University, new light was sought by means of questionnaires revealing the springs of thought and feeling and conduct. The teacher must become a naturalist. Observation of children replaced or supplemented formal textbooks on methods of teaching. In the place of a psychology of definitions, faculties, and mechanical associations appeared James's *Principles of Psychology* with its "Stream of Consciousness," classification of instincts, and laws of habit. The experimental and statistical methods of Cattell and Thorndike led to more exact knowledge of native ability, instinctive tendencies, and methods of learning. For measurement of ability the point of view of the naturalist proved inadequate. At one end of the scale came Cattell's tests for Columbia students, and at the other Seguin's form board, or similar devices, for the detection of feeble-mindedness. The movement was furthered by the pressing need of more exact classification of school children, as demonstrated by such studies as those of Ayres and Thorndike on retardation, and by the use of the Binet scale as adapted by Goddard, Huey, and Terman. However, adequate plans for remedying the evident inequalities in school grading could not be based on mere statistics of retardation or acceleration, or on lengthy individual tests of intelligence. The demand for specific measurement of accomplishment was met, with varying degrees of success, by the standardized tests and scales for arithmetic, composition, spelling, writing, reading; and the demand for economical measures of native ability by group tests which aroused so much popular interest when used in the army. The value of these instruments, as Captain Cuttle would put it, lies in their application. As a basis for a rigid classification and treatment of inferior and superior pupils, group tests tend to introduce the vicious educational determinism justly condemned by Bagley and others. But the possibility that through excessive zeal and overconfidence such tests may be pushed to extreme conclusions does not detract from their value as a means of tentative classification of pupils for further study and adjustment.

Influence of Medical Inspection

Medical inspection now covers far more than the control of contagious diseases. All types of physical deficiency are brought to view. Certain defects may be corrected without any particular change in the school routine. For other groups, such as the tubercular, cardiac, and anemic, special adjustment must be made; hence the special classes for cardiac children, the assignment of classrooms on the first floor to children who have serious heart trouble, open-air rooms or buildings for tubercular children, etc. From the standpoint of mental and physical efficiency there are few normal children. The exceptional child seems to be the rule rather than the exception. The United States Bureau

of Education as long ago as 1911 listed twenty-five different
types of children requiring special classes or schools or some
form of special adjustment.

Present Stage Experimental

Provision for exceptional children is still in the experimental stage. The great accomplishment thus far is the
recognition of the fact that there are in the schools various
groups of children who are unable to profit under the usual
class grading and instruction, and who are a hindrance to
the progress of their more fortunate schoolmates, and that
the welfare of the individual and of society demands radical
measures of readjustment. Among the most pressing
problems are: What are the groups for which special
provision should be made? What are the limits of these
groups? What is the reliability of the tests for selection?
What cases should be cared for in institutions? What
children should be assigned to special schools or classes?
What deficient or handicapped children should receive
permanent or temporary aid in order to keep up with the
regular class? How should teachers of exceptional children
be selected and trained? What teachers should receive
additional compensation? What modifications are required
in the course of study? What special methods of instruction? What equipment is needed? What form of administration and supervision? What vocational guidance should
be provided, and what follow-up methods should be used
after pupils leave school?

Special Schools and Classes for Incorrigible Children

During the decade 1890–1900 occurred the first organized
movement in the public schools toward provision for any
groups of exceptional children. Cleveland, Chicago, New
York, and Providence led in the establishment of classes and

schools for truants, disciplinary cases, and backward children. At first the different types of children were not clearly differentiated, a condition which has been in a great measure remedied through the general use of scientific tests and measurements. While provision for these classes of children has been greatly extended, it has by no means kept up with the demand. Compulsory attendance laws have placed in school many who do not desire to be there, and they have also increased the disciplinary problems of the school. Unruly pupils can no longer be sent home as a punishment or be subjected to expulsion. Through the extension of the school age the teacher can no longer look forward to the age of twelve or fourteen as the time of relief from the obstacles to her teaching. A certain measure of relief is found in truant, disciplinary, or industrial schools or classes. Excellent equipment for industrial training is sometimes provided. In practice, however, the educational opportunities are nullified by short-term commitments and by the abuse of the specious idea of parole. A term of punishment is not the equivalent of an education. In the numerous cases due to parental neglect, the punishment of the parents by fines is more effective than the punishment of the delinquent children. Truancy, irregular attendance, laziness, and unruly behavior are admitted factors in retardation and hence in creating subjects for exceptional treatment. Unfortunately, the incidence of these faults is not confined to the perpetrators. Statistics of retardation are relative, they measure the slowness of those who fall behind the main body, they do not measure the retardation of the entire body of school children. In the opinion of some, the disproportionate amount of time given to discipline of the unruly and to repetition for the nonstudious is the chief cause of our general educational inefficiency. As most savages, and many not savage individuals, will not work except under the spur of necessity, it may be assumed that activity in school tasks on the part of Aristotle's "most unruly of all animals," will always, in some measure, be contingent upon a memory, or an anticipation, of consequences. So long as the public attitude remains sentimental upon the subject of school discipline, officials will continue to go softly and permit the hard problems to strain the endurance of the teachers. Among future studies of exceptional children we shall look for one on the children who make themselves exceptional, and among studies of retardation a study of disciplinary problems as a cause of general retardation.

Provision for Mentally Defective Children — Need of Earlier Selection and of Institutional Care for Lower Grades

The segregation of mentally deficient children in special classes and the study of these children have demonstrated some extremely significant facts. There are in the public schools a number of children, estimated at from two to four per cent, who are of too low a grade of mentality to profit by the regular course of study. Claims of parents and some physicians that these children should not be deprived of the advantages of association with normal children are without valid foundation, as these children have but little association with the others, and are but slightly impressed by the usual social environment. Normal environment to them is one that is adapted to their mental status. The selection of the mentally deficient is no longer a matter of guessing or of demonstration after years of failure in regular classes. Tests of the psychologist and psychiatrist are now of sufficient accuracy to permit the proper classification of these children before entering school. Selection at this stage prevents many wasted years and permits greater efficiency in teaching normal children. Though the mentally deficient child learns, in general, in the same manner as the normal child, his progress is inordinately slow and requires special stimulation, and as his period of possible growth is not extended, conditions demand that special training begin as early as possible.

Many children — estimated at one half of one per cent — now in the public schools, having proved unable, even in special classes, to gain the rudiments of an academic or vocational education, there has naturally arisen the demand that the public schools be relieved of this burden which is unprofitable from every standpoint — social, economic, or educational. As yet we are lacking in laws regarding the care of feeble-minded and epileptic and in a sufficient number of institutions of the type of Waverly, Vineland, or Whittier, providing adequate social life.

Need of Grading

Special classes for mental defectives have done great service in the public schools in relieving the regular classes and in demonstrating the necessity for the complete or partial segregation of certain types. At first these classes were ungraded. The next step in evolution, as yet only partially carried out, is grading. Only the supernormal child, and to some extent the child of normal mentality, has the will, initiative, and intelligence to attack and organize projects when the successive steps are not clearly differentiated. An ungraded class of mentally defective is a promiscuous group. In chronological age it may include the extremes of school age. The mental status may range from imbecility to the shrewdness and cunning of the high-grade moron. Without the normal tendency to inhibition, both sexes, mixed, display their special problems from infantilism to adolescence. Children with the training of refined homes are in contact with the uncouth, the untrained in personal habits, and the

moral pervert.   The fluent in speech are classed with the
inarticulate.   While some children receive scanty lessons in
reading, writing, and spelling, others can scarcely attain the
recognition of a few simple words and cannot write their own
names.   Stringing beads or cutting paper is the limit of some,
while others, under direction and constant oversight, may
use a sewing machine, or construct toy houses and animals.
Social games find an eager though awkward response from
part of the group, while others are incapable of responding to
social stimuli or to simple rhythms.   To all these differences
of age, sex, general intelligence, habits, morals, speech,
academic attainments, social response, and coördination,
may be added various handicaps such as defective vision or
hearing, chorea or other nervous diseases, malnutrition,
physical deformity, or cardiac fault, and the impossibility of
grading is evident.   Only by the grouping of classes and by
the formation of special schools for mental defectives can it be
brought about that the children may be appropriately
grouped and provision be made for definitely progressive
training along simple academic and vocational lines.   The
special class will find its field among the backward children
including those cases of mental deficiency that are not
sufficiently pronounced to warrant segregation.   Such classes
will be flexible, permitting ready interchange with the
various classes of the school.

The Need for Clinical and Sanitarium Schools

Special schools for observation, readjustment, and re-
education serve only a limited field in connection with
hospitals, universities, or private venture.   As an adjunct
to the public school system they will become an invaluable
means of salvage.   They are needed in order to provide
adequate means for diagnoses in difficult cases of maladjustment, for the recovery of physical and mental balance, and

for the discovery of latent ability. Children, as well as their parents, sometimes must get away from home to get a new viewpoint.

Classes for the Physically Handicapped — Deaf, Blind, and Crippled Children

The history of classes for deaf, blind, and crippled children in the public schools shows a gradual transition from private to public responsibility. Children who were evidently incapable of profiting by the ordinary routine of school work and who were handicapped as regards the possibility of becoming self-supporting were regarded as objects of charity. Attendance in institutions depended upon the willingness of parents to relinquish their unfortunate children. As yet not all compulsory school laws include these groups. The admission of these children into the public schools has been furthered by the improved technique in the special methods of teaching and by a new social viewpoint regarding the handicapped members of society. As it is not desirable for the deaf to associate only with the deaf, the blind with the blind, etc., it is important that normal associations with the home, the school, and society be formed as early as possible.

Chicago led the way in admitting the blind to day schools in 1900. The classes for the physically exceptional children are as yet limited to a few of the larger cities. It is hardly possible to make provision for this type of children in the communities where there are not enough pupils to form a class. However, with the enlarged experience in transportation of pupils and the wide area that can be covered with a motor bus it may be possible in future greatly to extend facilities.

Crippled children need specially planned desks and are usually unable to move from room to room. The blind and deaf children are able to move from room to room and should associate with normal children as much as possible, the work of the special teacher supplementing the instruction in the regular classroom. The outstanding feature in the education of the blind is the recent adoption of the Braille as the universal type. This will greatly increase the range of reading material. Not less important is the differentiation between the blind and the partially blind, and in case of the latter the substitution of very large type for the point letters. In the sight-saving classes, introduced in Boston and Cleveland in 1913 and a little later in New York, pupils are enabled to use effectively and safely the remnant of sight which they possess.

Not less important than a plentiful supply of books in point type for the blind is a supply of books printed in the large type for the semi-blind. Teachers of sight conservation classes spend a large part of their time in reproducing selections from the textbooks in large hand or in reading aloud the books which the children are unable to use. Much time and money could be saved if more textbooks were printed in large type for the sight conservation classes. The Howe Publishing Society for the Blind of Cleveland has rendered great service in this direction, but the expense of these special editions, together with the limited demand, points to the need of national aid similar to the subvention of the press for the blind.

While it is desirable for deaf as well as blind or crippled children to associate with normal children, so far as possible, it is more difficult to assimilate the deaf in a regular school. Without the power of hearing, the children can gain little from the ordinary schoolroom. The power of lip reading and of articulate speech requires many years of highly technical instruction. For this reason, day schools for the deaf have been more favored than separate classes. The newest feature of instruction in these schools is the cultivation of the so-called "residual hearing." Many pupils hitherto treated as totally deaf are enabled to supplement lip reading by experience of music and auditory language. The selection of pupils subject to physical handicaps has called attention not only to varying degrees of physical disability but to the wide range in mental capacity. In accordance with the general tendency to more and more differentiation it has become necessary to form special classes of mentally defective blind, deaf, or crippled children.

Limit to the Segregation of Exceptional Children

The advantage of the segregation of certain types of children is unquestioned. Those who are mentally and morally unfitted for association with other children, who are incapable of profiting by such association, are better provided for in special schools. For other types of children, as has been demonstrated, special classes are needed with more or less association with the regular classes. The deaf, the blind, and crippled children and those suffering from tubercular and certain other diseases need facilities and additional care which usually involves separate classes. What provision should be made for children who are backward in their studies, who are handicapped by illness, by irregular attendance, ignorance of the English language, defective speech, etc.? Various measures are employed for these large, constantly changing groups of children. In some cities innumerable types of classes have been formed, in others an attempt is made to solve the problem by flexible forms of grading or by the assignment of special teachers to the schools, to render aid to special groups or individuals. The special class work may be organized and controlled from without the school or it may be managed within the individual school itself. Organization of work for schools suffering from defective speech may be taken as illustrative of the treatment of backward children or those suffering from remedial defects.

Correction of Speech Defects as an Illustration of Organization of Aid for Exceptional Children

The first classes for speech improvement were organized in New York in 1909. Special teachers are very generally employed for this purpose in elementary and high schools. Defective speech has been recognized as one of the most serious handicaps.   In degree it reaches from entire inability to speak, or distressing stuttering, to lisping and other minor defects. Speech work may be organized by assigning teachers to go from school to school, or the teacher may remain in one school and teach groups of children from various other schools, or a certain school may be selected to make a specialty of speech training and children from a distance may be assigned to this school as regular pupils. The second plan is superior to the first in providing better facilities in the way of classrooms and equipment; the third is the more valuable from the educational standpoint.   Let us take speech work as a type illustration of method of organization of work for exceptional children. Select a teacher who is an expert in phonetics and the psychology of speech. Then have her assigned to a school under the charge of a principal who is interested and informed upon the subject.   Daily drills are given to various groups for short periods, and the regular lessons are but slightly interfered with.   All the teachers of the school are trained in phonetics and are interested in following up the work of the special teacher.   All of the pupils become interested in the improvement of speech, and an atmosphere of helpfulness is created for the children who have the greatest speech difficulties. It is realized that speech is not, as popularly understood, a matter of direct imitation, but that it is learned by trial and error as are other habits. The cruder methods of training in oral English are gradually replaced by more direct methods. The general interest in the correction of speech defects leads to the effort to prevent speech difficulties, and the procedure of the classroom is adjusted accordingly. Early lessons in reading no longer permit the breaking up of the children's habits of natural speech. Children who cannot speak are taught to produce sounds correctly, and correct speech habits are cultivated. Those with faulty articulation or a tendency to stutter are corrected. All the problems of reading, both oral and silent, of spelling, of oral and written composition, are attacked from the standpoint of psychology of speech. In this way not only are many speech difficulties eliminated and special class work rendered unnecessary, but all the pupils of the school are gaining in language power through the improved methods of teaching. The influence of the special speech teacher is felt throughout the school. The general attention to special training and reading according to the principles of psychology of language and of modern phonetics take care of the slow readers and spellers except in extreme cases where supplementary aid is needed. Foreign children are cared for along the same lines.

Differentiation by Schools

While one school may be giving special attention to the problems connected with speech, other schools may expand along different special lines, with classes for the blind or semi-blind, deaf, crippled children, tubercular, etc. Where the pupils can move about freely from room to room there is nothing to prevent their being taught in regular classes, while receiving special help along the line of their handicaps or deficiencies. What is needed is not so much special classes and teachers with special licenses, as teachers of adaptability who will study the special problem of children. It should be possible for a principal to assign teachers to any groups of children needing special aid, and it is not necessary that these children all be blind or deaf or crippled or mentally deficient or truants. The training of teachers for such special work has made great progress, particularly by means of short courses given in normal schools and by various associations. The training of the teachers in service is of the utmost importance. The school is the best laboratory. Growth should be expected of all teachers; instead of fixity in position, there should be flexibility in assignment. Any intelligent teacher, principal, supervisor, or superintendent who has reached a stage of arrested development along certain lines should be given a new type of work to do, making it necessary to undertake new studies. Assignments of this kind would result in the care of exceptional children becoming a great boon to the entire system.

Gifted Children

Scientific measurement has demonstrated that many pupils are not working up to their capacity, and has made it possible to detect children of promise. It has focused attention upon these children and has aroused the suspicion that in limitation to the progress of the mass the children of superior ability are not getting a square deal, and society is failing to train its leaders. The newer view of democracy in education is that opportunity should equal ability.

Various experiments in grading were aimed at breaking the "lockstep," which was exposed by Superintendents Harris and Shearer. Their object was to enable pupils of ability to move through the grades more readily than others. Individual instruction was the basis of the Pueblo plan and of the more recent Dalton plan. The Batavia plan employed assistant teachers. Cambridge adopted a system of short circuit by means of parallel grades. New York provided "opportunity classes." Distinct from time-saving plans was the movement to revive and enrich the curriculum to appeal to the interests and aptitudes of pupils and to conform to the demands of society. Dewey's *School and Society*, the Chicago experimental school, and the Gary plan are landmarks in this movement. The junior high school has its wide range of choice for pupils beyond the sixth grade. The problem is attacked from another angle by project methods and the socialized recitation, which aim to stimulate initiative and to secure the coöperation of pupils in organized undertakings, each according to his ability.

The extended use of intelligence tests indicated a curve of distribution with a superior group corresponding to the lower group which had been the first object of attention. The possibility of selecting children of decidedly superior ability involves the responsibility to utilize talent in the interest of the individual and of society. Should not the schools make special provision for gifted pupils as well as for the backward or deficient? Should these selected groups receive individual or class instruction? Should they be placed in special classes or receive special attention in regular classes? Should the aim be merely rapid advancement or more intensive study, with additional subjects? Experiments in all these directions are under way. Attempts to do continuously two years' work in one have not met with undoubted success. The groups do not prove to be homogeneous. Children of approximately the same intelligence quotient differ in health, in nervous stability, in memory, in will, in training, and in interests. Some cannot keep up the pace, and fall out by the way. The advisability of merely doing the same things as other children in less time is questioned. At present, the trend seems to be in the direction of more intensive work, with supplementary studies in foreign languages, art, and science.

Danger of Unfair Discrimination

A great drawback to the extension of special opportunities for certain groups of children is that such measures frequently result in the withdrawal of opportunities from other groups. The selection of the best teachers for special classes leaves the weaker teachers for the regular classes. Workshops, laboratories, and other special facilities may be limited to certain groups. Smaller classes for special types of children may result in larger classes for the normal children. A striking illustration of the reactionary incidence of an apparently progressive movement is found in the junior high school. This type of school has naturally aroused great interest. New and improved buildings, the best teachers, induced by higher salaries, wide range of electives, earlier introduction of secondary studies, offer opportunities for pupils after six years in school; but what about the first six years? The advocate of the junior high usually assumes that the elementary schools will be taught and supervised by women only, at lower salaries than in the higher school. The over-age boy as well as the specially bright boy will be entirely deprived of the influence of men during the entire period of elementary education. Such attractive features as shopwork are postponed. It is a question whether the advantages to be had after six years in school will be an adequate return for the six dreary years.

Are the schools as a whole gaining in efficiency through the movement to form new schools and classes after every discovery of a new type of child? Is there not danger that the normal children, if there are any, are failing to receive their due measure of attention? For the success of special schools and classes it is necessary to enlist the most successful and interesting teachers. As these teachers are drawn by higher salaries and are given a new status, they do not return to the regular schools, which not only lose their best teachers but the advantage of the specialized training and experience. Adjustment of the course of study to the capacity of pupils and the demand of modern life is frequently apt to be confined to new and favored types of schools and special classes. The enrichment of the curriculum in spots tends to impoverishment elsewhere. If selected groups must be favored by having the best and sunniest rooms, superior equipment, and smaller classes, the unselected groups must work under less favorable conditions. Is there no way to organize work for exceptional children in such a way that the advantages gained by having superior teachers, special training and experience, flexibility in courses of study, and favorable conditions could be shared with the unexceptional children?

There can be no question that the exceptional child is the gainer by having exceptional advantages. That the gain is commensurate with the outlay is open to question. The homogeneous group is a fiction. A class selected according to one defect or quality may vary in all other respects. This is the outstanding feature of special classes and schools. There is no limit to the process of differentiation.

Need of Integration as Well as Differentiation

Our school systems, then, are undergoing a continued process of differentiation with an inadequate integration. From the main system, as new demands arise, a new subordinate system is created, with supervision, teachers, budget, etc., independent of other school functions. The apparent simplicity of each new system vanishes as the exceptional children provided for are found to have all the other exceptions. Schools become not organizations but collections of classes. Different types of classes are under the charge of their special directors or supervisors. Minute details are determined by the director who spends the money for supplies, admits and discharges pupils, and generally directs, at a distance, the work of the teacher. In any special class except those for low-grade mental defectives and for pupils too weak or crippled to move from room to room, the pupils may profit by taking most of their lessons in regular classes. Here they are taught by teachers who do not receive added compensation for this additional work — the special teacher frequently receives a "bonus." Special classes for exceptional children have served a good purpose in proving the existence of groups of children who need special attention ; they have also served to prove their limitation as a final solution of their special problems. Various tendencies, some already mentioned, point in a more promising direction.

The Exceptional Child a Social Problem

The problem of the exceptional child belongs not only to the public school but to the community at large. To begin at the beginning : in some form or other the facts of heredity, the ideals of eugenics, and an enlightened birth control must in time diminish the proportion of handicapped and deficient children. The local and national policy of prenatal care aims that all children shall be well born and free from avoidable taint and weakness. The accidents and dangers of birth are guarded against by restrictions regarding midwives and by the offices of the district nurse. The prevention of blindness is making marked progress through treatment at birth and through a campaign of education regarding the preservation of sight. The dangers of infancy are being minimized by labor and maternity measures, clinics, day nurseries, pure milk supply, and by the education of mothers. Through the activities of Boards of Health and associated physicians, contagious diseases are brought under control, with a consequent diminution of the number of children physically and mentally handicapped by such diseases. The Schick treatment, for instance, bids fair to eliminate diphtheria, as smallpox has been eliminated. Many children are retarded not only by the remedial handicaps with which they enter school, but by the loss of time and strength through surgical and medical treatment. Already the forces of the schools, the Red Cross, psychiatry, medicine, dentistry, etc., are being mobilized to meet this evil at the threshold of school life. Adenoids and tonsils, teeth, nutrition, nervous disorder, are attended to before admission to school.

Figures of retardation are frequently employed as an index of school efficiency. Such an inference would be justified if all children entered school with equal capacity, with equal powers of endurance, and with similar environment. It is wrongly assumed that they get an equal start by beginning at the same age. The most cursory examination of a first-year class shows that some pupils are immature and others could have earlier learned to read without injury. It is not difficult for the psychologist to determine approximately the mental age of a child five or six years old. This estimate is now accepted in a few cities as the basis for admission to school.

During the first school year children tend to retardation not only through vaccination and other diseases naturally or artificially acquired and through various difficulties of adjustment, but by entering the class late in the term, upon their arrival at the compulsory age. Discouragement and lack of concentration naturally follow, and the result is an addition to the number of exceptional children. The first school day should be the same for all beginners. Upon entering school all children need the care of the most sympathetic, the most intelligent, and the best trained teachers. Instead of withdrawing the best teachers to take classes of exceptional children, an enlightened policy will place them in the first years to reduce the number of exceptional children. If any bonus is required for exceptional ability, scientific training, and hard work, it should go to the teachers in the first year.

The New School

During the child's attendance at school every effort should be made to avoid the need for treatment in special classes. Difficulties of adjustment should be overcome as far as possible by special assistant teachers, by school visitors, and by the coöperation of hospitals and clinics. The educational guidance begun in the schools will be followed up to aid the adjustment of the exceptional children to economic society, and the industries themselves will be adapted to the ability of the workers. Henry Ford has demonstrated that productive work for the blind, the crippled, the deaf, and other defectives can be found in industrial establishments. School and society must combine to secure the economic independence of all who are by any means able to win the means of support.

The freedom and initiative sought for in the pupils will be tolerated and encouraged in teachers and principals. No two schools will be alike. Principals will no longer be clerks, but educators, with power over the assignment of teachers, the formation of classes, the making of the course of study, and the special aids for all types of exceptional children.

The problem of grading is shifting from the grading of children to the grading of studies. The plan generally followed thus far has been to grade the children according to age and then divide up the studies accordingly. The critical point in the application of plans for individual instruction and for the teaching of exceptional children is the selection and grading of material. What are the reactions and habits of most value to individuals and society? What forms of activity may be left to the processes of growth or imitation and what require formal instruction? What factors are common and basic in various social activities, requiring opportunity for frequent practice, and valuable alike for bright and slow pupils? What factors can be left for the bright pupils alone? With the more exact analysis and grading of material, greater success may be anticipated from the various forms of individualized instruction. Perceptible progress has been made in the practical analysis and grading of spelling, grammar, and arithmetic. The power to read affords an instrument of growth that is largely overlooked. As a by-product to other studies success in reading is not assured. For the bright child nearly all knowledge is attainable through reading. Books become the best teachers. Even in the case of the dullest children, the cultivation of the language arts provides the key for the moderate accomplishments attainable.

The advance in the education of exceptional children will keep pace with the advance in the education of all children. More scientific training of teachers, greater skill in instruction, broader school curriculum, better gradation of studies, a generous supply of reading material and other equipment, smaller classes, better textbooks, special aid at any time for pupils needing assistance, will prove to the advantage of all types of children. With the best efforts of teachers and school authorities, the care of the exceptional children requires the coöperation of the home and nearly every form of social agency. The school must be the focus of community effort.

REFERENCES

BEST, HARRY — *The Blind;* Macmillan, 1919.

GROSZMANN, MAXIMILIAN P. E. — *The Exceptional Child* (Extensive bibliography, pp. 719–746); Scribner, 1917.

HOLLINGSWORTH, LETA S. — *The Psychology of Subnormal Children;* Macmillan, 1920.

JENNINGS, HERBERT S., WATSON, JOHN B., MEYER, ADOLF, and THOMAS, WILLIAM I. — *Suggestions of Modern Science Concerning Education;* Macmillan, 1918.

MONROE, PAUL — *The Cyclopedia of Education;* Macmillan, 1911–13. (See articles and bibliographies under "Exceptional Children," "Special Classes," "Education of the Deaf," "Education of the Blind," "Speech Defects," "Supernormal Children," etc.)

National Association for the Study and Education of Exceptional Children — *Reports.*

TERMAN, LEWIS M. — *The Intelligence of School Children;* Houghton Mifflin, 1919.

WHIPPLE, GUY M., and OTHERS — *Classes for Gifted Children;* Public School Pub. Co., 1920.

CHAPTER XIII

THE EDUCATION OF WOMEN

BY

WILLYSTINE GOODSELL

TEACHERS COLLEGE, COLUMBIA UNIVERSITY

CHAPTER XIII

THE EDUCATION OF WOMEN

Educational Situation at the Close of the Century

In the closing years of the nineteenth century signs were not lacking that the long struggle to secure equality of educational opportunity for women was almost won. Like a deep-moving tide, the movement had slowly risen and grown in power, sweeping, in the latter decades, over obstructions and drowning the protests of alarmed conservatives. The dark prophecies of opponents of the cause that the exacting intellectual demands of higher education would undermine the health of young women, reveal their innate mental inferiority, rob them of all feminine charm, and lead them to neglect home and children in a feverish pursuit of Greek roots or the intricacies of quadratic equations, had proved to be without foundation. Young women had demonstrated to the satisfaction of all but the most captious critics that they could enrich their minds without impoverishing their hearts and could pursue a course in the liberal arts without sustaining a mental and physical breakdown. Public opinion in 1897 was distinctly more favorable toward college education for women and even toward their further professional training than it had been a generation previous, when Vassar was established as the first great milestone in the liberal education of American womanhood. When Matthew Vassar, with high faith in the possibilities of women and with praiseworthy courage in the face of no little public disfavor, opened the doors of a college for women, whose standards were never to fall below those of the best colleges for men, his firm declaration of faith revealed clearly enough the nature of the criticisms that had been leveled against his farseeing experiment:

It is my hope, indeed, it has been the main incentive to all I have already done or may hereafter do or hope to do, to inaugurate a new era in the history and life of woman. I wish to give one sex all the advantages long monopolized by the other. . . . This, I conceive, may be fully accomplished within the rational limits of true womanliness and without the slightest hazard to the attractiveness of her character. We are, indeed, already defeated before we commence if such development be in the least dangerous to the dearest attributes of her sex. We are not the less defeated if it be hazardous for her to avail herself of her highest educated powers when that point is gained. We are defeated if we start upon the assumption that she has no powers save those she may derive or imitate from the other sex. We are defeated if we recognize the idea that she may not, with every propriety, contribute to the world the benefit of matured faculties which education works. We are especially defeated if we fail to express by our acts our practical belief in her preëminent powers as an instructor of her own sex.

No doubt the breakdown of prejudices against the higher education of women, so marked in the final decade of the nineteenth century, was hastened by rapid changes in economic conditions that were sending millions of women into gainful employment and thousands into the professions of teaching, medicine, and law. Clearly the time was passing when fathers and brothers assumed as a matter of course the burden of supporting unmarried or widowed female relations — not only daughters and sisters but aunts and cousins, untrained to self-support. The theory that economic independence was as honorable a state for women as for men and its converse almost as discreditable, having once been launched upon a dubious world, appeared to be gaining strong headway. Furthermore, the relation of sound education to economic advancement began to be perceived with respect to women as it had long been understood in the case of men.

The educational opportunities open to women at this time were varied and generous indeed when compared with those of their grandmothers. A few statistics may not be out of place here as evidence of the very general utilization of these advantages by girls and women. In 1897 the public secondary schools of the country enrolled 235,988 girls and the private secondary schools 54,415, — a total of 290,403. It is noteworthy that for several years the number of girls utilizing the advantages of high school education had exceeded that of boys by many thousands. In 1897 the percentage of girls in public high schools was 57.64 as compared with 42.36 per cent of boys. The normal schools had, from their foundation, made a stronger appeal to young women than to men, chiefly for economic reasons. Therefore it is not surprising to learn that, in the year under consideration, there were 30,592 women students in public normal schools as compared with 12,607 men. When we turn to higher education, we find that there were enrolled the following numbers of women students:

Coeducational universities and colleges	16,526
Grade A colleges for women (14)	3,913
Grade B colleges for women	10,929
Total	31,378

To this number should be added 12,891 women in schools of technology, including agricultural and mechanical arts colleges, technical schools, and schools of applied science. The admission of women to the graduate schools of eastern universities was comparatively recent at this time. Yale and the University of Pennsylvania had led the way, opening certain of their graduate departments in 1892. Owing chiefly to the generous efforts of President Low, Columbia University, in 1900, admitted women to its nonprofessional graduate schools of political science, philosophy, and pure science. But the graduate schools of Harvard, Princeton, and the seaboard state universities of the South were almost without exception barred against women.[1] Despite the cautious policy of the East there were in 1897–98, 2173 women enrolled in graduate schools of coeducational universities and 225 in similar departments of women's colleges. In that same year the A.M. degree was conferred upon 171 women and the Ph.D. degree upon 37 women. Significant of the ever-growing interest of America in the higher education of women is the fact that during the twenty-year period from 1890–1910 the rate of increase of men students in institutions for higher learning was 214.2 per cent, while that of women students in coeducational universities was 438 per cent and in women's colleges was 348.4 per cent. As early as 1897 there were nearly one third as many women as men in collegiate departments of universities or in colleges and in twenty years there were destined to be more than three fifths as many women students as men.

Not so easily, however, was public opinion persuaded to a belief in professional training for women. In America, as in Great Britain, this cause was but partially won at the close of the last century. The enrollment of women in professional schools in the year 1897–98 was as follows:

PROFESSIONAL SCHOOLS   NUMBER OF WOMEN STUDENTS

Medical Schools	
Regular	1121
Homeopathic	360
Eclectic	81
Physiomedical	21
Total in Medical Schools	1583
Schools of Dentistry	150
Pharmaceutical Schools	131
Training Schools for Nurses	6705
Schools of Theology	193
Schools of Law	131

[1] The *Report of the U. S. Commissioner of Education* for 1897–98 shows that one woman was pursuing graduate study in North Carolina and one in Florida.

Inequalities in the Educational Opportunities of Women

Although the long struggle to obtain equal educational advantages for women had overcome its most serious obstacles by the close of the nineteenth century, it would require a determined optimist, with eyes closed to the facts, to maintain that such equality already existed. A glance at the conditions prevalent in higher and professional education for women will serve to dispel such an idea.

With respect to gifts and bequests to promote higher education, the women's colleges, including the coeducational universities, lagged far behind the men's. In 1896–97 the benefactions to the latter institutions totaled $7,608,144, whereas those to 157 women's colleges (Grades A and B) reached the small total of $647,338. It may rightly be objected here that the men's institutions far outnumber the women's and this fact would go far to account for the disparity. Nevertheless this does not wholly account for so marked an inequality as is evidenced by the apportionment in 1896–97 of such benefactions among four eastern colleges for women and an equal number of eastern universities for men.

MEN'S UNIVERSITIES	AMOUNTS RE-CEIVED 1896–97	WOMEN'S COLLEGES	AMOUNTS RECEIVED 1896–97
Yale	$445,055	Smith	$ 13,935
Harvard	445,906	Mt. Holyoke . .	113,746
Columbia	275,053	Wellesley . . .	11,149
New York University	457,154	Vassar	10,000
	$1,623,168		$148,830

Nor is this sharp disparity peculiar to the year 1896–97, for in the following year the list of benefactions to four eastern colleges for women and four for men is as follows: [1]

[1] It was necessary to change the list of institutions, since Yale, Smith, and Wellesley received no gifts.

MEN'S UNIVERSITIES	AMOUNTS	WOMEN'S COLLEGES	AMOUNTS
Harvard	$1,236,985	Radcliffe	$112,000
Columbia	354,417	Mt. Holyoke	136,582
University of Pennsylvania	406,202	Vassar	109,999
New York University	344,558	Elmira	100,000
	$2,342,162		$458,581

Of course this inequality may be explained in large part by the fact that the alumni of men's universities are a rich and influential body, whereas the alumnæ of women's colleges are not. Moreover, the age and prestige of the older universities, such as Harvard, Yale, Princeton, and Columbia, make a powerful appeal to wealthy men beneficently inclined toward education. But it nevertheless remains true that the gross discrepancy is in part due to the relative feebleness of the public interest and faith in the higher education of women at that time and, to a less degree, at present. In the New York press, in 1922, a man long interested in colleges for women urged public-spirited citizens to assist the alumnæ of these institutions in their heartbreaking effort to raise endowment funds, pointing out that by far the greater part of all gifts for higher education in America passed into the treasuries of universities for men, already richly endowed.

A further inequality with respect to women's education was evident in the matter of scholarships and fellowships for graduate study and research. In 1890 a fund of $23,360 was available for graduate scholarships for men; but not one scholarship had then been instituted for women. However, a scholarship fund of $1200 was available for either men or women students in state universities. In the same year (1889–90) the fellowships open to men amounted to $70,798, those for women to $2300. A fund of $14,950 was also available for fellowships for both sexes.

But far more important than these minor inequities was the curtailment of women's opportunities for professional education as well as for practical training in the professions. In 1897 few women were enrolled in theological schools and indeed relatively few were open to women. Of the 155 theological schools listed in the *Report of the Commissioner of Education* for 1897–98 only 27 reported an enrollment of women students. Somewhat better conditions prevailed in the law schools, of which 83 were listed in the *Report*. In 44 of these schools 147 women were pursuing courses in law; but it is noteworthy that no woman student was enrolled in the most distinguished schools of the country — in Harvard, Yale, and Columbia — since those institutions were locked, bolted, and barred against them. Moreover, as late as 1902 only twenty states had admitted women to the practice of law. When we turn to the profession of medicine, we find that women were pursuing courses in 90 of the 158 medical schools listed, most of these being connected with state universities. But again we find that certain of the finest medical schools in the country — Yale, Harvard, Columbia, Rush Medical School in Chicago, and the University of Pennsylvania — refused to receive women. More serious, however, than the fact that the professional training furnished by the nation's leading schools was not available for women was the state of popular opinion with regard to the woman who aspired to be a doctor, a lawyer, or a minister. Unquestionably such an aspirant was looked upon as a more or less ridiculous freak of nature. This widely prevalent attitude toward professional women operated to hinder, if it did not prevent, their success in their chosen work. Especially is this evident in the field of medicine. Women who had done creditable and even distinguished work in medical courses, and looked forward with hope to the practice of their profession, soon discovered that very few hospitals were willing to receive them as internes; thus their practical training in hospital wards and in clinics was seriously curtailed. Moreover, up to this time no woman physician had been appointed on the medical staff of a single public hospital or asylum. So flagrant was the discrimination against women that Dr. Mary Jacobi drew up a bill, which was introduced into the New York Legislature in 1897, providing that the State Board of Charities should consist of two women and three men, instead of a board of three men as then constituted. In so doing Dr. Jacobi believed that she had taken "the surest way in which to obtain the appointment of women physicians in all public institutions and the admission of women students to the hospitals."

Unfortunately, discrimination against women in the professions was not confined to medicine, law, and theology. In the field of education it was strikingly apparent that the higher administrative positions were almost wholly in the hands of men. In 1901 only two women in the United States held the position of State Superintendent of Public Instruction, in the states of Colorado and Idaho, and only 12 that of city superintendent. However, 284 women at this time were county superintendents, most of these positions being held in western states. In but 13 states — all save one (Louisiana) in the West — were women eligible to all school offices, although they might hold all *local* offices in 18 additional states. Moreover, women had equal suffrage with men on all school questions in only four far-western states. This situation is all the more significant when we remember the very real interest most mothers have shown in the education of their children. Add to this the fact that at this time the women teachers in elementary and normal schools overwhelmingly outnumbered the men, while in public secondary schools 52.7 per cent of the instructors were women, and the tremendous power of the traditional American theory that the administration of education properly belongs only to men will be appreciated. In her second visit to the United States in 1908, Miss Sara Burstall, Head Mistress of the Manchester High School for Girls in England, vigorously expressed her views on this question :

The subordinate position of women in educational institutions in America shows itself more and more clearly the more one studies; the higher up the scale one goes from the kindergarten to the university the worse is the position of women. Organization, initiative, administration, government, are in the hands of men. . . . This condition of things, in a country where women occupy a far better position generally than anywhere in the world, and where they are given the precedence in all kinds of ways, is very remarkable. We do not remember to have seen it noticed by students of American education. Americans themselves take their own system as natural and proper, and they are in general not acquainted with the work of English women in education. It is perhaps only a woman concerned in administration in England who would feel the difference, but as the writer progressed from place to place it was more deeply impressed upon her, especially the difference in matters of government. It was discussed with Americans, and from the conversation the view gradually emerged that Americans do not consider administration as the natural and proper work for women. They feel it to be essentially men's work, though they admit that the exceptional woman may and does do it well.[1]

But the inequalities in the professional opportunities of women in education did not stop with administrative positions. A marked disparity also existed with respect to appointments to college and university faculties. In 1897 there were but 902 women teaching in the collegiate departments of universities and colleges for both sexes, as contrasted with 6750 men; and only 53 women instructors were in the professional departments to these institutions. To these numbers should be added 1834 women professors and instructors in Grade A and

[1] *Impressions of American Education in 1908*, p. 275.

B colleges for women. Commenting, in 1902, upon the declaration of a prominent educator that there appeared to be "a scarcity of women possessed of the proper qualifications and training for the highest positions in college work," President Harper of the University of Chicago expressed serious doubt concerning the correctness of the statement. On the contrary, he declared it to be his belief that the women being graduated with the doctor's degree from the best American universities were, "in almost every particular, as able and as strong as the men." Rather did he attribute the situation to the fact that to women few places on college faculties are offered. He writes as follows:

The fact is that to women there do not come the opportunities to show their strength which come to men. In colleges and universities for men only, women may not find a place upon the faculty. In a certain great state university, in which there are as many women students as men students, women are represented in the faculty by a single individual, and she has been appointed within the last three years. In some of the women's colleges, women find a place. In others, second-rate and third-rate men are preferred to women of first-rate ability. The number of faculties of colleges and universities on which women have appointments in any number is very small, and even in certain institutions in which women have gained secure footing there is often greater or less distress among the men of the various departments if even one or two women are appointed. And yet, is it possible that the heads of our state institutions — institutions which are established for the people and conducted with the people's money; institutions which are professedly democratic beyond all others — deliberately refuse to recommend the appointment of women even when they have attained equal rank with men in scholarship and efficiency? So far as I can ascertain, during the past year the appointments of women, east and west, even in coeducational institutions, have numbered very few — fewer, perhaps, than ever before. Is this progress? Or is it rather a concession to prejudices which, instead of growing weaker, are growing stronger? I venture to ask the regents of our state universities and the trustees of our coeducational institutions to consider this question; and I think it not inappropriate to suggest for the consideration of the trustees of certain women's colleges the question whether, in this matter, they have given to women the full opportunity they deserve.[1]

[1] *Report of the U. S. Commissioner of Education for 1902*, Vol. I, pp. 661–662.

Educational Progress in the Last Twenty-five Years
(1897–1922)

The foregoing discussion may serve to make plain that the twentieth century was confronted with not a few unsatisfactory and difficult situations in respect to the education and training of women and the opening to them of new opportunities for congenial work. Nevertheless the first two decades of the century have witnessed steady progress, not alone in the fields of secondary, higher, and professional education but in the inception of new educational movements for securing a more satisfactory education for women. Increasingly, educators have come to perceive that the schools owe something more to the girl, as well as the boy, than the imparting of useful information or even the development of a "cultivated" mind, in the historic meaning of the word. Discontent with a too bookish education has become widely prevalent since the opening of the century and has expressed itself in a variety of practical experiments and new educational organizations.

Progress in Secondary and Higher Education

The advances made in the long-established schools are shown chiefly in three ways: (1) in an enormous growth in numbers, (2) in the enrichment of school and college offerings, (3) in a differentiation of secondary and higher education to meet the needs of students of widely different interests and plans for future gainful employment. The movement to furnish an education adapted to students of varying needs began before the end of the last century, as is evidenced by the industrial, manual training, and commercial courses introduced at that time in some public high schools. This tendency has gained strong headway during the last twenty-five years and has resulted at present in a rich and varied offering in at least the fully accredited, four-year secondary schools of our larger cities and towns. In 1917–18, as shown in the *Biennial Survey of Education* published by the United States Bureau of Education, 95.12 per cent of the 13,951 high schools reporting were offering an academic course; 21.17 per cent, a commercial course; 13.13 per cent, a technical or manual training course; 8.78 per cent, a teacher-training course; 14.42 per cent, an agricultural course; 20.54 per cent, a home economics course; and 1.79 per cent, a trade training course. The proportion of girls enrolled in these various departments makes plain the fact that the historic academic course, surrounded as it is with an aura of prestige, is still by far the most popular department with women students and the trade-training course the least. The percentages follow:

COURSES	PER CENT OF TOTAL NUMBER OF GIRLS ENROLLED
Academic	73.71
Commercial	17.60
Technical or Manual Training	.98
Teacher Training	2.39
Agricultural	1.19
Home Economics	10.19
Trade Training	.56

It is a significant fact that, although the proportion *of all students* electing the academic course has decreased from 80 per cent to nearly 70 per cent since 1911, nevertheless the vocational courses are not winning their way very rapidly. The public high schools of the United States are still predominantly engaged in preparing students to meet college entrance requirements. It may truly be said that in general "there has been a greater tendency for the schools to offer vocational courses than for students to enroll in such courses." This statement applies more fully to girls than to boys, since the proportion of high school boys entering gainful occupations continues to be higher than that of girls.

With respect to the number of students enjoying the advantages of high school education it may be said that the increase in the last twenty years is notable when compared with that of European countries. Of the army of 1,645,171 secondary students in the schools reporting in 1918 it is a little surprising that 940,315, or 57.2 per cent, were girls. Twenty years before (1898), there were but 260,413 girls enrolled in public high schools, constituting 57.9 per cent of the total enrollment. It would appear, then, that the percentile increase of girls over boys in our high schools has not continued during a period of two decades. Even at present a larger proportion of boys than of girls enters college from each type of high school. The figures are 39 per cent of boys and not quite 22 per cent of girls. Probably most young women who continue their education beyond high school attend commercial or normal schools.

Turning to higher education, the progress in respect to the number of women students is no less striking. In 1898 there were 32,485 women in the collegiate departments of universities and colleges, whereas in 1919–20 there were 128,677 — an increase of more than 296 per cent in twenty-one years. The proportion of women to men in the collegiate departments of these institutions has likewise increased during this period from 52.9 per cent to 60.5 per cent. At this rate of increase the enrollment of women in collegiate departments in universities and colleges may equal that of men in another twenty-five years. No less marked is the growth in numbers of women students in graduate departments from 1555 in 1898 to 5909 in 1918, a gain of 280 per cent. In this latter year there were 69.5 per cent as many women taking graduate work as there were men.

Professional Education

Significant, also, is the steady growth in numbers of women in the professional departments of universities, colleges, and technological schools. In 1898 there were but 983 women enrolled in these departments, whereas twenty years later there were 2830 — a gain of more than 187 per cent — and this in the face of no little discouragement. However, it must be admitted that women are not flocking in large numbers into the historic professions of law, medicine, and theology nor into the schools that prepare for those professions. In 1919–20 (the latest year for which statistics are yet available) there were but 888 women taking medical courses, 1171 taking law courses, and 874 taking courses in theology. It is certainly surprising that law should attract more women than medicine, which has long been supposed to be a profession making strong appeal to the nurturing instincts of women. No doubt the small number of women preparing for this work may be partially explained by the great physical demands made upon both the student and the practitioner in medicine, the extended period required to establish one's self in the profession, the restricted facilities open to women in hospitals and clinics, and the popular distrust of, if not prejudice against, women physicians on the ground of incomplete practical training. Nevertheless the World War gave a very real impetus to the tendency on the part of medical colleges to open their courses to women. At the present time they are admitted to sixty of the ninety medical colleges in this country. Between 1914 and 1918 several of the largest medical schools in the United States took action to admit women. The list follows :

Medical School of the University of Pennsylvania in 1914
Tulane University in 1915
College of Physicians and Surgeons of Columbia University in 1916
Bellevue Hospital Medical College in 1917
Medical School of the University of Maryland in 1917
Medical College of Virginia in 1917
Harvard University Medical School in 1918

The enormous stream of young women entering the normal schools and the number in the teaching profession have shown signs of lessening during the last five years. The small salaries paid to women teachers the country over, as well as the attractive new vocations opened to them during the World War, are largely responsible for this situation. Yet there were 116,887 women enrolled in the normal schools of the country in 1918 as compared with 68,698 in 1899 — a gain of more than 70 per cent. One of the crucial problems in American education to-day is the professional training of thousands of young women, between the ages of sixteen and twenty-five, who are teaching in the rural schools of our country, not only with no professional preparation for their great task, but with a totally inadequate general education. This situation is almost wholly responsible for the high percentage of illiteracy revealed during the World War by native-born army recruits from the rural sections of the country. A realization on the part of the more enlightened public of the menacing nature of such conditions, threatening as they do any wholesome development of democratic institutions and ideals, has led to the organization of a powerful movement for the improvement of rural education. One of the foremost objectives of this movement is the professional preparation of teachers — mostly young women — for work in country schools.

Little progress has been made in the last quarter-century with respect to the advancement of women to administrative positions or their appointment to professorships in university faculties. The fact that the lower ranks of the teaching profession are largely recruited by women is truer to-day than it was twenty-five years ago. Most of the boys and girls in elementary schools are taught by women, and more than 66 per cent of the instructors in secondary schools are women. Apparently this situation awakens surprise and consternation in the minds of foreign educators, on the ground that such a practice tends unduly to feminize education. Amusing, as well as revealing, is the fulmination of Professor Armstrong of the Mosely Commission, which visited the United States from England in 1904:

> To put the matter in very simple terms, it seemed to me . . . that the boy in America is not being brought up to punch another boy's head, or to stand having his own punched in a healthy and proper manner; that there is a strange and indefinable air of femininity coming over the men; a tendency toward a common, if I may so call it, sexless tone of thought.

This cursory glance at the progress made in the professional training of women would be manifestly incomplete without brief reference to the splendid strides made in the field of the education of nurses during the last quarter-century. This profession for women has been thrice blessed by coming under the able leadership of certain remarkably gifted women, among whom Professor M. Adelaide Nutting of Teachers College, Columbia University, is an outstanding figure. Guided by leaders of unusually broad and far-seeing vision, the vocation of the trained nurse has been lifted into a noble profession, requiring years of intelligent preparation both in theory and practice. In increasing extent is this profession appealing to women with college degrees or at least with a few years of college education. Space is lacking to write of the truly impressive advances made in the training of nurses, but certain of these cannot be passed over. First should be mentioned the recognition on the part of universities of the growing prestige of nursing as a profession having a considerable body of theoretical and scientific knowledge. This is evidenced by the organization of departments of nursing in connection with sixteen leading universities in America. In addition there are fourteen universities and colleges having some affiliation with schools of nursing and twelve offering courses for graduate nurses, chiefly in public health nursing. Another advance may be seen in the differentiation of courses and of types of work in the field of nursing. About 70 per cent of graduate nurses are engaged in private practice, a condition somewhat analogous to that in the profession of medicine. Approximately 18 per cent are occupied in hospitals as instructors, supervisors, directors of schools of nursing and of hospital nursing service. Twelve per cent of the nursing profession are working in the significant new field of public health nursing, as visiting nurses, as nurse assistants in medical supervision in the public schools, as community nurses in rural districts, and as nurses in industrial establishments. The Department of Public Health of New York City employs about seven hundred nurses to assist in the protection of health.

The growth in schools and in numbers of the nursing profession is imposing. The number of schools of nursing accredited by state boards of examiners in 1922 was 1577. The total number of women students in schools of nursing in 1920 was 54,953 and the number graduated that year was 14,980. According to the census of 1920 there are 149,128 trained registered nurses in the United States — an increase of 87 per cent in ten years.

Educational Movements of the Last Quarter-Century

During the last twenty-five years one educational movement after another has been organized, looking to the improvement of different phases of education, and most of these have directly influenced the education of girls and women. Prominent among them should be mentioned the home economics movement, the movements for vocational education and vocational guidance, the Girl Scout movement, the movement for improved civic education, the movement to elevate social work into a profession, the physical educational movement, and the movement for more enlightened sex education.

The Home Economics Movement

No doubt the growing popularity of household arts education for girls, during the last decade of the nineteenth century, was in large measure due to the fact that comparatively few young women received training in domestic affairs from their mothers, as had once been universally the case. Ignorance of both the theory and practice of home management was becoming general among girls who entered gainful employments at an early age or who passed from high school to college. Add to this the fact that an impressive body of scientific knowledge concerning food values, textiles, household sanitation, child hygiene, and allied subjects was rapidly being added to the practical training in domestic arts, and it can readily be understood that this phase of education was bound to make for itself an important place in schools educating women. In the opening years of the twentieth century, courses in household economy had been organized in the colleges of agriculture and mechanical arts the country over. About the same time the movement spread to the industrial schools and normal schools. It is not surprising, then, to learn that in 1909–10 cooking and sewing were taught to girls in 95 elementary school systems, 207 high schools, and 142 higher institutions, including state universities.

A powerful impetus was given to this movement by the passage of the Smith-Lever Act in 1914 and the Smith-Hughes Act in February, 1917 — legislation which revealed the nation-wide interest in the more extensive education of girls in household economy. The first act provided large federal grants to the states for diffusing practical information relating to agriculture and home economics among the people of the rural sections. This work has been undertaken and organized by the land grant colleges and has resulted, so far as the feminine portion of the population is concerned, in a notable increase in the number of girls' garden clubs and canning clubs and in much useful instruction in the household arts given by county agents to women in farming districts. The Smith-Hughes Act went a step farther and provided for the better preparation of teachers of agricultural, trade, industrial, and home economics subjects. This work was placed under the control of a Federal Board of Vocational Education, and liberal annual appropriations were provided by the act to such states as complied with its conditions.

In 1918 the *Report* of the United States Bureau of Education contained the statement that the rate of extension of home economics courses in public high schools had been about one thousand per year. The tendency has been to make this work elective to high school girls while it is required in the upper grades of the elementary schools. More than one hundred thousand girls were enrolled in the home economics departments of our high schools in the year 1918, constituting 10.19 per cent of the total enrollment of girls in high schools. Although this percentage is small, it must be remembered that many girls in other high school departments elect courses in home economics, thus increasing the number who benefit by this instruction by scores of thousands. Moreover, the rapid growth of home economics in rural school programs has led many normal schools to require a minimum course in the subject of all students. For several years past there has been a marked tendency to establish practice homes, in detached houses or in apartments, where girls, in high school or college, may obtain admirable practical training in household economy. Some of these practice homes have even been able to secure the loan of a baby to be cared for by the resident students as part of their course in child hygiene. The quickened interest in child welfare that is spreading throughout the country is manifested in the establishment of child welfare courses in most departments of home economics in colleges and universities.

Movements for Vocational Education and Vocational Guidance

One of the most significant of all the movements for the betterment of women's education, by making that education more responsive to their needs, is the vocational education movement. Apart from the organization of the Women's Educational and Industrial Union in Boston in 1877, little was done to train women for wage earning in the nineteenth century. It was in the early years of the twentieth century that this new movement had its rise, and the interest in its aims and accomplishments, as well as in the problems growing out of its attempts to furnish well-considered vocational training to girls, has been steadily on the increase. The first attempts to grapple with the question led to the establishment of trade schools for girls in the large industrial cities of the East. A pioneer in this field was the Manhattan Trade School for Girls opened in New York in 1902. A few years later similar schools were organized in Boston, Worcester, Philadelphia, Chicago, Milwaukee, New Orleans, and other cities. Despite this favorable beginning, however, the whole movement for vocational education of youth was for several years more concerned with the training of boys than of girls. This is shown by the fact that in 1910 of the 193 trade schools listed in the *Report of the Commissioner of Education* a very small proportion were established especially to train girls.

In 1907 a promising forward step was taken in the organization of the National Society for the Promotion of Industrial Education, which, early in its history, showed an active concern in the extension of vocational education among girls. At the convention of the Society held at Grand Rapids in October, 1913, it was decided that stronger emphasis should be placed upon the vocational training of women. At this convention an assistant secretary, newly appointed "to make a special study of vocational training for women who are wishing to prepare for self-support and women who are already self-supporting," made her first public appearance.

Reference has already been made to the Smith-Hughes Act of 1917 creating a Federal Board for Vocational Education to coöperate with the states in promoting vocational training in trades and industries as well as in agriculture and home economics. By January 1, 1918, the conditions of the Smith-Hughes Act had been accepted by each of the forty-eight states of the Union, and plans for state organization of vocational education had been submitted and approved. At the present time federally aided courses in vocational education have been organized in all the states, and provision has been made for the training of teachers of vocational subjects. In 1922 the Federal Board for Vocational Education reported the establishment of 1001 trade or industrial schools, including evening, part-time, and all-day schools. In these schools were enrolled 216,541 women students — a gain of more than 260 per cent — since 1918. If this rate of increase continues, the terse comment of an American financier that Germany before the war educated her youth for a skilled vocation while the United States educated hers for a job will be pointless before many years.

Closely related to the vocational education movement is that for the more intelligent guidance of youth in the choice of vocations. The huge labor turnover among ignorant young girls, as well as the drifting of girls into the so-called "blind alley trades," clearly testify to the existing need for such guidance. The vocational guidance movement, inaugurated by Mr. Frank Parsons in the Boston Civic Service House in 1901, has spread to well-nigh every state in the Union and has led to the establishment of a vocational guidance department in connection with many of the public school systems of our larger cities. It is an encouraging index of the thoroughgoing methods of the leaders of this movement that surveys have recently been made of the vocational opportunities and conditions existing in industrial cities, with a view to discovering the essential facts regarding the physical and hygienic conditions of girl workers, the influence of the occupation upon their character and growth, the opportunities for beginners, and, above all, the relation of the occupation to vocational education within the school.

Education for Citizenship

Another strong trend in the direction of relating education more intimately to daily living is seen in the movement for better civic education in the schools. Although education for citizenship is no new demand in America, yet there has been profound dissatisfaction in recent years with the results achieved by the schools. This dissatisfaction received clear expression in the preliminary report of the Commission on Reorganization of Secondary Education, appointed by the National Education Association in 1911. The Commission declared that facts, theories, and activities that do not rather directly contribute to the student's appreciation of methods of human betterment have no claim to a place in a course in citizenship: "Under this test the old civics, almost exclusively a study of government machinery, must give way to the new civics, a study of all manner of social efforts to improve mankind." From the beginning of the movement it has fortunately been taken for granted that girls are as much in need of this instruction as boys; and the extension of suffrage to women has but made this need more apparent.

There appears to be fairly general agreement among educators that any plan for educating girls and boys in the duties of citizenship shall include some form of direct experience with governmental activities, either by way of organization of a school republic or by contact with a variety of social organizations by means of which the community is maintained. Moreover, it is coming to be more clearly understood that the teaching of good citizenship "presupposes teachers who are themselves notable examples of good citizenship." Who can maintain that the army of women teachers in our schools, newly enfranchised as they are and hardly yet awake to the larger life beyond the walls of their sheltered homes, are in any adequate degree prepared to undertake this splendid task? It is idle to expect nation-wide results from this movement for better civic education until the country as a whole is educated to the point where it regards teaching as a responsible profession to which no person will be admitted without broad and thorough preparation.

The Movement for Education of Social Workers

In the closing years of the nineteenth century the multiplication of social agencies to serve the destitute, the unemployed, the sick, the aged, and the mentally and physically defective led to a pressing demand for persons suitably equipped to carry on this work. At the same time the number of permanent salaried positions open to properly qualified men and women greatly increased. Little by little social work came to be regarded as a profession for which a thorough preparation was necessary. In the National Congress of Charities, held in 1893 and again in 1897, experienced social workers urged that training schools for social work be organized to meet a growing need. The first venture in this new field was made in the summer of 1898 when the New York Charity Organization Society instituted a training class which became, in 1901, the Summer School for Philanthropic Workers and, in 1904, the New York School of Philanthropy. Since this school was established four other cities have taken similar action. The Boston School for Social Workers was organized in 1904, the St. Louis School of Social Economy in 1906, the Chicago School of Civics and Philanthropy in 1907 (an outgrowth of an earlier venture called the Chicago Institute of Social Science), and the Pennsylvania School for Social Service in 1910 in Philadelphia. During the academic year 1913-14 approximately 900 students were enrolled in these schools and 167 received certificates of graduation. Much stress is rightly placed by the leaders in social education upon field-work. The student is placed with some governmental agency or with the recreation department of the settlements or is assigned investigational work in methods of social inquiry.

From the inception of this movement it has been recruited in large measure by young women. Its attraction seems to have been especially strong to those of fine intellectual equipment. No doubt the opportunity to care for the needy, the defective, the unfortunate has proved attractive to many women to whom teaching made little appeal. In the academic year 1922-23, 191 students took courses at the New York School of Social Work, of whom only 18 were men. It is hardly too much to say that this promising new domain of work bids fair to be overwhelmingly a profession for women.

The Physical Education Movement

Although the recent awakening of popular interest in sounder physical training and hygienic instruction of young people is not primarily concerned with women, yet it is altogether possible that the contemporary movement for an improved and greatly extended course of physical education may benefit girls even more than boys. The reason for this statement lies in the fact that the vigorous bodily development of women has been even more neglected in the past than that of men. In a *Report on Pittsburgh Vacation Schools* written in 1906, the president of one of the city vacation school systems declared that the systematic neglect of the physical education of girls was our "first sin of omission." He deplored the fact that girls were given "the sweet, sentimental books they like to read" and were permitted to spend their leisure hours in sewing or gossiping. Everywhere he saw an attempt to develop girls according to a passive, conventional, formal ideal instead of educating them to "a healthy freedom and alertness of mind and body."

Although the period from 1880 to 1897 has been characterized by one somewhat overenthusiastic writer as "a time of active growth and diversified expansion" in physical education, it is perhaps more true to the facts to say that this phase of education has, with some notable exceptions, been grossly neglected in the United States up to the time of the World War. The revelations of physical unfitness in a high proportion of the drafted army recruits startled the American public unpleasantly but efficaciously. During the last five years progress in the direction of affording girls and boys in the public schools better hygienic instruction, more effective physical training, and more thorough health supervision has proceeded apace. Between 1915 and 1918 eight states of the Union enacted laws providing for state-wide physical education. Most of this legislation reveals an encouraging tendency to interpret physical education in a broad and comprehensive way. The New York program provides for medical inspection, instruction in the important facts of hygiene, and "physical exercise as a health habit, including gymnastics, elementary marching, organized supervised play, recreation, and athletics." The programs of the other states are no less comprehensive. It is noteworthy that all of these state laws, with the sole exception of that of Nevada, provide for compulsory physical education throughout all the public schools. If the widespread public concern with regard to this aspect of education be not permitted to die down, soundly planned systems of physical education will have been established in every state of the Union before many years have passed. It is to be hoped that these programs will take into consideration the special needs of women and make a carefully adapted course in physical training and preventive hygiene compulsory upon every girl. Should this ideal be realized, the nation will see, before the close of a generation, the complete disappearance of the weak, anemic, listless woman, so frequently commented upon by foreign visitors not many years ago.

Progress in Sex Education

The question of how best to educate young people to a better understanding of the facts and problems of sex has engaged the attention of educators for more than a decade. Yet it required the rude shock of war to lift "the veil of false modesty from the question of social hygiene and sex education." Before the World War thrust certain ugly facts and conditions upon the attention of parents, public opinion in America was not ready to sanction any thoroughgoing program of sex education in the public schools, and hardly in the colleges. Especially was this true in the case of girls, about whom still hung a mid-Victorian tradition that they must be reared in complete innocence, which, of course, meant ignorance. Of late years, however, some of this prejudice on the part of parents and the public in general has broken down. In 1918 Congress created the Interdepartmental Social Hygiene Board, charged, among other duties, with the disbursing of $300,000 annually for the years 1919–20 to such universities, colleges, or other higher institutions of learning as, in the judgment of the Board, were qualified for scientific research designed to develop more effective educational measures in the prevention of venereal diseases. Appropriations have been made to thirty colleges, universities, and normal schools in order to assist these institutions in developing departments of hygiene which shall include instruction "emphasizing with appropriate and due proportion and with proper tact and persistency the serious importance of venereal diseases, their causes, carriers, and prevention. . . ."[1] The schools are urged at the same time to stress the other important facts and applications of general hygiene, individual hygiene, group hygiene, and intergroup hygiene.

Even more important and far-reaching has been the movement to introduce courses in sex education in high schools. In the year 1919 the Bureau of Education and the division of venereal diseases of the Public Health Service coöperated in an effort to contribute to the solution of this difficult problem. These organizations have held conferences in eleven eastern states and have prepared a series of four monographs on various aspects of the problem of sex education, which have been sent to more than five thousand educators requesting them. Very wisely the leaders in this movement

[1] Quoted in *Report of the U. S. Commissioner of Education*, 1920, p. 65.

have committed themselves to the principles that (1) the object of sex instruction is development of positive ideals of physical vigor and social uprightness; (2) sex instruction should be placed in a normal setting as part of the regular curriculum; (3) programs must be based largely upon successful experiences of individual teachers.

If this encouraging beginning leads to intelligently planned programs of sex education in the public schools, carried out by teachers eminently qualified for this important work, it will be impossible to measure the social benefit that will result from this effort. Girls, no less than boys, are in crying need of enlightenment and individual help in regulating sanely their own sex natures and in adjusting themselves to social situations involving the other sex. Surely the successful regulation of this most difficult of human relationships should not be left to chance and to the sordid gossip of the street and the playground. Nevertheless popular opinion seems loath to relinquish one of the last of the ancient tabus, and the education of parents and the public in general must proceed much further before marked advance can be made in the direction of sex education in the public schools. Conditions are somewhat better in the higher institutions of learning. A recent questionnaire sent to one hundred colleges and universities educating women made inquiry concerning how much, if any, instruction in sex hygiene and sex problems was offered. Of the sixty institutions replying, forty are furnishing such instruction to women through lectures on sex hygiene.

The Girl Scout Movement

This brief survey of progressive tendencies affecting the education of women cannot close without mention of the promising movement to organize the young girls of the country under the banner of the Girl Scouts. Avowedly modeled

after the Girl Guides of England, the Girl Scouts were first
organized in the United States in 1912, under the magnetic
leadership of Mrs. Juliette Low. The earliest troops were
formed in Georgia but the movement has rapidly spread
from state to state and in recent years from coast to coast.
In 1919, seven years after its first small beginnings, 41,225
girls between the ages of ten and eighteen were enrolled as
Girl Scouts, while many thousands more were still in the
"tenderfoot" stage, not having passed the tests for admission
to scout troops. Leaders of the movement point out that
neither home nor school are so planned as to give the growing girl "a place of her very own, where she can be herself, and where she can do the things she wants to do."
This gap in the life of the girl the new organization seeks to
fill.

The fundamental purpose of the Girl Scouts is declared
to be "to promote the virtues of womanhood by training
girls to recognize their obligations to God and country, to
prepare for duties devolving upon women in the home, in
society and the state, and to guide them in ways conducive
to personal honor and the public good." Since this organization is planned to give the girl wholesome, out-of-door
occupations and sports in her unemployed hours, it is helping to solve the puzzling question of how to educate girls
and boys to a worthier use of leisure. It has been said that
the "girl problem," no less than the "boy problem," is essentially a leisure-time problem. The Girl Scout organization
shows girls how "a good time" can be enjoyed even without movies and boys. Then, too, its activities and ideals
win the girl's heart and draw her by natural methods to a
more sensitive appreciation of social interrelationships
and a deeper realization of her responsibility for the public
good. Educators cannot but respect the purposes and
achievements of this powerful movement.

Twentieth-Century Problems

When due credit has been given to those forward-looking educational movements of the last twenty-five years, it may not be out of place to summarize very sketchily a few of the problems that loom up on the present-day educational horizon. Upon examination many of these will be found to center about the crucial question of how to educate women for congenial work and financial independence while fitting them to be home makers in the larger sense of that word. For the last twenty years social writers have repeatedly pointed out that the higher education of women and their professional training and success are disinclining them for marriage and the cares of housekeeping and child rearing. Gloomy statistics of the low marriage and birth rates among college-bred women are hurled at those who have faith and hope in women's full and free development. Needless to say, little attempt has been made to discover whether these rates are appreciably higher among the sisters and cousins of the same social class as these college women. In other words, no satisfactory study has been made to determine whether low marriage and birth rates are not equally characteristic of the prosperous middle classes from which college students are drawn. Alarmed at the showing of statistics, some educators are urging that college and high school curricula be profoundly modified to include compulsory courses in cooking, sewing, household management and sanitation, child care, and the like. Moved to revolt by this attack upon their strongholds, the heads of liberal arts colleges for women are bitterly opposing such plans as subversive of the broad, general culture for which women have so long been striving.

At the same time another powerful group of educators, including such leaders of thought as Professor John Dewey and Dr. Charles Eliot, are insistently demanding that the higher education of women be brought in touch with the vocational needs of the community — that preparation for a life career and genuine culture are by no means alien to each other. Loud and long has been the controversy over this question and the end is not in sight. With respect to those girls who must enter wage-earning occupations at an early age, the problem of vocational education assumes a different aspect. Is it of much use to train scores of thousands of girls for skilled vocations when factories and other establishments are busily engaged in reducing the work of laborers to a few routine operations that can readily be mastered in a few hours? This is obviously one of the most difficult of all the questions that confront the believer in vocational education of girls. Needless to say it is bound up with the larger and more intricate question of the mechanization of industrial life, with its unfavorable reaction upon the worker. A lesser problem, although a real one, has to do with the matter of educating girls of the laboring class for the dual occupations of paid worker and home maker. If educators accept the doctrine that women must be trained for two spheres, then a considerable part of the program of the girl in a vocational school must be given up to courses in household economy. This will manifestly result in lessening her efficiency in her chosen vocation and thus will eventually handicap her in competition with men upon whom no such dual requirement is laid.

One of the most serious problems that confronts the twentieth century in the education of its womanhood is concerned with the development in women of a more informed interest in community, national, and world affairs, together with a deeper sense of civic responsibility. Self-centered individualism is not solely a feminine defect but it is still more characteristic of women than of men, owing to the more restricted nature of their social and political experience. Until the schools have more clearly and resolutely envisaged this problem, little will be accomplished toward its solution. When the social sciences and their practical applications are accorded a central position in the curriculum of school and college a long stride will have been made toward the development of the responsible woman citizen.

Finally, the question of educating girls and women to a truer appreciation of the real values of life yields in importance to no other problem.   If women are to make a peculiar contribution to society, they must be alive to the incompleteness, the pathos, the possibilities of human life.   They must be led to a sensitive appreciation of beauty, of truth, of the essentials of human progress.   On the other hand, they must be helped to perceive the ugliness, the gross materialism, the inhumaneness of our twentieth-century civilization in many of its economic aspects.   An education which opens women's eyes to social life as it is and as it might be will stir, it is to be hoped, the nurturing instincts of women and their deep-rooted feeling for the value and importance of every human life.   These emotions, duly enlightened and regulated by understanding, may accomplish much to make this chaotic world a better place to live in.

REFERENCES

ADLER, FELIX — "Differentiation of College Education for Women"; *Journal of the American College Association*, Vol. V, No. 3, 1912.

Association of Collegiate Alumnæ — *Publications*, 1897–1922.

BEVIER, ISABEL, and USHER, SUSANNAH — *The Home Economics Movement;* Whitcomb and Barrows, 1906.

BURSTALL, SARA A. — *Impressions of American Education in 1908;* Longmans, Green, 1909.

COOLEY, ANNA — *Domestic Art in Women's Education;* Scribner, 1911.

DOCK, LAVINIA L., and STEWART, ISABEL M. — *A Short History of Nursing*, Ch. X; Putnam, 1920.

CHAPTER XIV

EDUCATION IN THE SOUTH

BY

EDGAR W. KNIGHT

UNIVERSITY OF NORTH CAROLINA

J. P. Anderson

CHAPTER XIV

EDUCATION IN THE SOUTH

Introduction

The story of public education during the last quarter-century in those states which had formed the Confederacy is a unique and somewhat remarkable record. But an adequate understanding of it or of the present educational status and problems of the South requires a view not only of the actual educational situation twenty-five years ago but also of the social, economic, and political conditions which had prevailed there for two or three decades following the Civil War. A summary of that situation and an account of those conditions become therefore an important part of the story here to be related.

The Continuing Effects of the Civil War — Educational

The chief need of the South twenty-five years ago was a full and working agreement on education. The principle of universal education at public expense had not yet passed into conviction there. It was still in the academic stage, the topic of the educator and theorist. It had not yet become the interest of the citizen. Compared with the United States as a whole, the Southern states were very backward in education. Public schools were deplorably poor and ineffective. The average annual per capita expenditure for public education in 1897 was $2.62 in the country at large, but in the South it was less than ninety cents and in some Southern states it was less than fifty cents. The amount raised per taxpayer was twice as large and the amount

371

raised for each child of school age was three times as great in the country at large as in the Southern states. The amount of taxable wealth back of each child of school age in the South was only one fifth or one sixth as great as that in the North and the West, where the proportion of adult males to the school population was also fifty to one hundred per cent greater than in the Southern states; and the number of children of school age to every hundred persons of the total population was greater in the South than in any part of the United States. The average monthly salary of teachers in the United States was nearly fifty per cent larger than in the South, where it was less than twenty-eight dollars. In Alabama, Tennessee, and Mississippi the average was only twenty-four dollars and in North Carolina it was only twenty-one dollars. Between 1860 and 1900 the average annual salary of teachers in the South had actually decreased. In some parts of the South teachers received no more for their services than was received for the hire of those who worked under conditions of penal servitude.

Courses of study had somewhat expanded, but poorly equipped teachers and the lack of supervision rendered such courses ineffective and chaotic. The schools were imperfectly graded and methods of teaching were wasteful and deadening. School equipment was likewise poor. The grounds were often one half acre or less in size and the average value of rural schoolhouses as late as 1900 was only one hundred dollars. The average value of school property per child of school age was only one fifth that of the United States. One fifth of all the schoolhouses in North Carolina and Virginia were log, a condition fairly typical of all the South. In Tennessee as late as 1907 one seventh of the schoolhouses were log. In Virginia in that year only 168 of more than 7000 schoolhouses had modern provisions for ventilation. The school term in the South in 1897 was only

93 days, while the term for the entire country was 141 days. In North Carolina it was only 60 days. In some places teachers were employed for half the term in winter, and different teachers in the summer taught the same schools the remainder of the term. Teachers were generally untrained, sometimes very indifferent, and often held in low esteem by the public. From one half to four fifths of them held second- and third-grade certificates, usually the lowest then issued. Eighty per cent of nearly 2800 teachers in Florida held such certificates in 1897, and only 317 of them were graduates of normal schools.

Normal schools and other agencies for training teachers were few and standardless. Certification standards were low and often varied among the counties of the same state. The status of the teacher was so ridiculously low that few promising young people could be persuaded to enter the work. Less than 60 per cent of the school population was enrolled in school and less than 40 per cent was in average daily attendance. Only one pupil out of ten of those enrolled reached the fifth and only one in seven the eighth grade. There was not a public high school of standard grade. Textbooks were often nondescript, and their selection was unintelligent and haphazard and generally optional with local authorities. The public, under such conditions, could not view the schools with pride or even complacency.

The unit of practical school administration in the South twenty-five years ago was the small and weak district. There were no creditable and substantial county school organization and supervision. County superintendents were generally colorless and deficient in leadership, employed for part time and poorly paid for that. The positions usually went to briefless young lawyers, broken-down preachers, country editors, too often as a reward for political service. Each local school was left to itself without aid or counsel from county or state. Its trustees were often chiefly interested in keeping the school near their homes and in employing their relatives or friends as teachers. The policy of multiplying schools had been ruinous. State departments of education were less real than nominal, as a rule little more than clerkships or pitiful political appendages. State superintendents were seldom educational statesmen and leaders but politicians, lawyers, soldiers, or patriots. Rarely were they selected for professional fitness, and the conditions of the office generally made them clerks.

No Southern state had any compulsory attendance legislation although thirty-two of the United States had enacted such laws. The subject was often favorably discussed by groups of school workers and resolutions favoring such legislation were adopted. But bills introduced into the legislatures usually met with the specious argument that the school system was not ready for such a step. Lack of sufficient physical equipment for schools often gave such argument respectful hearing, but the force of the industrial revival then gaining in the South undoubtedly was strong. Practical state-wide legislation on the subject did not come for many years. The state superintendent in North Carolina in 1898 recommended "a mild form of compulsory legislation to begin with," but action was delayed. When compulsory attendance legislation was finally enacted in the South, it was usually optional in character and in some of the states required a majority vote of the electors in the county or district to adopt; and when adopted, the law required attendance only for a minimum term and with exemptions so numerous as to render it ineffective.

Child labor laws were slowly enacted in the South, where, with the rise of cotton factories, boys and girls of school age quickly became a part of that pathetic industrial force known as child labor. Industrial reforms were needed as an essential part of necessary educational progress. But a warfare was waged between the system of child labor on the one side and industry, the parent, the child, and even democracy on the other; those who worked for such reforms conceived them and education as two important phases of the movement for a more nearly democratic order. In 1900 nearly thirty per cent of all the operatives in the cotton mills of Alabama were under sixteen, and in the entire South one fourth of them were under that age. Eighteen per cent of the textile operatives in North Carolina and probably 30,000 in the entire South were under fourteen years of age. The number of children under twelve in factories was probably 20,000. As late as 1900, fully sixty per cent of the operatives in the spinning departments of cotton factories in the Piedmont region were less than sixteen years of age.

These facts reflect not only an unwholesome educational situation in the South twenty-five years ago, but a stubborn and unyielding obstacle to the later development of education there. The chief burden of the painful industrial readjustment of a population then moving from the conditions of agriculture to those of manufacture were too often laid on the child, by argument that legislation restricting the labor of the child was paternalistic and invasive of parental function. Under these conditions, then, why should the South provide money to build schools for the children while the influence of growing industry continued to shut so many of them up in factories? Moreover, thousands of humble families, accustomed to agricultural failures and a vicious crop lien despotism, seemed to see in the new factory instant escape from rural isolation, barrenness, and poverty. What they failed to see, however, was that redemption from these evils by this means would often drive them to others they knew not of, to pitiless helplessness of fixed dependency. Urbanized industrial tenancy was to become and to remain almost as troublesome to the development of schools as farm tenancy has been. Few, even of more exceptional virility, without the aid of adequate child labor and compulsory attendance legislation, could hope to rise out of the enfolding powers of such a system which has consciously served to hold its humble and timid agricultural and industrial forces in a state of arrested development.

Illiteracy was widespread not only among the negroes but among the native whites in the South. Of the native white population ten years of age and over more than twelve per cent were unable to read and write, while in some of the Southern states, especially North Carolina, Louisiana, and Alabama, the percentage was approximately sixteen per cent — one native white person in every six above the age of ten being unable to read and write. The average rate of illiteracy among the native white population for all the other states of the Union was less than three per cent. The menace of illiteracy among the native white population in the South had decreased from 22.7 per cent in 1880 to 12.2 per cent in 1900. But the extent of illiteracy continued a disgrace. Notes of denial and resentment were often heard, but they became less and less occasional as the knowledge of the real significance of illiteracy increased. But the menace could not be removed until frankly faced by the people of the South, until indifference to it rather than illiteracy itself came to be recognized as the greater reproach to that region.

Education in the South had failed to develop and advance as its friends had hoped during the quarter-century following the close of reconstruction. Except in the towns and cities which were stimulated to action by aid from the Peabody Fund, public schools were in bad plight, and even there progress was slow. Public education had not yet been accepted in the South. It was still poverty stricken, bore the odium of bad rule and partisan politics, and was otherwise in disrepute. In consequence, indifference to it was so deadly as to equal outright hostility.

Economic Effects

One of the most immediate causes of these conditions was economic desolation. The Southern states had come out of war with a loss of the greater part of their white adult males and an almost complete loss of their accumulated capital. Factories, public buildings, railroads, houses, barns, farm implements, and seeds had been destroyed. Banks had been ruined. The entire labor system had been demolished, and the negroes, unable quickly to adjust themselves to their new economic status, had preferred restless roving to helping to rebuild the waste places of the South. Public finances were in a perilous condition, with state treasuries depleted and credit abroad lost. Reconstruction had followed and robbed the South of what war had spared. Federal officers were often dishonest, cases of fraud and extravagance were numerous and flagrant, corrupt and ignorant officials and legislatures not only looted treasuries and public funds but imposed enormous taxes and ran their fingers deep into the pockets of posterity by piling up bonded debts totaling more than $300,000,000. Everywhere there was widespread economic depression. Tariff laws oppressive to the South but favorable to the East and pension laws which took many millions from the South to the North combined with other influences to make recovery slow.

The wealth of the South thus lost had been considerable. In 1860 with nearly one third of the population of the United States and less than one fourth of the white population, the South had produced more than one half of the agricultural wealth of the entire country, and this in spite of the handicaps of the many economic disadvantages of slave labor. Moreover, the ante-bellum Southern states had greater industrial ambition and success than has generally been assumed. In 1860 they had an investment of more than $175,000,000 in nearly 25,000 factories of one kind and another. Between 1850 and 1860 they had increased their railroad mileage from 2335 to 10,713, a quadruple gain, exceeding by 400 miles the combined railroad mileage of the New England and Middle States, where a gain of only 91 per cent had appeared in that industry during that decade. This development of railroads in the South represented an investment of more than $220,000,000, which had come principally from southern sources.

In 1860 the South had nearly five and a half billions of the slightly more than twelve billions of the total assessed property valuation of the entire country. The wealth of the South (including the wealth represented in the slaves) had exceeded by $750,000,000 that of New England and the Middle States. But ten years later the wealth of the latter group of states exceeded that of the South by nearly eleven billion. The taxable wealth of the entire South in that year was less than that of New York and Pennsylvania. In 1860 South Carolina had ranked third in wealth in the United States but thirtieth in 1870. Georgia had gone from seventh to thirty-ninth place during that decade, Mississippi from fourth to thirty-fourth, and Alabama from eleventh to forty-fourth. Meantime, values were greatly increasing in other sections of the country. As illustration, South Carolina in 1860 had an assessed property valuation greater by $68,000,000 than the total valuation of Rhode Island and New Jersey, but in 1870 those two states had wealth valued at $685,000,000 more than that of South Carolina. These figures reveal the economic losses in the Southern states. The outcome of four years of war and a decade of reconstruction was complete economic collapse, a catastrophe from which the South has been able only in recent years even partially to recover.

The first problem, therefore, had been to restore the agricultural life of the South — a region of poor roads, poor schools, millions of acres of unused lands, multitudes of mortgages, and no money to finance economic recuperation. The principal resource must be cotton, the demands for which made it the best money crop. During most of these years the South knew nothing but cotton, and the force of agricultural tradition and custom was powerful. Diversity as the remedy for adversity was yet unknown. Efforts to resume economic life consisted in an endless chain of borrowing living expenses while the cotton crop was being made. Lack of crop diversification, lack of working capital, and the system of share farming, cropping, and crop liens, which developed as a result, formed a vicious cycle of economic despotism.

Southern banks borrowed credit from remote sources, usually the North, on the assurance that it would be used only to produce cotton. The coming crop was security. The local merchant borrowed from the Southern banks and in turn gave credit to the local farmer on the same stipulation and promise to raise cotton. The crops were thus mortgaged, often before they were planted, and their value was usually spent before they were harvested. Under the crop lien system the raising of foodstuffs was not encouraged, and prices paid for provisions under this system ranged from 75 to 100 per cent higher than the cash prices. When the cotton was picked, the farmer was forced to sell it, no matter what the price, to the merchant who had "run" or "grub staked" him during the year. The merchant repaid the Southern banks, which in turn repaid the Northern banks, with high interest collected at every point. When this cycle was completed, it was necessary to start it all over again. Slavery did not disappear in the Southern states, therefore, with the emancipation of the negroes. This peculating scheme of crop liens kept them in economic bondage for many years.

Racial Conflict

The racial conflict was another obstacle to schools during the last quarter of the last century. Viewed from the purpose, the process, or the result of reconstruction, the negro had been the center of interest. The issue of mixed schools during that régime had been disastrous to education in the South. The negro's ignorance later played into the hands of the politicians, served to lower political morals, and in time to produce political stagnation, and to make him a barrier to educational advancement generally. The thoughtful white leaders of the South were friendly to him then and have remained his best friends. They considered him educable for work, for improvement, and for useful citizenship. They knew that the right kind of education was the only safe remedy for his condition. And their expenditure of 109 millions out of all too meager school funds for his education between 1870 and 1900 is one of the creditable commentaries on the sober educational opinion of that section. Nevertheless, his exploitation by demagogues and designing politicians during most of that time made him an influence of mischief. Before progress in education could come this had to be removed.

Other Obstacles to Progress

Other obstacles to education which were inherited from the war and reconstruction were defective educational legislation and unsound school organization. Conflicts between the constitutional provisions for schools and legislation enacted under them were often troublesome. Sources of school support were decreased or often entirely cut off by constitutional restrictions. Moreover, the blight of partisan politics was deadening. Few features of public school work escaped its ill effects. Unscrupulous men in offices and local political bosses had learned during reconstruction how to exploit the schools for partisan purposes. Schools came to be regarded as the spoils of political victory instead of opportunities for promoting public well-being, and in many places in the South they have not yet been fully emancipated from this influence.

These are some of the reasons for the low condition of public education in the South twenty-five years ago. It had had its rebirth in poverty and destitution. During its early years it had been nurtured and cherished by a few friends and by fewer zealous but often visionary philanthropists. Often it had been the victim of a very feeble leadership. Occasionally it had been betrayed by petty politicians who were moved less often by principle than the desire to gain partisan advantage. Frequently it was subordinated to pernicious and deadening sectarian dogma. These and other handicaps of inheritance and environment forced public education in the South into a life-and-death struggle until near 1900. Before it could overcome these obstacles and approach a promising maturity and position of increasing respectability new foundations had to be built.

The incentives and basis for educational reform depended first on a substantial increase in economic wealth. The relapses of war and reconstruction had to be outgrown, the orderly processes of production and of exchange had to be resumed, the South had to recover her economic stability. This was to be gained slowly. After 1880 the dominance of agriculture, especially of cotton raising, began to yield place to manufacturing. In that year the value of manufactured products was less by $200,000,000 than that of agricultural products, but by 1900 the products of manufacturing and of mining interests exceeded those of agriculture by nearly $300,000,000. And between 1880 and 1900 the products of Southern factories increased by more than 220 per cent. Capital invested in cotton mills alone increased during that period from $22,000,000 to $113,000,000.

The resources and the deposits of national banks increased nearly 400 per cent each, and their capital was more than doubled during these two decades. Railroad mileage increased 112 per cent, and the true value of all property nearly doubled. During the decade from 1890 to 1900 the total taxable wealth of the South increased nearly fifty per cent. This vast industrial change from field to factory meant the presence of a great social change. Industry was coming more and more to be a force in Southern life. Material wealth was rapidly increasing and formed for the first time since 1860 a substantial basis for an increase in school revenues.

The Reconstruction Period

The race issue which had checked the cause of schools for many years was finally to serve as a powerful influence for educational progress. The single purpose of reconstruction had been to give the ballot to the negro; and the operation of the reconstruction acts of Congress, which formed new governments and created a new political people in the South, was incidental to this one object. Passionate political feelings had been involved at every step of the process. In 1867 Congress had forced negro suffrage on the South when only six of the Northern states permitted it. This sudden and indiscriminate gift of the voting privilege to men entirely unprepared for its intelligent use had produced a régime of riot and rascality during which schools and other means of progress had fallen victim to the vengeance and cupidity of adventurers and malefactors.

But before the last state had been restored to the Union the process of undoing reconstruction was under way. Conflicts over the elimination of the negro from politics were fierce and demoralizing. Open bribery, intimidation, stuffing ballot boxes, the manipulation or falsification of election returns, and the use of tissue ballots had developed into high arts. In one election in South Carolina the number of votes cast was nearly twice the number of the names on the poll books. The imposition of the poll tax and the creation of "shoestring" election districts to include sections of dense negro population served to eliminate negro votes or to render them ineffective. By these and other devious ways the dangers of negro domination were somewhat averted during a decade or more following the close of reconstruction. Moreover, a new political movement in some parts of the South threatened division among the Democrats and encouraged the factions in skillful attempts to control the negro vote which had always been purchasable and which was now powerful and dangerous because it was uncertain. The wits of the factions bidding for the negro vote were pitted against each other. In one election, in order to insure their votes, the poll taxes of the negroes were paid by one political faction. The other faction placarded all public places with the extraordinary announcement that poll tax receipts would be accepted for admission to the circus which was to give its performance on election day, and the negroes preferred the show to the polls. But such elimination methods as these were unpleasant. New and less crude devices wearing at least the color of legality had to be found for eliminating the negro from politics. Open and avowed suppression of the negro vote appeared safer and more respectable than fraud and chicanery, even though the legal devices found for contravening the purpose of the Fifteenth Amendment were not lacking in artful subterfuge.

Mississippi led off in 1890 and was shortly followed by other states. The payment of all taxes legally demanded for the two preceding years was set up as one prerequisite for the privilege of voting. Another was the ability of the voter to read and properly to interpret, under the close scrutiny of white election officials, any section of the Constitution. These requirements eliminated large numbers of negro votes and greatly reduced the chance of negro voters to qualify. Finally, the famous "grandfather clause" practically guaranteed the supremacy of the white vote by giving the privilege of voting to those citizens or the descendants of those citizens who had the privilege prior to January 1, 1867, without regard to property or educational qualifications. The vote of the negro thus quickly dwindled into negligible proportions and his political equality became more nearly extinct in law than it had long been in fact. The final stage of the unfortunate reconstruction controversy closed, therefore, in a complete reversal of the purpose and process which marked its beginning. Meantime, however, the schools had been subordinated and often sacrificed to less worthy interests and the education of both whites and blacks had fallen pitiably into neglect. Public energies which should have been spent for schools and for rebuilding Southern civilization were necessarily used to wrest the government and political power from the blacks and their allies. And in some Southern states educational conditions were less wholesome at the close of the century than they had been in 1860.

The Beginnings of Educational Progress

Thus the race issue which for more than two decades after the war had been a very large factor in retarding education became after 1890 one of the strongest influences in promoting it. When the states set up the constitutional requirement of literacy as a qualification for the privilege of voting, to apply ultimately to both races, even for the avowed purpose of eliminating or restricting negro suffrage, they were automatically committed to the enlargement of public educational opportunity. A premium was thus placed on education, and attention was sharply drawn to the imperative necessity for enlarged educational facilities. In the same constitutions which disfranchised the negro or in legislation enacted under such constitutions, requirements were soon made for improving the schools. In Mississippi special taxes were required to increase the school term to four months; in South Carolina the state tax for education was increased so as to provide an annual school revenue of as much as three dollars per child enrolled; in Louisiana provision was made for restoring to the school fund the interest on the lands squandered during reconstruction, and the right of local taxation equal to the state tax for schools was also given the people. Provision was made in Alabama for an increased state school tax, and local taxation for schools was authorized in North Carolina and Virginia.

Restless discontent among the people of the strictly rural sections of the South and radical political changes which marked the closing decade of the last century were other influences which were to hasten the spirit of educational reform. The class consciousness of the farmers had been awakened and had expressed itself through several organizations which were consolidated as the Farmers' Alliance and Industrial Union in 1889. The principal cause of the movement was economic: it sought to win for the farmers conditions under which they might enjoy a just share of their own creations. But it was also concerned with social and political reform. The necessity of the education of the masses was insisted upon by the Alliance which, in resolutions on the subject, held that the uneducated were "always at the mercy of the better informed" and the members were urged to use their influence to secure better educational facilities for their children.

This unrest of the farmer was extraordinary. He had always been accounted so instinctively cautious and conservative that the practical politician had not looked for much shifting in the political allegiance of rural voters. Their isolation had made it difficult to move them suddenly by any impulse sufficient to break party lines and to cause a cleavage from traditional party connections. Dissatisfaction with conditions and with existing leadership, however, produced radical political changes and led to the formation of several political parties. Some of these were the Union Labor Party in Arkansas, the Young Men's Democracy in Louisiana, and the People's Party, also known as the Third Party and the Populist Party. The last named, the strongest of them all, developed organized strength throughout the South and in some cases broke up political associations of a generation and upset the calculations of the most astute politicians. The educational influence of this movement of revolt and of liberation was very evident in Alabama and North Carolina in the nineties, and in all the Southern states it soon became the fashion for all parties to pledge themselves to public school support. By 1900 they were coloring their political platforms with strong declarations of devotion to the cause of public education.

Another foundation for educational upbuilding appeared in a new type of leadership, developed largely through the union of the so-called middle and aristocratic classes. The former through an increase in economic wealth had become more thrifty and influential, and stimulated through the challenge of an awakening democracy they became ambitious for and able to secure some part in public affairs. In ante-bellum civilization the nonslaveholding whites had not had large place in the essential councils of the South; they had not filled many important offices nor were they allied with the landed and slaveholding classes who had monopolized political power — a monopoly which represented also the supremacy in social and administrative ability.

But the conditions of the new order after Appomattox and reconstruction, by which both the aristocrats and the common people and their property had been depleted, fused both classes more effectively than the South had ever known. The menace of negro power, common suffering, and the bearing of a common burden served to unite them; and in the distribution of political responsibility the South was soon to know no distinction of classes. It was to be democratized in part at least by this fusion of the white people. The South was, happily, to maintain those old dignities and reverences which power and social usage always develop; but to these was to be added another deep force — a quickened sense of responsibility and of liberality toward those who had been unprivileged. By these means aristocracy was to pass and the plain people were to begin to share in the privileges of government. There was to be an upward movement among the masses, now drawn more closely together and led to seek through ambition and industry and the unity of their civic heritage the means of opportunity for all.

The restoration and the preservation of the best in Southern life became a passion with this new leadership as it became conscious of opportunity and power. It viewed with impatience the educational weaknesses of the time and insisted that the truth about the schools be told. It attacked demagoguery and attempts to exploit the public mind with vain boasts of exaggerated achievements. It secured response to the needs of the people through interest in an extension of public school opportunities, which always becomes necessary and inevitable as democracy becomes a reality. The program of this new leadership was the rehabilitation of the South, and in it the desire to enlarge educational opportunity became a form of civic and patriotic piety, even a common faith. The chance for democracy was thus made brighter as the unprivileged and the poor and the privileged and the rich joined hands to build a common school system for all the children.

Thus was prepared the way for educational advance in the South. There had come an increase in wealth. The race issue in politics had been eliminated. The rural people had been awakened, and a new type of leadership had appeared. Many of the stubborn and mischievous difficulties, which for years had stood as a deadly upas to enfeeble social growth, were now in large part removed, and by effort no less heroic and courage no less indomitable than that exhibited during the war. The South now felt a new challenge, a new sense of duty, made more ringing and clear by the conditions of the new order. This sense of responsibility had been personified in Robert E. Lee; it was felt deeply and voiced loudly by leaders of later years, and hereafter it was to lie close to the heart of the New South. And fidelity to it was to bring after Appomattox victories more decisive for Southern well-being than any that preceded it.

Educational Propaganda

By the beginning of the present century conditions were ripe and the way prepared for marked advance. Only the organized agencies of propaganda were now needed and these were to appear in large part in the work of the Conference for Education in the South and in the movement represented by the Southern Education Board and the General

Education Board.   The first of the organizations, also known as the Southern Conference Movement, the Southern Educational Movement, and the Ogden Movement, grew out of a small conference held at Capon Springs, West Virginia, in the summer of 1898 and known as the Conference for Christian Education in the South.   Rev. T. U. Dudley, Bishop of Kentucky, an alumnus of the University of Virginia, late Chancellor of the University of the South, Sewanee, Tennessee, was elected president.   At the second conference, held the following year at the same place, the name was changed to the Conference for Education in the South and Dr. J. L. M. Curry, general agent of the Peabody and the Slater Boards, was elected president.   The third conference also met at Capon Springs and Mr. Robert C. Ogden, of New York, one of the most sympathetic friends public education in the South ever had, was elected to the presidency and served in that position for many years.   To his generous enterprise, resourcefulness, and administrative wisdom much of the success of the conference was due.   For several years he invited numerous people in the North who were interested in education to attend these annual meetings as his guests and for their accommodation provided special trains. In this way influential people of the North became acquainted with those of congenial spirit in the South and thus gained a safer knowledge of the perplexing problems and needs of Southern life.

Formal resolutions of the early conferences were significant.   They dealt with the importance of thoroughness of elementary instruction, longer school terms, better qualified teachers, and better buildings and equipment, traveling libraries, and industrial education.   Impressive also is this resolution of the second conference :

Resolved, That the education of the white race in the South is the pressing and imperative need, and the noble achievements of the Southern

Commonwealths in the creation of common school systems for both races deserve not merely the sympathetic recognition of the country and of the world at large but also give the old and high-spirited colleges and universities of the South a strong claim upon a generous share of that stream of private wealth in the United States that is enriching and vitalizing the higher education of the North and West.

It is of importance to remember in this connection that private, denominational, and state higher educational institutions in the South were then very poor. Most of them were forced to struggle for existence. Between 1898 and 1903 benefactions to institutions of higher learning in the United States had amounted to more than $61,000,000, but little of this money had reached the South. All the Southern colleges combined had at the latter date only 15 millions of the $157,000,000 of productive funds held by the colleges of the United States. Out of eight and a half millions of volumes in college libraries in the United States only one and a quarter million were found in the South. The colleges of the South had only about $1,000,000 invested in scientific apparatus against a total valuation of $17,000,000 for the entire country in 1903. The physical equipment of the colleges of the United States at that time was worth nearly $150,000,000, but less than $9,000,000 of it was found in the South. The total annual income available for higher education in Alabama, Georgia, Kentucky, Louisiana, Mississippi, the Carolinas, and Virginia was $19,000 less than the annual income of Harvard.

Succeeding meetings of the Conference for Education in the South were held in Winston-Salem, Athens, Richmond, Birmingham, Columbia, Lexington, Pinehurst, Memphis, and other cities in the South. At the instance of the conference, the Southern Education Board was organized in 1901 to aid in the development and the wise direction of educational sentiment, and to help secure larger policies for education, by appealing to the resources of taxation and local forces for self-development. The Board neither held nor distributed funds. Extensive and systematic field work was planned with Dr. J. L. M. Curry as supervising director and President Edwin A. Alderman, then of Tulane University, President Charles D. McIver, of the North Carolina Normal and Industrial College, and President H. B. Frissell, of Hampton Institute, as district directors. President C. W. Dabney, then of the University of Tennessee, was selected as chief of the bureau of investigation, information, and publication; and the services of Dr. P. P. Claxton, then of the University of Tennessee, and Professor J. D. Eggleston, Jr., of Virginia, were secured for the bureau of publicity which was established at Knoxville.

The plans and purposes of this novel campaign for education met with the instant approval of the press of the South and the practical support of the leading people at that time engaged in school work in that section. Able advocates of better schools came forward and enlisted their services in the movement: college and university presidents and professors, lawyers, business men, officeholders, and other builders of public opinion. The most practical school questions were discussed in the meetings which were now held throughout the South — better buildings, increased school funds, improved teaching, improved legislation for schools, and more effective educational organization and administration generally. People gathered in schoolhouses, churches, courthouses, public halls, in city and country alike, to hear discussions of the ways and means of improving education for their communities. Popular education was the theme before multitudes, and enthusiasm for it spread widely and grew intimate with the people. Meantime, the General Education Board was formed (1903) for the purpose of wise and systematic coöperation with the

Southern Education Board, to investigate, collect, and present actual facts concerning educational conditions in the South, and to render financial assistance within the discretion of its trustees and the limits of its resources. Its services to education in the South have been large and varied and have formed a wise and effective demonstration of method.

The work of the General Education Board in the South has been in four main directions. Through the United States Department of Agriculture it has made large contributions for the promotion of practical farming, under an agreement begun in 1906. Demonstration farms are employed under supervision of demonstration agents whose work has been far-reaching. State demonstration agents also conduct work among boys and girls under actual farming conditions through boys' and girls' clubs. The promotion of secondary education constitutes another important service of the board which appropriates to the state universities or the state departments of education sums sufficient to pay the salaries and traveling expenses of high school experts. Through this means hundreds of secondary schools have been built and maintained in recent years. In addition to these services the board has made gifts for higher education in the South, as well as in other sections of the country, to increase endowments and equipment. It has also contributed largely to the support of negro schools, mainly those for the training of teachers, and has contributed towards the expenses of two rural school supervisors who work under the direction of state departments of education in each of the Southern states, for the promotion of better educational, economic, and social conditions of the colored people. Other services of the board have been rendered to medical education, schools of education, and the financing of studies or surveys of state school systems.

The Educational Advance

The work of these agencies had a powerful and practical influence immediately on educational development in the South. Active campaigns for better schools and for improved educational facilities generally were promoted, beginning in North Carolina in 1902, in Virginia in 1903, in Georgia and Tennessee in 1904, in South Carolina, Alabama, and Mississippi in 1905, in Arkansas, Florida, and other states in 1908. Most of these campaigns were continued for several years with fruitful results. Improvements appeared in many ways: the educational provisions of the constitutions and laws were revised and strengthened; in a decade school revenues were increased by 100 to 200 per cent; the improvement of schoolhouses was marked; by 1910, the annual school term was lengthened to 121 days; and the enrollment and average attendance increased. Illiteracy decreased, local taxes for schools multiplied, teachers' salaries increased considerably in comparison with those paid in 1900, progress was made in the training of teachers through state-supported normal schools and teacher-training agencies in institutions of higher learning, and the certification of teachers was put on a better basis. The revival movement also gave impetus to the development of high schools, which began to be established in rural communities as an integral part of the state school systems. Interest in the consolidation of the smaller into larger and better graded and better equipped schools began to grow; rural libraries increased; school-improvement and parent-teacher associations were formed; child labor and compulsory attendance legislation expanded; and supervision through a better type of county superintendent began to show improvement.

By 1915 the average annual school term had lengthened

to 130 days. The average term for the United States in that year, however, was approximately 160 days. The average annual salary of all teachers was $328 in the South and $543 for the country at large. The average annual expenditure per child of school age was $8.50 for the South and $22.19 for the United States, and the value of school property per capita of school population was $18 and $79, respectively. Approximately 72 per cent of the school population in the South was enrolled, as against 74 per cent in the United States; nearly 69 per cent of the enrollment (50 per cent of the school population) was in average attendance in the South as compared with 76 per cent of the enrollment (56 per cent of the school population) in the country as a whole. Out of 8906 public high schools reporting a four years' course of study in the United States in 1915, with an enrollment of 1,362,514 pupils (about five per cent of the school population), only 1466 such schools with 150,607 pupils (about two per cent of the school population) were in the South. A recent study of the United States Bureau of Education (*Bulletin*, 1922, No. 11) reports in the Southern states 1575 secondary schools, public and private, approved by the state departments of education and accredited by the state universities. Eight counties in Arkansas, twelve in Florida, sixty-four in Georgia, one in Mississippi, two in Tennessee, four in Louisiana, and two in Virginia are more recently reported as having no public high school of standard grade.

Most of the Southern states still rank low among their sister states. Measured by attendance in elementary and in high school, in length of term, and in expenditure (per child of school age, per child attending, and per teacher for salaries) they ranked among the forty-eight states in 1918 as follows: Texas, 36th; Florida, 37th; Virginia, 39th; Tennessee, 40th; Louisiana, 42d; Georgia, 43d; North

Carolina, 44th; Alabama, 45th; Arkansas, 46th; Mississippi, 47th; and South Carolina, 48th. In that year the waste as a result of nonattendance, due largely to lack of adequate child labor and compulsory attendance laws, was about 33 per cent, with 25 per cent as the corresponding figure for the United States. The percentage of the school population enrolled in high schools of all grades was 9.3 in the United States and 5.1 per cent in the South. The increase in teachers' salaries generally has been substantial, but the average annual salary now paid public elementary and secondary teachers in the South is less than four fifths of the average for the United States.

The explanation of this low educational position is not hard to find. With limited funds the Southern states must provide two systems of education for large numbers of children scattered over wide areas. They have relatively a larger school population than the other sections of the country. For each thousand adult males in these states there are 1279 children of school age, while the corresponding average in the North is 789 and in the West about 600 children. Moreover, the estimated average true value of all property for each child of school age in the South is approximately one third that of the Northern states and one fourth that of the Western states. In addition, there is the disadvantage of sparsity of population in the South. North Carolina, Tennessee, and Virginia are the only Southern states having more than ten white children, and none has an average of ten colored children, of school age to the square mile. Moreover, the policy of separate schools is accepted as permanent. In the Northern states the average density of school population is from three to ten times greater than that of the South, and in the Western states, where the school population is small, it is largely concentrated in the irrigated regions, rich river valleys, and mining towns and is not so widely distributed as in the South.

No fair account of recent educational progress in the South can be given, therefore, without taking these difficulties into account. Those states are rapidly finding their duty, however, not in the measure of their resources for school support but rather in the measure of their needs for it. With less than normal power they have had to bear abnormal burdens. Between 1900 and 1915 the increase in public school expenditures for the United States was 180 per cent, but in the South it was 280 per cent; and the policy of increased expenditures for the enlargement of educational facilities is rapidly coming to be accepted as permanent. The estimated public school maintenance expenditures for the present school year (1922–23) for the states reporting are: Arkansas, nine millions; Florida, ten millions; South Carolina, eleven millions; Georgia, fifteen millions; North Carolina, twenty millions; Louisiana, twenty millions; and Virginia, twenty-two millions. Virginia to-day has public school property valued at nearly thirty-three millions, an increase of nearly 400 per cent since 1910; and the value of schoolhouses erected in North Carolina during the present school year is twenty-five millions, nearly twice the total value of all school property in that state in 1918. The public schools of Alabama between 1918 and 1921 made 74 per cent as much progress as in the period from 1890 to 1918, as measured by the Ayres index numbers for state school systems.

The tendency to improve administrative organization of public education has not, however, made the same progress in the South as in the country at large. Of the nine states in the Union still retaining ex officio state boards of education, four are Southern states — Texas, Florida, Mississippi, and North Carolina — and all the Southern states except Tennessee still elect their state superintendents of schools by popular vote. In seven of these states, county boards are elected by popular vote; but Texas, Florida, Mississippi, South Carolina, and Georgia continue to elect county superintendents of schools by that method. These latter officers are appointed by the county boards of education in North Carolina, Arkansas, Louisiana, and Alabama; by the county courts in Tennessee; and by the state board of education in Virginia. In theory the county, but in practice the district, with many of its traditional functions, is the unit of local school administration. There is a hopeful tendency, however, toward making the county the unit for the support and direction of public schools. Of significance also is the intelligent manner in which several Southern states have recently approached these administrative problems through commissions to study and report on educational conditions.

With the enactment of a compulsory attendance law in Mississippi in 1918 the last of the Southern states became committed to the policy of requiring children between certain ages to attend school for all or some part of the school term. This movement had begun in the South in 1905 with the passage of initial legislation on the subject in Tennessee. North Carolina followed in 1907, Virginia in 1908, Arkansas in 1909, Louisiana in 1910, South Carolina, Texas, Florida, and Alabama in 1915, Georgia in 1916, and Mississippi in 1918. Revisions, extensions, and improvements have been made in some of these states since the introductory enactments, though such legislation is still local and optional in character and very defective, lacking the full force of public approval needed for its complete success.

Child labor legislation, theoretically closely related to compulsory attendance laws, is found in all the Southern states. But reform is needed here also. Some of the states have made beginnings in legislation and practices designed to protect dependent and delinquent children. Perhaps one of the most advanced and complete plans not only in the South but in the country at large is that set up in North Carolina in 1919, providing for county boards of public welfare and a juvenile court in every county with jurisdiction over all delinquent, neglected, and dependent children under sixteen years of age. Improvement has appeared also in general health regulations and the physical examinations of school children and in renewed efforts, largely as a result of the war, to eliminate illiteracy, with which the South is still shamefully burdened.

Other hopeful signs of educational progress appear in the tendency to improve the status of the public school teacher by raising and standardizing the qualifications to teach and by making provision for the teachers to meet the requirements by enlarging teacher-training facilities. The tendency is toward state rather than county certification and toward accrediting approved university and college diplomas and accepting credentials of teachers from other states.

The Task for the Future

To furnish the kind and amount of education now needed in the South further reform and reorganization seem necessary. More emphasis must be placed on expert educational leadership and direction throughout. The traditional ex officio state boards of education need to be replaced by boards of representative men and women who are recognized for their sane and progressive attitudes toward, and demonstrated ability to promote, public school work. The demand likewise is for a change in the selection of the state superintendent. He is potentially the most strategic officer of the average American state, and the duties of his office require a high order of business and executive ability and professional skill which can never be guaranteed by popular election and which are rarely ever at home with those characteristics which usually commend men to political leaders and party bosses. The choice of a state superintendent of schools should not be limited to the narrow bounds of the state, which is necessary when selection is by popular election. There is needed also a more enlightened county board of educational control, chosen from the citizens at large, for reasonably long terms, and with powers and duties similar to those of city school boards, and selected for recognized ability to direct the large enterprise of public schools in the county rather than for political reasons. A new conception of the office of county superintendent is also urgently needed in the South. Popular elections have no proper place in filling such an office, the duties of which are executive and professional in character. The local district system, still powerful in the South, needs likewise to be replaced by the county as the principal unit of support, organization and administration, and supervision. The proper and adequate education of the negro, one of the most confusing problems now facing the Southern states, is dealt with in Chapter XV.

The Southern states have always been primarily agricultural, and approximately 80 per cent of the people still live in rural sections, with farming as their occupation. The permanent prosperity and well-being of the South, therefore, depend upon the prosperity and well-being of the rural population. For this reason the strategic point in the South's future growth appears in the kind of provision that is made for the education of the rural people. Differences between the educational advantages provided for the children of the country and those provided for the children of the towns and cities are glaring. The rural school has not yet been standardized and modernized or touched by that spirit of improvement which has been marked in urban education, but the increasing interest in the consolidation of the small and ineffective schools into larger, better organized, better supported, and more closely supervised schools, is one of the hopeful signs of improvement. The building and maintenance of modern roads and highways, the encouragement of progressive methods of agriculture, the improvement of public health, are uniting with the movement for better rural schools to make rural life in the South more wholesome and inviting. Only by these means can real and lasting progress there be promoted. No material prosperity will be of advantage if the level of citizenship and public wholesomeness is not thereby advanced through education.

The material wealth of the South has grown great and apparent. The value of manufactured products is twice as great as that of the entire United States in 1880. During the last two decades the value of farm property has increased more than 400 per cent and the value of farm products nearly 600 per cent. The value of mineral products is six times as great as ten years ago. These facts not only reveal the industrial change but they furnish illustration of how intimately is the South related to the life of the whole country. The Southern states are no longer poor. In recent years they have made such a giant stride from poverty to prosperity that they are now able to do almost anything for public schools, public roads, and public health. The World War, moreover, not only revealed the weaknesses of education there, but it also helped the South to find herself. Under the impetus of the call to fight, to give, and to do for others what she had not felt fully able to do for herself, she found fresh hope and new energies. The call for food for our own and the soldiers of Europe, the campaign against waste, and the drives for the Red Cross and Liberty Bonds, led the South to thoughtful consideration of new enterprises and of old ones undeveloped. More nearly complete remedies for her short-comings were thus revealed.

The measure of the South's conscience on schools and other means of intellectual progress must be taken neither from her impatience with unsympathetic and unintelligent criticism from without nor from her ability to build schools, but rather from her constantly growing need for education. Just as the chief problem of the South twenty-five years ago was to secure complete agreement on education, so to-day her chief need is *to educate*. The task to-day is little less conspicuous than then for its magnitude and difficulty. The task now is to build schools on a sound basis of financial support, professional direction, and supervision, so as to furnish every child equal educational rights — "the opportunity 'to burgeon out all that there is within him,'" to use the sentiment of the late Aycock, North Carolina's educational governor. Then, and then only, will the people of the South be enabled to observe fully, faithfully, and intelligently, their constantly enlarging relationships and, in the paraphrase of Jefferson, the earliest of the South's educational statesmen, to understand what goes on in the world and keep their part of it going right.

REFERENCES

COCHRAN, T. E. — *History of Education in Florida;* Lancaster, Pa., 1922.

Conference for Education in the South — *Proceedings.*

GARNER, JAMES W. (Editor) — *Studies in Southern History and Politics;* Columbia University Press, 1914.

General Education Board — *Public Education in North Carolina;* New York, 1921.

KNIGHT, EDGAR W. — *Public Education in the South;* Houghton Mifflin, 1922.

KNIGHT, EDGAR W. — *Public School Education in North Carolina;* Houghton Mifflin, 1921.

Blue Book of Southern Progress; Manufacturers' Record Pub. Co. (Baltimore), 1922.

MURPHY, EDGAR G. — *Problems of the Present South;* Longmans Green, 1918.

NOBLE, STUART G. — *Forty Years of the Public Schools in Mississippi;* Teachers College, 1918.

PAGE, WALTER H. — *The Rebuilding of Old Commonwealths;* Doubleday, Page, 1905.

Peabody Board — *Proceedings of the Trustees.*

REISNER, EDWARD H. — *Nationalism and Education since 1789;* Macmillan, 1922.

United States Bureau of Education —
   Bulletin, 1912, No. 27, History of Public Education in Arkansas.
   Bulletin, 1915, No. 12, History of Public Education in Alabama.
   Bulletin, 1919, No. 14, An Educational Study of Alabama.
   Reports of the Commissioner of Education.

Virginia Public Schools — *Report of the Education Commission,* 1919.

CHAPTER XV

EDUCATION OF THE NEGRO

BY

Stuart G. Noble

TULANE UNIVERSITY

CHAPTER XV

The Education of the Negro

Introduction

The history of the education of the negro since his emancipation falls into two periods. In the first, a period of experimentation embraced by the years 1865 to 1895, two facts were clearly demonstrated: (1) that Northern philanthropy without the aid of federal or other public funds could not support the burden of educating some two or three million colored children; (2) that literacy alone could not accomplish the regeneration of the race. Upon the experience of the first era was based the procedure of the second. During this period, embraced in the quarter-century that has just elapsed, Northern philanthropy has tended more and more to coördinate its efforts and to direct its activities toward assisting the war-broken Southern states to assume their proper burden in educating all the children of all the people. During this period also the message of Samuel Armstrong and Booker Washington has been largely accepted and spread abroad as the gospel of regeneration through industrial training.

The Education of the Negro a Southern Problem

Nine tenths of the total negro population of the United States, according to the census of 1910, are to be found in the South. About thirty per cent of the total population of the South is of the colored race, while less than two per cent of the population of the Northern states was so reported at that date. More than half the population of Mississippi

405

and South Carolina are negroes. While there is a large number of negroes living in the North and West, an increasingly large number within recent years, the bulk of the negro population lies south of the Ohio and the Potomac.

The problem of negro education is thus essentially a Southern problem. And, since the support for white and colored schools comes from a common source, whatever conditions affect the growth and efficiency of the public school system in any Southern state affects the growth and efficiency of both white and colored schools. Economic retardation, for instance is largely responsible for the backwardness of white as well as of negro schools. A brief survey of the social and economic conditions that have handicapped the Southern states in their efforts to solve their educational problems may here be in order.

To begin with there is the handicap of adult illiteracy, which in 1890 affected fifteen per cent of the native white population and almost two thirds of the negro population. Thanks to the efficiency of such schools as have been available, negro illiteracy in the country as a whole has been reduced to 22.9 per cent and native white illiteracy to 2.5 per cent in 1920. The reports on illiteracy tend to show that there was a higher percentage of illiteracy among negroes in the South than in the North or West, and a higher percentage in the rural than in the urban communities of the South. In other words, illiteracy is greatest where opportunities for schooling are most meager.

Sparseness of population is undoubtedly one of the greatest handicaps under which the South is at present laboring. The factor of sparseness becomes all the more acute when it becomes necessary to provide separate schools in the open country for white and colored children. No state in the South in 1918 had as many as ten negro children to the square mile; Arkansas, Texas, and Florida had no more than three to the square mile. Compare these averages with those for several Northern states, where the negro population was a negligible quantity. Massachusetts had 107, New Jersey 98, Connecticut 61 children to the square mile. This means that it takes eight times as large a territory in the South as it does in the North to provide enough children for a small one-teacher negro school.

The South is also handicapped by a lack of wealth. It has been estimated that in 1912 there was in the eleven Southern states an average of $3449 per child of school age. Among the agricultural states of the Middle West we find Iowa with wealth to the amount of $13,473 per child and Illinois with wealth to the amount of $10,808 per child. In the ten years that have elapsed since these estimates were made there has been a considerable increase in the wealth of the South, but not by any means enough to bring the South abreast of the states of the North and West.

The reason for the backwardness of negro schools is to be found not altogether in the hostility of the whites toward negro education. It may best be accounted for by the same reasons that explain the backwardness of the white schools. Although the past quarter of a century has witnessed an enormous increase in the wealth of every Southern state, it must be remembered that by 1910 some of the states had not yet recovered from the devastation wrought by the Civil War.

The Hampton Idea

The story of the progress of negro education in the last twenty-five years takes us back to 1897, four years after General S. C. Armstrong laid down his work at Hampton. Since educational practice in this generation owes so much to the theory first enunciated by this fervent advocate of negro education, it may be well to set forth the cardinal

principles for which he stood. In 1868 he undertook to
found at Hampton, Virginia, a school after the manual
labor plan prevalent in many parts of the United States
before the Civil War. In certain respects, however, his
theory of education was broader than that of the manual
labor schools of an earlier date. He held that pupils should
engage in manual labor not merely to defray a part of their
school expenses or to learn a trade, but to develop mind and
character. The moral value of industrial training, he said,
was a sufficient justification of it, and character the chief
outcome of the labor system. His idea can best be indicated
by a quotation which dates from 1870:

> The education needed is one that touches upon the whole range of life,
> that aims at the formation of good habits and sound principles, that
> considers the details of each day, that enjoins in respect to diet, regularity,
> proper selection, and good cooking; in respect to habits, suitable clothing,
> exercise, cleanliness of persons, and quarters, and ventilation, also industry,
> and thrift; and in respect to all things, intelligent practice and self-
> restraint.
>
> In all men, education is conditioned not alone on an enlightened head
> and a changed heart but very largely on a routine of industrious habits,
> which is to character what the foundation is to the pyramid. The summit
> should glow with a divine light, interfusing and qualifying the whole mass,
> but it is only upon a foundation of regular daily activities that there can
> be any fine and permanent upbuilding. Morality and industry generally
> go together.

The institution established by General Armstrong was
chartered as Hampton Normal and Agricultural Institute,
a name which suggests the character of the instruction that
was to be offered. The founder seems to have grasped the
significance of adapting instruction to the needs of an
agricultural people. That he had a clearer understanding of
the social situation which confronted him than most of his
contemporaries future developments in negro education
were to demonstrate. He understood the limitations of the
race, and the industrial training which he offered at Hampton
was designed to provide such social and economic experience

as the race on the whole needed most. Since Armstrong's death, through the able administration of Hollis B. Frissell the institution for a period of twenty-five years has enjoyed a season of remarkable prosperity. The new administration has carried forward to fulfillment the purposes of the founder and demonstrated the effectiveness of industrial education in racial uplift. In 1922 Hampton was offering training in upward of thirty trades, including household arts, manual arts, and agriculture. In 1917 its equipment was valued at about $2,000,000, and its endowment was in excess of $3,000,000. By the same date it had turned out 1782 graduates, 539 of whom were engaged in teaching.

Booker T. Washington

The Hampton idea has not been confined to a single institution. It has spread throughout the South, has influenced the trend of industrial education in other parts of the United States, and has been carried by missionaries to China, Ceylon, Africa, and Rhodesia. In 1881 there went from Hampton to the little village of Tuskegee in Alabama a young negro who had caught the vision of General Armstrong and had been fired by his zeal. To this man, Booker T. Washington, the negro race is indebted for elucidating, defending, and propagating the idea of social uplift through industrial training. Washington found a hearing not only in the North, where philanthropists gave him liberal contributions to develop Tuskegee Institute, but he secured what he prized equally as much, the indorsement of his principles by leaders of the white race in the South.

He had observed, as had J. L. M. Curry and others, that the opposition of the Southern white people, prevalent in certain parts of the country during the Reconstruction Period, had now subsided into supine indifference. So long as they were not taxed to support it they did not care what kind of education the negro obtained. They might sneer at the abortive results of the so-called "colleges," but Southern white people no longer actively opposed the efforts to educate the negro. Washington had sagacity enough to see that Northern philanthropy could not support the burden of educating the entire negro race. Hope for federal aid in this enterprise had been dissipated by the failure of the Blair Bill a decade earlier. The only hope for the negro lay, as Washington saw it, in aro' 'ng the Southern people to the point of providing substantia   'd from state and local funds. As he expressed it :

> One of the chief hindrances to the p. 'ess of negro education in the public schools in the South is in my opinio. 'ue to the fact that the negro colleges in which so many of the teachers ؛ \ prepared have not realized the importance of convincing the Southern 'hite people that education makes the same improvement in the negro t.. ' it does in the white man ; makes him more useful in labour, so much be   er a citizen, and so much more dependable in all the relations of life, tha. 't is worth while to spend money to give him an education. As long as t ؛ Southern white people remain unconvinced by the results of the educa..o'i which they see about them that education makes the negro a better man 'or woman, so long will the masses of the negro people who are dependent upon the public schools for their instruction remain to a greater or less extent in ignorance.

By the year 1895 Booker Washington had established a substantial institution at Tuskegee after the pattern of Hampton, and had attained a place of national importance in education. His enthusiastic advocacy of industrial training, however, had brought him into open conflict with able leaders of his own race who mistook his emphasis on this form of education for a condemnation of academic instruction and of higher education of the negro in general. Washington was equal to the controversy. In 1897 he answered his critics as follows :

> I am convinced that whether the negro receives much education or little, whether it be called high or low, we have reached the point in our development where a larger proportion of those who are being educated should, while they are receiving their education or after they have received it, be taught to connect their education with some industrial pursuit.

Booker Washington repeatedly expressed himself as not opposed to professional education or to any form of higher education of the negro, but as favoring most the form of education that would best equip the colored population to make their way materially and socially in their rural environment.

As the chief exponent of industrial education, he received both praise and criticism. Some members of his own race construed his advocacy of this form of education as the barring of the door to higher education against exceptional negroes. Industrial training to some appeared the forging of the fetters of slavery again upon the negro, which would subject the race to manual labor forever. To others the practical ideals of physical well-being and economic gain, so frequently stressed by Washington, seemed too materialistic. To clarify the matter it may be well to examine several excerpts from his works which contain the gist of his theory.

Mere hand training, without thorough moral, religious, and mental education, counts for very little. The hands, the head, and the heart together, as the essential elements of educational need, should be so correlated that one may be made to help the other.

How well I remember the feeling of stimulus and satisfaction inspired by the sight of a perfectly made bed, the pillows placed always at the right angle, and the edges of the sheets turned over according to rules of neatness and system. The work of the farm had a similar influence upon my views of relative values in education. I soon learned that there was a great difference between studying about things and studying the things themselves, between book instruction and the illumination of practical experience.

Their classroom work in spelling, mathematics, grammar, and English composition comes effectively into play. They find out that a carpenter has a small chance of getting ahead unless he can use his head intelligently. He writes out a contract, for example, to put up a four-room house, on the basis of three cash payments — when he takes the job; when the roof is on; and when the house is turned over to the owner. This contract is read aloud to the instructor, who asks the other members of the class to criticise it. One of them points out a flaw which would allow the owner to 'crawl out' of his bargain on a technicality. Another is pleased to discover that the arithmetic is so faulty that the estimates of the cost of material would land the contractor in the poor-house.   Then the student begins to see that his so-called academic teaching is as important in his calling as his skill with the plane, the saw and the miter-box, and that he cannot hope to become a good carpenter unless he is also a diligent scholar.

These excerpts express the ideas which Washington repeated time and again in his books, in his speeches, and in his contributions to periodicals.   He represents his work as a "training for conditions" and as "welding theory and practice."   To him, as to General Armstrong, industrial training had a moral value.   Good habits in thinking and behavior were to be formed in an environment that would insure their future functioning.   If there was much emphasis of material success it was because a low standard of living was largely responsible for the negro's moral shortcomings. He had in mind not the "talented tenth" of W. E. B. Du Bois, but the masses of his race living, and destined to live, the lives of a simple farming people in the rural South. Accused of fixing an industrial mold for a colored caste, he replied that he was merely adapting instruction to the needs of his people.   For more than thirty years, with tongue and pen, he preached the gospel of regeneration through industrial training.

Before the end of the past century the drift toward industrial education had definitely set in.   Leading thinkers upon the subject, men like J. L. M. Curry and A. D. Mayo, were at that time preaching it throughout the North and South.   An investigation, conducted by the *New Orleans Times-Democrat* in 1897, showed that the majority of the presidents of the negro colleges and most of the missionary bishops having colored institutions under their control were in favor of it.   Several religious boards operating negro schools introduced industrial training in some form or other about this time.

The idea has now been definitely accepted as one of the essential principles in the education of the negro.   Industrial education has furnished the common ground for the coming together of the three interested parties, the Northern philanthropist, the negro, and the Southern white man. An agreement on principles having been reached during the past decade, the basis for an effective system of public education has been laid. The problem of providing a simple form of industrial training that may be widely and cheaply distributed is now being solved by the county training schools and by the industrial supervisors provided by the Jeanes Fund.

The Public Schools

In the past twenty-five years the chief gains in negro education are to be found not in statistics indicating progress, but in the unmeasurable growth of a sentiment among Southern whites favorable to such education. Booker Washington, who knew the South better perhaps than most observers in the field, said that the Southern people were not so much opposed to negro education as indifferent to it. If they could be brought to see the advantages of increased productivity, community health, and social betterment to be derived from the education of the negro, Washington did not doubt that they could be won to the cause. In this conviction he was not alone. Able leaders of the South, such as Bishop Atticus G. Haygood, Dr. J. L. M. Curry, and Bishop Charles B. Galloway, urged their people time and again to make a more generous provision for the negro schools.

With the opening of the new century we find a number of hopeful signs of the development of a favorable sentiment. Representative Southern men, speaking before the Southern Conference for Education in 1903, expressed the opinion that the Southern whites wished to do well by the negro "in spite of the difficulties." This Conference, which held yearly meetings for a decade or more, did much to awaken the

Southern people to their responsibility for public schools for both races.   In 1912 the Southern University Race Commission was organized, composed of professors representing eleven Southern universities.   The purpose of the Commission is to study race relationships with a view to bringing about a permanent adjustment of differences.   The Southern Sociological Congress began about this time to call together the outstanding representatives of both races for the study of their common problems.   For a decade the Southern Student Conference, held each summer at Blue Ridge, North Carolina, by the International Committee of the Young Men's Christian Association, has been conducting classes in the study of the race problem.   Dr. W. D. Weatherford, the leader of the Conference, has done much through his writings and speeches to develop a healthy spirit of coöperation between the races.   Other hopeful signs of better feeling are to be found in the coöperation of the states and local units with agents of the General Education Board and the Jeanes Fund, and in the contribution of public and private funds by white people to the county training schools and to the Rosenwald Schools.

The tendency of the Southern states to pass compulsory education laws is also a wholesome sign.   The chief argument of the demagogues against compulsory attendance was for years the argument that it would bring negro children into schools, promote literacy among the negroes, and perhaps lead to negro domination in politics.   Before 1890 no Southern state had a compulsory law.   By 1908 Virginia and North Carolina had secured the passage of such laws. At present every state has compulsory attendance, but in one or two the local option feature still prevails.

Opportunities for education in both white and colored schools are, as has been previously pointed out, and for the reasons indicated (Chapter XIV), somewhat more limited in the Southern states than in the North and West. While instances of superior advantages may be noted in exceptional communities of every Southern state, on the whole it must be admitted that schools for both races, when compared with schools in other sections, are decidedly backward. If schools for white children are poor, the schools for negroes are poorer.

State superintendents of education, reporting to the United States Bureau of Education in 1912, painted a sorry picture of the condition of negro rural schools. One of them wrote:

There has never been any serious attempt in this state to offer adequate facilities for the colored race. The average length of the term for the state is only four months; practically all the schools are taught in dilapidated churches, which, of course, are not equipped with suitable desks, blackboards, and other essentials of a school; practically all the teachers are incompetent, possessing little or no education and having had no professional training whatever, except a few weeks obtained in the summer schools; the schools are generally overcrowded, some of them having as many as one hundred students to the teacher; no attempt is made to do more than teach the children to read, write, and figure. . . . It can probably be truthfully said that the negro schools here are gradually improving but they are still just about as poor and inadequate as they can be.

The Rural School Supervisor of South Carolina, W. K. Tate, reported:

Among the negro rural schools which I have visited I have found only one in which the highest class knew the multiplication table. The teacher is attempting to use the books and follow the course of study provided by the State Board of Education and intended primarily for white schools.

A statistical summary of the negro schools in Mississippi for the decade ending in 1910 concludes as follows:[1]

In the negro schools we see a few of the marks of progress, but we cannot say that they have advanced very far. In the last ten years there has been a substantial increase in the enrollment and average attendance. The number of teachers has increased 17.5 per cent, but has by no means kept pace with the enrollment. The average negro teacher now has to teach four children more than he did in 1899, and receives for it ninety-two cents more a month. He is now attempting the Herculean task of teach-

[1] See Noble's *Forty Years of the Public Schools in Mississippi with Special Reference to the Education of the Negro.*

ing sixty-seven children, or almost twice as many as the average white teacher is required to teach.   Were it not for the fact that such a small percentage of the enrollment is in daily attendance, colored teachers would be able to accomplish little indeed.   As things now stand, we can hope for but the most meager returns.

The writer of the foregoing, summarizing a chapter on the apparent lack of progress of the negro masses, says:

For the masses, however, the lack of progress indicated by the statistical studies of this chapter is typical. . . .   In view of the meager equipment of the rural schools, the short terms, the formal courses of study, the ill-trained and poorly paid teachers, it would be marvelous indeed, if greater results were forthcoming.   It is trite to say that the virtual stagnation of fifty-six per cent of the population of Mississippi constitutes a menace to the social and economic health of the state.   Better facilities and specific training leading to moral and economic efficiency will alone improve the situation.

The field agent of the Slater Fund described the situation in 1912 as follows:

In the states of the lower South the physical equipment of colored schools is far below what it is in Virginia and North Carolina.   In many cases in Georgia and Alabama, for instance, schoolhouses are not provided by the public.   Only the teacher's salary comes from that source.   In South Carolina there are 2,354 public schools for colored people, but there are only 1,442 public schoolhouses.   The county boards of Georgia own only 208 colored schoolhouses, worth on the average $166 each. . . . Alabama reports for colored people only 975 schoolhouses owned by the state, local communities, and towns and cities. . . .

TABLE

ENROLLMENT, ATTENDANCE, TEACHERS, IN NEGRO SCHOOLS
IN SOUTHERN STATES

Reports of the U. S. Commission of Education

YEAR	CHILDREN 5 TO 18 ENROLLED AT SCHOOL		NUMBER OF TEACHERS		PER CENT 5 TO 18 ENROLLED		PER CENT ENROLLED IN ATTENDANCE	
	White	Negro	White	Negro	White	Negro	White	Negro
1917–1918	6,277,840	2,063,177	174,980	36,920	77.0	69.0	68.0	63.0
1908–1909	4,909,283	1,712,137	122,941	30,334	74.8	56.3	66.3	65.2
1898–1899	4,261,309	1,560,070	98,710	27,313	72.3	57.7	65.1	62.9
1889–1890	3,402,420	1,296,959	78,903	24,072	66.3	51.6	63.6	62.7

From these excerpts and from the accompanying table of statistics of public schools in the Southern states the reader is enabled to get a more or less satisfactory view of the facilities for negro education. The study of negro education made through the Phelps-Stokes Fund and published as a bulletin of the United States Bureau of Education in 1917 makes certain other observations worthy of notice. It calls attention not only to the inadequacy of the material equipment of the schools, to the short terms and irregular attendance, but to overcrowding, to the poorness of instruction, and to the crying need for proper supervision. In three typical counties of Alabama were found eighty colored schools with a seating capacity of 3794, an enrollment of 6391, and an attendance of 5832. It is shown that 70 per cent of the teachers in schools of the black belt have themselves never attended school beyond the sixth grade. It is further shown that little progress had been made in adapting the state-prescribed course of study to the needs of negro children of the rural masses, and that supervision other than that of the Jeanes Fund agents was to be found only in cities and in exceptional communities.

The period between 1902 and 1914 was a period of remarkable development for secondary education in the South. But, of the schools established, by far the greater number were for the use of the white race. Only a small number of Southern cities and towns have developed high schools for negroes. The Phelps-Stokes study listed sixty-four public high schools for the colored race in the entire South, and mentioned two hundred other schools which enrolled a few secondary pupils. The best schools of either elementary or secondary grade are to be found in the cities. There the advantages for each race are more nearly equalized; better teachers are secured, higher salaries are paid, and more supervision is provided.

Much improvement in the public school system has undoubtedly been made in the last half-dozen years. With the return of prosperity all the states of the South are in much better economic circumstances than ever before. There is considerable evidence that this prosperity is bringing to the negro schools a larger proportionate share of the public revenues. The assistance of the philanthropic boards of the North is calling forth the effort of the South. All this is a good augury for the future of negro education.

The Jeanes Industrial Supervisors

The Jeanes Fund, established by the bequest of Anna T. Jeanes of Philadelphia, undertook in 1908 to send industrial supervisors into the negro schools of the rural districts, where instruction at best was meager and facilities for teaching were unspeakably poor. Begun in a small way, the number of supervisors has been increased year by year until in 1921 there were 272 engaged in 269 Southern counties. These traveling teachers visited that year 8900 schools and raised for school improvement $395,000. Working under the direction of the county superintendents, they encouraged the feeble efforts of rural teachers, introduced simple home industries into backward schools, gave talks on sanitation and cleanliness, promoted the improvement of schoolhouses, and organized clubs for the betterment of school and neighborhood.

The supervising teachers are trained in industrial work, domestic and agricultural. They are prepared to show the rural teacher how to teach sewing, cooking, gardening, laundering, and sometimes nursing, basket making, carpentry, and farming. A county superintendent describes the work of one of the earliest of the Jeanes workers as follows:

He commenced at once to organize in each colored school visited a school improvement association, coöperative corn and cotton clubs, where the school children and patrons cultivated the grounds, taking lessons in agriculture at the same time, agreeing that the proceeds arising therefrom should inure to the benefit of the school, in equipping the same and extending the length of the school term, introducing manual labor, both for boys and girls. . . .   The schoolyards have been cleared off and planted in trees and flowers, corn and cotton clubs organized, work done on the little farms, and manual arts and domestic science introduced into most of the schools, where wood work, raffia, straw basket making, and sewing are being learned by the children. . . .

At the outset the Jeanes Fund bore the entire expense of the supervisors, but within a year or two some of the counties assumed a part of the burden of support, and others assumed responsibility for the whole cost. The Jeanes workers are appointed by the county superintendents and are members of the county teaching body, just as other teachers are. Here we have a splendid instance of an enlightened philanthropy assisting Southern public school authorities to help themselves.

County Training Schools

County training schools for negroes were first organized in 1912. The beginning was made by four Southern counties in coöperation with the Slater Fund. As stated at the time of organization the purpose of the schools is :

1. To supply for the county a central school offering work in advance of that offered in the common rural schools.
2. To lay emphasis on thorough work in all common school studies.
3. To give industrial training, laying particular emphasis upon subjects pertaining to home and farm.
4. To prepare boys and girls to make a good living and lead a useful life by knowing how to care for the home, to utilize land, to make home gardens, to raise their own meat, poultry, products, milk products, etc.
5. To prepare young men and women to become rural and elementary school teachers. . . .

The chief motive for the founding of these schools is to be found in the last of the purposes just mentioned — the training of rural school teachers. The schools are organized as public institutions, the title of all property being held by the county, state, or district. They are under the supervision of the county superintendents just as other public schools. Aid from the Slater Fund to the amount of $500 for teachers' salaries is provided on condition that $750 be appropriated from public funds for salaries.

The average length of term of the negro rural school in the South is considerably shorter than that of the white school. Negro children are not able to cover the ground covered by white children of the same age. The average negro pupil in the rural districts is retarded from two to five years. Economic necessity forces a large number out of school at an early age. Whatever vocational work is offered in the school must be introduced earlier than in the white school if it is to reach anything like a fair proportion of the pupils. For these reasons it is recommended that the county training schools be organized upon the five-two-three plan, that is, five years of primary work, two years of elementary work, and three years of secondary work.

In the suggested course of study for the county training schools, published in 1917, industrial work is introduced in the third year and continued throughout the remainder of the ten-year course. Beginning with weaving of mats and other useful articles from pine needles, corn husks, and other native materials, the work for girls advances into sewing and darning, making of hats, cooking of plain meals, preserving, care of beds, dressmaking, nursing, and home making. The work for boys is differentiated from that of the girls in the fourth year and proceeds with chair caning, the use of simple tools, cobbling, harness mending, whitewashing, repair of farm implements, blacksmithing, concrete mixing, etc.

The aim of the secondary school is largely vocational. Three courses are offered: (1) a home-makers' course for girls, (2) a farm-makers' course for boys, and (3) a rural teacher-training course. The stress placed upon the industrial subjects in this school as well as in the primary and elementary grades is in accord with the theory of adapting the curriculum to local needs.

The committee on course of study does not neglect the minimum essentials, the three R's, history, current topics, hygiene and sanitation, civics, moral training, and physical exercise.

The report of the Slater Fund for the session 1920–21 shows that by this date 142 counties in fourteen Southern states had established county training schools. In nine years the number of teachers had increased from 20 to 840, the average yearly salary from $267 to $640, and the total receipts from $11,000 to $1,007,000. In 1920–21 there was a total enrollment in county training schools of 35,317, of which number 2347 were in grades above the eighth. The General Education Board has since 1915 coöperated with the Slater Fund in providing equipment, workshops, and teachers' homes. The schools draw pupils from all parts of the counties in which they are located. Boarding facilities are sometimes provided; but, in general, the schools are handicapped by lack of dormitory facilities.

Through the medium of the county training school it is hoped to make up one of the chief deficiencies of the negro schools. The supply of trained teachers for the country schools is in this way to be provided, and industrial training in an elementary form is thus to be carried to the remotest country districts.

Activities of the General Education Board

The General Education Board of New York City out of its ample funds has, since 1902, the date of its organization, made increasingly liberal contributions toward the support of negro education in the South. In the states of Alabama,

Arkansas, Florida, Georgia, Kentucky, Louisiana, Maryland, Mississippi, North Carolina, South Carolina, Tennessee, Texas, and Virginia, the Board is coöperating with the state departments of education in the development of better schools, and better economic and social conditions in the rural sections. The undertaking is in charge of state agents for negro rural schools, whose salaries and traveling expenses are paid by the General Education Board. The agents coöperate sympathetically with county superintendents and with interested white and colored citizens in promoting the welfare of negro schools. The Board has also rendered material assistance to the Jeanes Foundation by contributing to its work of assisting counties to employ supervising industrial teachers. It has also coöperated with the Slater Fund in providing equipment for schools and in contributing toward the building of teachers' homes. The Board, through the state departments of education in 1918, aided fifty-nine summer schools for negro teachers. These schools were manned by 478 teachers and enrolled 6157 students. Summer scholarships at Hampton and Tuskegee have also been provided for a number of deserving and specially qualified teachers. The success of the policy of the General Board of Education in training the Southern public school authorities to help themselves is proved by the fact that Texas has recently taken over the entire expense of the state supervisor of negro schools.

The Rosenwald Fund

The crying needs of the negro schools have been for trained teachers, supervision of instruction, and material equipment. Other agencies have undertaken to train teachers and provide supervision. No means for providing better schoolhouses had been secured until Booker Washington interested Julius Rosenwald of Chicago in the enterprise. In the last eight years, through the assistance of Mr. Rosenwald, it has been possible to erect in fourteen Southern states over fourteen hundred negro schoolhouses. Most of these are of the one- and two-teacher type, but fifty of them cost $10,000 or more, and one of them as much as $104,000. Aid to the extent of $300 for the building of a schoolhouse may be obtained from the Rosenwald Fund by any community duplicating this amount either from public funds or from private contributions. The Rosenwald Fund coöperates with the public school systems just as the other philanthropic agencies are doing. The state departments of education supervise the building of the schoolhouses. It is stipulated that at least two acres of land must be provided before the building is begun, and that due consideration be given in the construction to lighting, heating, ventilation, and sanitation. Plans and specifications are furnished by the Rosenwald Fund. These school buildings undoubtedly furnish the best facilities available for education of the colored youth in the rural districts of the South.

Private Schools

The *Report of the United States Commissioner of Education* for the year 1897 lists 178 secondary and higher institutions for the education of the colored race. This number included the land-grant agricultural colleges and several state-supported state normal schools. Of the 170 institutions located in the South the greater part were under the control of denominational or other philanthropic boards. Practically all of them had elementary, secondary, college, and sometimes professional departments.

It is safe to say that this was not a complete list of the private institutions for the education of the colored race. Twenty years later, when the Phelps-Stokes study was made, there were discovered 655 institutions under private control, with a total enrollment of 83,679.   Only 266 of these institutions were classed as "large or important."   Of the total student enrollment, 70,654 were found to be pupils in the elementary grades; 11,527, pupils in the secondary grades; and 1588, pupils in the colleges and professional departments.

The period of our study is characterized by searching inquiry into the purposes, needs, practices, and products of the privately supported negro schools of the South.   Dr. J. L. M. Curry, agent of the Slater Fund, reported in 1895 that much of the money contributed by charitably disposed persons of the North and South to the support of negro schools had been largely misapplied.   Many of the higher private schools, he said, were "handicapped by high-sounding and deceptive names and impossible courses of study." Elementary, secondary, and college departments were often found under the same roof.   In the twenty-five nominal colleges he estimated that there were enrolled only about one thousand students.

In estimating the character of the instruction offered Doctor Curry said:

The general instruction heretofore given in the schools, it is feared, has been too exclusively intellectual, too little of that kind which produces intelligent and skilled workmen, and therefore not thoroughly adapted to racial development nor to fitting for the practical duties of life.

Professor Kelly Miller, a noted negro scholar, in an interesting study published in the *Report of the United States Commissioner of Education* in 1901, said:

The wild clamor for identity of plan and method without examining into fitness and adaptability shows a lack of self-knowledge, self-confidence, and self-respect.

Booker Washington in *My Larger Education* expressed himself on this point as follows:

One of the troubles with negro education at the present time (1910) is that there are no definite standards of education among the different schools. It is not possible to tell, for instance, from the name of the school whether it is teaching the ordinary common school branches, Greek and Latin, or carpentry, blacksmithing, and sewing. More than that, there is no accepted standard as to the methods or efficiency of the teaching in these schools. A student may be getting a mere smattering, not even learning sufficient reading and writing to be able to read with comfort a book or a newspaper. He may be getting a very good training in one subject and almost nothing in some other. A boy entering such a school does not know what he is going for, and, nine cases out of ten, he will come away without knowing what he got.

The Phelps-Stokes study, after commenting upon the fact that over 75 per cent of the enrollment in the so-called academies, colleges, and universities for negroes is to be found in the elementary grades, adds:

Unfortunately, most of the schools with college courses are seriously handicapped, not only by inadequate funds but also by the small number of pupils prepared to study college subjects. The facts presented in the chapter on college and professional education show that only three institutions have a student body, a teaching force, and equipment, and an income sufficient to warrant the characterization of "college." Nearly half of the college students and practically all the professional students of college grade are in these three institutions. Fifteen other institutions are offering college courses which represent a wide variation of standards. Not more than ten per cent of the pupils in these schools are in college classes.

To the private institutions of the South, limited as their equipments have been, and misdirected as their efforts too often have been, the colored race is indebted for practically everything that it has received in the way of secondary and higher instruction. A surprisingly large percentage of their graduates have been turned back into the schools as teachers. Practically all the trained negro teachers in either public or private schools have received their training in these institutions. From these schools have come many clean, honest workers, and many able leaders.

A committee appointed in 1900 by the Conference for Education in the South reported two years later that some of the schools established by sincere but mistaken individuals were not only utterly inefficient but "positively mischievous" in that they persuaded students away from the more deserving institutions.   Booker Washington contended in 1912 that no more private schools should be established and that philanthropic contributions should be used to strengthen the public schools.   A plan for coördinating the work of philanthropic boards was effected in 1914.   The inquiry conducted by the Phelps-Stokes Fund into the character of instruction offered in the private and higher schools for the colored race, published in 1917, has done much to clarify our notions as to plans and purposes, and has opened the way for a definitely formulated policy for the education of the negro.

Problems of Negro Education

The questions raised by the various inquiries have led to scientific study of the mental capacity of the race.   Ever since the emancipation of the negro many have entertained a doubt as to his ability to profit by schooling.   This doubt, it must be said, was based upon opinion rather than upon facts scientifically derived.   During the period which we are reviewing a number of psychological studies have been made.   The main fact that has been deduced by these researches is that the negro in the higher mental processes is on the whole somewhat inferior to the white race.   This is not to say, however, that all negroes are inferior in mental ability to all white people.   On the contrary, it has been ascertained that many full-blooded negroes have ability surpassing that of the median white man, and that there are some negroes of exceptional ability.   These facts should put at rest the much-protracted discussion as to the advisability of providing opportunities for higher education of the negro.   A small percentage of the race can profit by such instruction, and for this number opportunities should be provided.

Educational Values

A live topic for discussion has been the question of educational values. Many who have spoken upon the subject have expressed themselves either as favoring or opposing a certain form of education — academic instruction, higher education, or industrial training. In all such expressions, educational values are concerned. In a curriculum social efficiency should be the inevitable criterion. Each school subject should be weighed to determine the extent to which it will function in better living, and those subjects that promise to be most fruitful in the later lives of the pupils should be given the greatest stress.

Booker Washington has come nearer than any other individual of either the white or negro race to offering a scheme of values which proves acceptable to the various social elements concerned — the Northern philanthropist, the negro, and the Southern white man. His scheme is based upon the present needs of his race. From his writings it may be gathered that he prizes the following social interests somewhat in the order of their arrangement:

(1) *Economic independence.* This is interpreted to mean ability to earn a living, to acquire property, and to enlarge accordingly the circle of human wants. He makes this item fundamental to the other social aims since it leads to better health, better morals, and better means of enlarging the intellectual horizon.

(2) *Morality.* This is founded upon a religion that functions in good living.

(3) *Sociability.* Under this head he includes respect for the institutions of the white race, its government and religion; the establishment of cordial relations between the two races; the development of race pride, leading to the integrity of the race.

(4) *Health*. Including personal hygiene and sanitary living conditions.

Washington does not mention the intellectual or æsthetic elements. It is understood, however, that the intellectual element is considered as a means to the other elements. As for the æsthetic element, he thinks it is not fundamental, and, for the present, should have minor consideration. Negro leaders almost without exception accept Washington's values. Dr. W. E. B. DuBois, however, would emphasize in the higher institutions the æsthetic element in order that the leaders of the race may have access to the broadest civilizing influences. Northern and Southern leaders of both races have almost reached an agreement upon the basis of Washington's values.

The success of negro education, in whatever form and to whatever extent, depends upon a common agreement among the interested parties as to plans and purposes. The policy of the larger philanthropic boards in the North to work with and for the negroes through the established public agencies promises returns that will loom up large in future accounts of the education of the negro.

REFERENCES

DuBois, William E. B.—"The College-bred Negro"; *Report of the United States Commissioner of Education*, 1902, Vol. I, Ch. III.

Hart, Albert B.—*The Southern South;* Appleton, 1910.

Jones, Thomas Jesse—*Negro Education;* United States Bureau of Education Bulletin, 1916, No. 38.

Miller, Kelly—"The Education of the Negro"; *Report of the United States Commissioner of Education*, 1901, Ch. XVI.

Noble, Stuart G.—*Forty Years of the Public Schools in Mississippi with Special Reference to the Education of the Negro;* Teachers College, Columbia University, 1918.

Peabody, Francis C.—*Education for Life;* Doubleday Page, 1918.

WASHINGTON, BOOKER T. — *Character Building;* Doubleday Page, 1902.

—— *My Larger Education;* Doubleday Page, 1911.

—— *Working with the Hands;* Doubleday Page, 1904.

WASHINGTON, BOOKER T., DUBOIS, WILLIAM E. B., and OTHERS — *The Negro Problem;* Pott, 1903.

WEATHERFORD, WILLIS D. — *Negro Life in the South : Present Conditions and Needs;* Association Press, 1911.

—— *Present Forces in Negro Problems;* Association Press, 1912.

CHAPTER XVI

EDUCATION IN THE UNITED STATES POSSESSIONS

PART I

EDUCATION IN PORTO RICO

BY

J. J. OSUNA

UNIVERSITY OF PORTO RICO

CHAPTER XVI

EDUCATION IN THE UNITED STATES POSSESSIONS

I

EDUCATION IN PORTO RICO

Before the Occupation

When the United States took over Porto Rico as a result of the War with Spain, they found a civilization Spanish in character, with a very small percentage of well-educated people, the masses being poor, ignorant, and illiterate. This state of affairs was the result of four hundred years of Spanish rule. It cannot be said, however, that there were no schools during those four centuries, for there had been some educational activity in the island since 1511. The backward educational conditions were due to Spanish methods, as conditions in Porto Rico were no worse than they were in Spain, where even at the present time 65 per cent of the population is illiterate.

A study of those four hundred years of educational "activity" will reveal many excellent school laws and royal decrees and orders concerning education. The backward state was not due to lack of good laws, nor even to lack of advanced educational thought, but to failure to execute the laws or to apply the thought. In fact, it can be safely said that laws were frequently written and promulgated, which those in authority never intended to be executed. As a result, we find that, in practice, there was no definite organization of education during the Spanish régime; that whatever educational activity existed was the result of sporadic attempts here and there by the church, by private societies or clubs, by municipalities, by the government, and, above all, by private individuals of foresight and philanthropic spirit; and that all these attempts lacked a knowledge of conditions, of needs, and, therefore, of a definite end or aim.

When the United States took over Porto Rico, only one child out of fifteen of school age attended school. During the year ending June, 1899, there were reported 212 town schools and 313 rural schools. Excluding some municipalities for which the number was not reported, there were 426 rural barrios without any school whatever. The enrollment for the year was reported as 19,804 boys and 9378 girls, a total of 29,182; but only 14,720 boys and 7153 girls, or 21,873 pupils, were reported to be in actual attendance. The total number of children of school age, four to sixteen, who were then without school accommodation was reported as 268,630. The total expenditure for education was $288,098.

In 1898, there were two normal schools—one for men and one for women — and one public secondary school. All the other secondary schools were private. There was not an institution of higher learning. Public school teachers were poorly prepared in the two normal schools, which required merely an elementary school education for admission. The teachers worked independently of the system, each admitting pupils irrespective of age or grade of advancement. There were no school buildings that had been constructed solely for school purposes.

Such were the conditions when the United States took over Porto Rico and began its work of school organization.

Problems of the New Government

The task of establishing a graded American system of public instruction in Porto Rico was greater than one would imagine. There were many problems to be solved. The first of these was the reorganization of public education. This was not an easy task, for the teachers were not accustomed to working in an orderly, well-organized system and many of them considered directions given by the newcomers as dictation on the part of conquerors. The second problem to be attacked was the extension and financing of education. The school census of 1898 showed that the island had a school population of 322,393 (school age five to eighteen) and an enrollment of 29,172, or of only about nine per cent of the school population. The finances of the island were limited. To reach this multitude of school children, provide for the increase in population, and finance such a system was a tremendous task.

The third problem requiring immediate attention was that of equipment. The total lack of suitable school buildings was one of the most conspicuous features of the educational weakness of the Spanish régime, and one which impressed visitors from the North most unfavorably. Another problem which faced the American educators was that of co-education. An American people cannot appreciate this problem as thoroughly as can a Spaniard or a Latin American. In America the boys and the girls attend school together from the kindergarten to the university, women enjoy greater freedom than in any other country of the world, and there is no appreciable difference in intellectual, social, and moral standards between men and women. But when the Americans took possession of the island, they found a civilization in which it was thought morally wrong for boys and girls to go to school together, where woman by tradition was destined to submit herself to the will of man, and where there was a very different and marked contrast between the intellectual, social, and moral status of men and women. To establish the American coeducational system in such a society was to accomplish that which Spain and many other parts of Europe have not yet accomplished ; it was to step in a day over centuries of traditions, customs, and prejudices.

Perhaps the greatest problem which confronted the American educators was the adaptation of a standard American common school system to a Latin-American people, who were mostly of Spanish blood and traditions and whose vernacular was also Spanish. This problem was made still more difficult when the attitude of the people toward manual labor and the language question were taken into consideration. No one can appreciate the seriousness of these problems and the difficulties encountered so well as one who has lived among the people and who speaks, thinks, and feels with them and with the people of the United States as well. The new generation of Porto Rico, a bilingual people, will be able to appreciate these problems and look with admiration at the efforts put forth to approach these conditions wisely and will view with sympathy and understanding the many mistakes and failures made.

The Present System

The work of school organization was begun and, after an investigation of conditions, the school law of 1899 was issued. This law, however, was not practicable, as it left the control and administration of the schools in the hands of the respective municipalities, which were not in a position to carry on the administration of the schools. The failure of this first move was so evident that on the establishment of civil government the school system was centralized, and a commissioner of education was given ample powers in the administration of the schools.

To-day the organization, administration, and work of the Department of Education of Porto Rico is characterized by a high degree of centralization. The public school system is headed by the Commissioner of Education, who is appointed by the President for a term of four years or at his pleasure, with full power of appointment over all subordinates. The Commissioner is responsible to the Governor, who in turn is responsible to the War Department at Washington. Since the insular legislature enacts laws to be executed by the Commissioner, he is responsible to the legislature, although his tenure of office does not depend on that body. By law he is President of the Board of Trustees of the University of Porto Rico and Chancellor of the University. He appoints all his subordinates, and nominations made by local officers must have his approval. All expenditures for educational purposes, whether for insular, municipal, or university funds, are subject to his approval. The Commissioner, then, is the pivot around whom revolves the whole educational machinery, so that a good commissioner means a good school system, while a poor and inefficient commissioner means a poor and inefficient system of schools.

Elementary Education

The problem of school extension immediately demanded the attention of those intrusted with the organization of the schools. The task of providing educational facilities for the large number of children was begun. The first two years was a period of readjustment and only slight progress was made; but with the establishment of civil government a larger number of schools were instituted. However, at this time the estimated school population was 332,497, while the school attendance was only 15 per cent of that number. The increase of the school enrollment during the first few years of civil government was constant, but the problems of finance and adaptation were such that progress was necessarily slow.

When Dr. E. G. Dexter became Commissioner of Education, he adopted as the first of his aims, "To provide instruction in the branches comprising a common school education to all children of school age in the Island, this instruction to be both in English and in Spanish." His successor followed the same policy. The period from 1907 to 1914 was a period of earnest endeavor on the part of the Department of Education to reach the largest possible number of children of school age. Double enrollment was resorted to with the result that in 1914 the average enrollment per teacher was eighty-one. The total enrollment of the public schools reached as high as 207,101, the largest number of children ever enrolled in the public schools of the Island. It can be seen readily that under such conditions school work could not be thorough and that the program of school extension had been carried out at the expense of efficiency. Since 1914 the Department has abandoned the policy of double enrollment and has placed the emphasis on thorough work and adaptation of the system to meet insular needs.

In 1921 the educational situation was as follows: According to the census of 1920, the insular population was 1,299,809. The number of children of legal school age was 438,747, and the number of children of compulsory school age was 209,220. The total enrollment in all schools supported by public funds was 193,369. Of this number 119,947 were enrolled in rural schools; 62,126, in elementary graded schools; 4364, in secondary schools; 565, in the collegiate department of the University of Porto Rico; 1040, in the summer session of the University; 2987, in elementary night schools; 158, in night classes for technical instruction; 2018, in special needlework and embroidery classes; 39, in rehabilitation service; and 25, in the school for the blind. In addition, 6818 pupils attended private schools. The total number of different persons who attended either public or private schools at any time during the year was 200,087. The total enrollment in the public schools was 43.1 per cent of the total population of school age, and 90.3 per cent of the population of compulsory school age; but of the 209,787 children of compulsory school age, only 138,983, or 66.3 per cent, were enrolled.

The above data show the great progress that has been made in school extension since 1898. They also show how much still remains to be done. According to these data, 57 per cent of the total population of school age is not enrolled in any school whatsoever, and only 33.8 per cent of the children of school age are reached. It would seem that a large number of children have no opportunity whatsoever to secure an education. This information is rather misleading. Officially a child is counted of school age as soon as he is five years old, and he remains for thirteen years in the records of children of school age. During this period, most of the children receive a four-year rural school education or an eight-year elementary school education. Though they appear in the statistical records for a number of years as children of school age not attending any school, nevertheless they may have completed the courses which the government is able to offer and may be, therefore, by no means destitute of education.

In spite of the above, the fact remains that Porto Rico is not furnishing school facilities for 57 per cent of her school population and that 33.8 per cent of her children between the ages of eight and fourteen years are out of school. Ever since the establishment of the school system, the Island has had a compulsory school law. There is also to-day a child-labor law providing that no child under fourteen years of age who has not received a certificate from the Department of Education to the effect that he has finished the work required of the third grade of the rural or the eighth of the graded schools can be employed in any remunerative occupation during the hours public schools are in session.

Such laws have not been, are not, and cannot be enforced until the island provides school facilities for at least all her children of school age. Thousands of children of compulsory school age are running the streets to-day soliciting at every turn places in the public schools, but they have to be refused admittance because there is no room for them. Although great progress has been made in the extension of the school system since 1898, when only 9 per cent of the school population attended school as against 43 per cent to-day, and when only 4.7 per cent of the total population was in school as against 15.6 per cent to-day, yet the extension of the public school system so as to reach the largest number of school children is still the great problem confronting the Department of Education. Educational progress has been made in the last two decades and a half, but we have just begun to educate the masses of the people.

Secondary Education

The history of education in Porto Rico shows that, although elementary education was neglected, provision was always made for the education of the few in what may be called the secondary schools. History shows that at various times attempts were made to establish university courses. The idea of secondary education was always popular; not so, that of elementary education. It was hard for the educated classes to understand that the establishment of elementary schools should precede that of secondary schools.

When Dr. Brumbaugh began to establish the public school system, placing the emphasis on the extension of elementary education, he met with severe criticism from a few people who wished higher institutions of learning to be created before the elementary work was organized. Dr. Brumbaugh answered his critics that the greater duty was to the larger number and he pushed the elementary schools to the point of complete organization, giving the high school work only partial support. Outside of the Insular Normal School for the preparation of teachers, no support was given at first to collegiate and professional education.

Secondary education in Porto Rico includes the educational training given to those who have completed an eight-year elementary course or its equivalent. It is given in two styles of schools known as high schools and continuation schools. The high school in Porto Rico is the same as the traditional high school in the United States — the institution offering a four-year course of study beyond the elementary school course of eight grades. Continuation schools were established in towns which could not support a high school. These schools take the pupils upon the completion of the elementary school course and carry them, without the necessity of leaving home, one, two, or three years further in their educational career. Thus the continuation school originated as an extension of the elementary school course and not separate from it. Although emphasis is placed on manual training for boys and cooking and sewing for girls, yet the continuation schools are far from being prevocational and vocational schools, and do not fit the students for specific vocations. They are established mainly to provide further study beyond the eighth grade. From the continuation schools the students may pass on to the corresponding year in the regular four-year high school.

Higher Education

The one institution offering higher and professional education is the University of Porto Rico. It was established by act of the Insular Legislature, approved March 12, 1903.

At present the University consists of the College of Liberal
Arts, offering a four-year course beyond the high school and
leading to the bachelor's degree either in arts or in sciences;
the College of Pharmacy, offering two- and three-year courses
and leading to the diplomas of Graduate Pharmacist, and
Pharmaceutical Chemist, respectively; the College of Law,
offering a four-year course beyond the high school and leading to the degree of Bachelor of Laws; the Normal College,
offering two courses beyond the high school diploma — one
of two years, leading to the Normal Diploma, and one of
four years, leading to the degree of Bachelor of Arts in Education.   The Normal College also prepares teachers for the
rural schools by giving a one-year course to students who
have completed a part of their high school work.   The College of Agriculture and Mechanic Arts offers several technical courses to high school graduates leading to the degree
of Bachelor of Science.

The American Contribution

The school system of Porto Rico as a whole, from the elementary school to the university, is not well equipped with
buildings, laboratories, or general supplies.   When it is recalled that there was not a building erected for school purposes during the four centuries of Spanish rule, and that
many buildings in use at the present time have been erected
since 1898, the progress made in supplying suitable buildings
and equipment may be easily recognized.   Some advancement has been made in recent years in providing proper
school buildings and facilities for the children of Porto Rico;
but, as this work has practically just begun, the majority
of the children are still attending school in inadequate and
unfit rented buildings.

A visitor to Porto Rico of twenty-five or thirty years ago,
returning to-day, would find that amazing changes in the

life of the Island had taken place. He would see wealth among many different classes. He would find English spoken among the younger generation and signs of progress at every turn. But if he were to penetrate into all the districts of the Island, mix with all classes, and meet representatives of her 1,300,000 inhabitants, he would come to the conclusion that Porto Rico, as compared with the United States, is still an undeveloped country with an undeveloped civilization. However, if a visit were made not only to Porto Rico, but also to Cuba and to other Spanish-American republics, and even to Spain, the traveler would see many common characteristics in their civilizations; but he would also see many differences and contrasts, and the most striking of these, as far as Porto Rico is concerned, is the improved system of public education.

Present Needs and Problems

In spite of these changes in the culture of Porto Rico and in spite of the great progress made in public education, Porto Rico has lacked and still lacks a definite, specific cultural aim suited to the particular needs of the Island. The schools have been functioning with considerable success, but without knowing clearly what they were supposed to accomplish. The American public school system was brought here and established irrespective of the Island's traditions, environment, and aim for the future. The time is ripe to establish and define a goal for the public schools.

The public school system of Porto Rico should be reorganized. At the present time, the Island has an elementary school of eight years and a high school of four years. Why there should be such an organization when the majority of the children receive only a four-year elementary school education cannot be explained. There is no reason why the eight-four plan should exist in Porto Rico, except that it has been the prevalent organization in the United States; though even there the reasons for this organization are not clear. The present organization was borrowed from the United States, transplanted, and imitated, mainly to comply with academic requirements which would enable Porto Rican pupils completing elementary and secondary education to enter the colleges and universities of the United States. In other words, the interests and the needs of the masses of Porto Rican children have been and are being sacrificed for those of a very small number who may want to enter college or university. The schools should be reorganized to meet existing conditions.

The important problem still to be solved is that of an intelligent adaptation of the American school system and ideals to Porto Rican needs. Whatever adaptation has been accomplished has been the result either of common sense on the part of skillful teachers or of accident, but not of scientific investigation. The tendency has been to copy and imitate rather than to create. However, of late, these problems have been receiving the attention of the educators of the Island, and there is no doubt that a new day and a more scientific approach await the public school system of Porto Rico.

REFERENCES

Commissioner of Education, Porto Rico — *Annual Reports* since 1900; Bureau of Insular Affairs, War Department, Washington, D. C.

Osuna, J. J. — *Education in Porto Rico;* Teachers College, Columbia University, 1923.

CHAPTER XVI — *Concluded*

EDUCATION IN THE UNITED STATES POSSESSIONS

PART II

EDUCATION IN THE PHILIPPINE ISLANDS

BY

GILDO MASSO

THEODORE ROOSEVELT HIGH SCHOOL,
NEW YORK CITY

CHAPTER XVI — *Concluded*

EDUCATION IN THE UNITED STATES POSSESSIONS

II

EDUCATION IN THE PHILIPPINE ISLANDS

Introduction

This section will present a rapid survey of the educational developments that have taken place in the Philippine Islands during the quarter-century that has passed since the archipelago became an American possession. We shall define the educational policies of the American administration, and make a brief estimate of the success of each policy.

The Present Organization

Soon after the occupation, the American authorities in the Islands perceived the necessity of a series of fundamental policies to guide the work in the educational field. They were confronted by two alternatives; namely, (1) establishing a policy of centralized control for the sake of rapid progress of the schools, and (2) giving ample powers to the local authorities for the sake of rapid training in political powers. The first alternative was chosen. · Wide powers have been given to the highest school official with the result that a highly centralized school system has been created. The Director of Education, as the head of the school system is called, appoints the school superintendents, prepares all courses of study, makes contracts for the purchase of books and supplies, exercises general supervision over the school system, and has extensive powers in the establishment of new schools, the selection of teachers, and the construction of schoolhouses.

This policy of centralization has worked satisfactorily in bringing about an efficiency of management that otherwise would have been well-nigh impossible. It has been claimed that centralization promotes uniformity in types of schools, in courses of study, in textbooks, and in standards of school supplies, thus preventing a large amount of waste. Perhaps more important is the claim that centralization introduces expert leadership and service. These two claims have been amply substantiated in the Philippines. In other countries centralizing tendencies have been checked by the fear of bureaucracy and by the unwillingness of the people to surrender functions which they believe themselves competent to exercise. The first of these two objections has not held good in the Philippine Islands as regards school affairs, in view of the achievements of a centralized administration in creating a modern school system in a short period of time. As to the second objection, it may be said that as a result of the lack of experience on the part of the people in the management of school affairs, especially in the early days of the new régime, they have not as a rule objected to the present policy of centralization. As social progress advances, and as the Filipinos add to their training for and experience in handling their own affairs, it is to be expected and desired that the power of local educational authorities will be increased.

The organization of the school system is a matter in which uncertainty has at various times prevailed. The attempt has been made to set up an educational ladder of the American type with adaptations necessitated by local conditions. The result has been a 4–3–4 plan of school organization instead of the American 8–4 plan. In the United States itself the convenience of the 8–4 plan has long been questioned and the 6–3–3 plan advocated on the ground that it "not only makes better provisions for meeting varying educational and social needs, but can be defended as psychologically more sound than the 8–4 plan." The Philippine system wisely includes a four-year elementary school followed by an intermediate course of three years and a secondary course of four years. The system is crowned by a state university located at Manila which offers courses on a par with those offered in American universities.

The schools are open to all on a purely democratic basis. The fee system in use under the Spanish régime was abolished soon after the American occupation. Although with this policy of free public schools the educational system has grown rapidly, it is yet far from meeting adequately the needs of the country. There are now under 21,000 teachers of all classes of a little over 1,000,000 children. But this is only about one third of the school population, now estimated to be about 3,000,000.

Other American Policies

It will be well to discuss now the aims pursued by the American administration in setting up the present school system. The fundamental aim is the elimination of illiteracy by placing within reach of every child of school age the means of obtaining the rudiments of an education. The aim of the primary course, an official report states, is to give the boy and girl enough English so that they can read an ordinary book or newspaper, and gain a reading and writing habit. That the schools are gradually solving the problem of illiteracy is shown by the census reports. Using the term "illiteracy" to mean in the case of the Filipinos inability to read and write in any language — English, Spanish, or any local language or dialect — it was found in the census of 1903 that 55.5 per cent, or more than one half of the population over ten years of age, could neither read nor write in any language or dialect. We must bear in mind, furthermore, the fact that of the 44.5 per cent literate, only about one out of two was able both to read and write, that in all probability less than 10 per cent of the people of the Philippines could speak English or Spanish, and that therefore the majority of those reported as literate could read or write only in the native tongues. Fifteen years afterwards, according to the census of 1918, illiteracy had been reduced to 50.8 per cent and both English and Spanish were more widely used, English being spoken by larger numbers of the literate Filipinos than Spanish.

Difficult as the problem of reducing the appalling illiteracy is, it seems to be exceeded in complexity by the language policy inaugurated by the American administration. A unilingual system has been created with English as the medium of instruction, the purpose being to make English the common language of the Archipelago, to create a "bond of union for the numerous and more or less distinct language groups." There are eight languages in the Islands, each of which is used by not less than 500,000 people, and some seventy-odd more which are used by smaller groups. English has been chosen as the main integrating agency for several reasons. The great majority of the Filipinos are ignorant of Spanish, and it has been assumed that it will be as easy for them to learn English as Spanish. The native languages are numerous and diverse, and there is no literature worth while in any of them. English, on the other hand, is well suited for communication with the outside world and practically opens to those who command it the entire field of literature. Spanish is not spoken by the adjacent countries, while English is the common language of every port from Japan to Australia and Suez. Finally, English, as the common means of communication, will make for efficiency in government and for social solidarity. However, the Filipinos are still divided on the language question. One of the political parties recently demanded the use of Spanish as the official language of the government; while others, on the other hand, strenuously advocate the adoption of English for the same purpose.

The results of the language policy are thus described by the Director of Education in his annual report for 1914:

To date, progress in securing linguistic unity by spreading a knowledge of English has been steady; but slower than could be wished, because the Bureau of Education has never been able to offer instruction to more than one half of the total school population during any school year.

The slow progress of English is well shown by the census figures. In 1918 among the literate Filipinos of ten years and over there were 511,721 males and 245,742 females who spoke Spanish, while there were 569,501 males and 326,757 females who spoke English. English is advancing but gradually, and accompanying its advance there has been an increased study of Spanish. The latter phenomenon is attributed to the great increase and circulation of newspapers and periodicals whereby there is now much more reading of Spanish than formerly.

The Curriculum

The American educators in the Philippines made, in the opinion of the writer, a happy selection of point of view for the formulation of curricula. In the development of the school system they have constantly had in mind the local conditions and needs. As already stated, they devised a 4–3–4 plan of school organization instead of transplanting the American 8–4 plan. This organization fits well with the threefold policy of academic, vocational, and physical education which we shall now discuss in detail.

The annual report of the Director of Education for 1911

states that the aims of the instruction given in the four-year elementary course are

to enable the pupil to understand, read and write simple English; to give him sufficient knowledge of figures so that he can later protect his own interests in minor business dealings; and to provide him with a limited fund of information on the subjects of geography, sanitation and hygiene, government, and standards of right conduct. Furthermore, the course aims to give every pupil sufficient training in some manual occupation to enable him to better earn a livelihood in later years as a result of having attended the public schools.

This course is the same for all, except for variations in industrial work and adaptations to meet the needs of some of the more primitive peoples. Since 1909 differentiation has begun in the fifth grade, that is, in the first year of the intermediate course, and has been continued throughout the remaining two intermediate grades. Differentiated courses had been offered in the secondary schools since 1904; but it was decided to give them in the intermediate schools for two reasons; namely, the shortness of the period of schooling possible for the average pupil and the maturity of the boys and girls in the intermediate grades. Provision is made for five intermediate courses — a general course which leads directly and normally to the high school; a trade course which aims to prepare children to earn a living as artisans; a farming course which engages the pupils chiefly in gardening and agricultural work; a course in business to prepare for office positions; and a course in housekeeping and household arts which gives both theoretical and practical instruction and training in home making. There used to be a course in teaching upon which the Bureau of Education largely depended for its new supply of primary teachers; but in 1919, with the demand for better trained teachers and with more material available from the higher grades, the teaching course was eliminated from the intermediate grades.

In all these intermediate courses sufficient academic instruction is given to enable their graduates to pursue secondary studies successfully. The secondary courses aim definitely at the preparation of young men and women for leadership. It has been the belief of American educators in the Philippines that the ordinary course offered in the secondary schools of the United States is not well adapted to the needs of the Filipinos. Desirable changes have been made, consisting mainly in reducing the amount of instruction in foreign languages and science, in placing more emphasis upon spoken and written English, and in introducing a practical course in local commercial geography and economic conditions.

Attention has also been given to physical education, "so planned as to make it possible for all or practically all of the pupils enrolled in the public schools to receive physical training of some sort." This line of work includes health inspection, personal and social sanitation, and such activities as marching, calisthenics, dancing, impromptu games, and group athletics.

The boys and girls have received the same kinds of schooling and in the same schools, except that as a rule only boys take manual training and agriculture, and only girls take cooking and sewing. A marked departure from this policy of coeducation was made in 1917, when instructions were issued to segregate the boys and girls in the intermediate and secondary schools where the numbers attending were sufficient to make the plan desirable. The chief purpose of this step was to make it easier to carry on the special kinds of work prescribed for the different sexes.

Schools as Social Centers

Following present-day tendencies the educational authorities are gradually widening the sphere of public education so as to bring under the influence of the school not only the immature members of society, but also those who have reached adulthood. More and more the educational plants are being used for civic, educational, and social activities, such as night schools, public lectures, concerts, debates, receptions, dances, and athletic meets, meetings of parent-teacher associations, literary societies, and various kinds of clubs. Dental clinics, school dispensaries, school nurses, and other health agencies are as a rule under the auspices of the Junior Red Cross. The value of these activities to the people, especially to those living in the rural districts, cannot be overestimated.

School Support

The school system is at present financed by funds obtained (1) from Insular sources through annual appropriations; (2) from provincial sources through annual appropriations; (3) from municipal sources through a land tax and through internal revenue; and (4) from voluntary contributions. In spite of the fact that the provisions made for the support of public education have been comparatively liberal, they have not been sufficient to meet the educational needs of the people and to avoid many of the shortcomings already pointed out. Lack of adequate financial support is evidenced by the fact that during the period from 1908 to 1916 the average daily attendance increased 72 per cent, whereas school expenditures increased only 15 per cent. In the United States from 1877 to 1912 daily attendance increased 149 per cent while school expenditures increased 570 per cent.

Teachers and Equipment

The development of the school system has also been hindered by the lack of professional training of the majority of the teachers.   Indeed the teaching corps has been created almost *in toto* under the new régime; but because of the rapid growth of the school system most of the teachers have received their training, pitifully meager all too often, after entering the service.   The training agencies include normal schools, secondary schools, summer normal institutes, district institutes, teachers' meetings, reading courses, and supervision.

A third handicap that has prevented a larger measure of efficiency in the educational work has been the lack of adequate school buildings.   The government authorities soon after the occupation began to take steps to remedy this deficiency.   The school-building policy has not been, and rightly so, a definite policy.   It has changed in accordance with the dictates of experience and with altered circumstances, particularly as regards the sources of the money used.   Both Insular and local funds have been expended to erect schoolhouses.   It is a significant fact that the first act passed by the Philippine Assembly and the Philippine Legislature was Act No. 1801, known as the "Gabaldon Act" and approved in 1908, which appropriated the sum of one million pesos for the construction of school buildings in the barrios, or outlying hamlets.   Three years later a second act was passed appropriating another million pesos for the same purpose.   Since the members of the then newly formed Philippine Assembly were all elected by direct vote of the people, these two laws showed popular confidence in and gave great moral support to the school system.

In the matter of school-building construction, many errors were made at first.   For example, in the first buildings constructed there were faults in their adaptation to conditions in a tropical climate and to the particular conditions of the sites in which they were put up.   In all these particulars there has been a large measure of improvement, and now all over the Islands the Filipinos point with pride to their modern and beautiful school buildings.

Publicity

A practice of the American school authorities which has produced far-reaching effects is that of keeping the people well informed, through various channels of publicity, in regard to educational projects and results. In this way coöperation and favorable popular sentiment for the schools have been secured. There was at first a great deal of apathy and ignorance to overcome, mainly due to the unfavorable social, political, and economic conditions which prevailed in the early days of the new régime. But the impetus with which the educational work was assumed, the publicity which it received, and the results soon obtained could not but impress upon the people the earnestness of the new administration in the solution of the existing educational problems. A recent report — the *Wood-Forbes Report* — commenting on the attitude of the Filipinos towards education says:

> Their support and aid in the building up of public education is beyond praise. They have sacrificed much that their children might be able to go to school, and the interests of an entire family are often subordinated to sending the selected member to a higher school or university.

Results

Such a spirit has made possible the educational progress that is sketched in the preceding pages. We have seen that a well-organized school system has been set up, the most conspicuous feature of which is a unilingual policy intended to meet urgent and permanent needs. Curricula have been devised which in various ways take into account the local needs of the people. The schools are free and open to all, and are fast removing the blot of illiteracy. They are constantly extending their sphere of influence, and the best provisions possible under the circumstances have been made in the matters of financial support, training of teachers, and construction of school buildings. In a quarter-century, and through the concerted efforts of Americans and Filipinos, a modern school system has been established in a country of 3000 islands and 11,000,000 people.

REFERENCES

Census of the Philippine Islands, 1903, Vol. 2; 1918, Vol. 2; Bureau of Printing, Manila.

Director of Education — *Annual Reports*, 1908–1921; Bureau of Printing, Manila.

General Superintendent of Public Instruction — *Report to the Secretary of the United States Military Governor, May 27, 1901;* Bureau of Printing, Manila.

Philippine Commission — *Annual Reports*, 1903, Part 3; 1908, Part 2; Government Printing Office, Washington.

Special Mission to the Philippine Islands — *Report to the Secretary of War (Wood-Forbes Report)*; Government Printing Office, Washington.

Superintendent of Public Instruction — *Annual Report for 1902;* Bureau of Printing, Manila.

INDEX